CRASHING THE NET

CRASHING THE NET

The U.S. Women's Olympic Ice Hockey Team and the Road to Gold

MARY TURCO

To Jan, McLinda, Kristin and Justin,
Best wishes to a family who
appreciates the love of athletics, in
particular ice hockey. With love
from your friends in Vermont
and Dartmouth, Mary + Jack Turco
June 21, 2003

HarperCollinsPublishers

English translation of haiku on page vii reprinted by permission of translator Kristen Deming. Additional permission from Koji Suzuki and the *Japan Times*.

"Cammi Granato" reprinted by permission of Nike, Inc.

HarperCollins books may be purchased for educational, business, or sales promotional use. For information please write: Special Markets Department, HarperCollins Publishers, Inc., 10 East 53rd Street, New York, NY 10022.

FIRST EDITION

Designed by Pagesetters, Inc.

Library of Congress Cataloging-in-Publication Data

Turco, Mary.
    Crashing the net : the U.S. women's Olympic ice hockey team and the road to gold / Mary Turco. — 1st ed.
      p. cm.
    ISBN 0-06-019264-X
    1. Hockey for women — Social aspects — United States. 2. Women hockey players — United States — Social conditions. 3. Winter Olympic Games (18th : 1998 : Nagano-shi, Japan) 4. Sports for women — Social aspects — United States. 5. Women athletes — United States — Social conditions. 6. Sex discrimination in sports — United States. I. Title
GV848.6.W65T87 1999
796.962'082'0973—dc21   98-51503

---

99 00 01 02 03 ❖/RRD 10 9 8 7 6 5 4 3 2 1

To my mother and father,
Agnes Thornton Garden and Douglas Garden,
with love and appreciation

Haiku

I'll be a wicked woman!
Breaking each patch of ice
I tread on.

—MIZUE YAMADA
   Translated by Kristen Deming and Koji Suzuki
   JAPAN TIMES, FEBRUARY 12, 1998

CONTENTS

Acknowledgments xi

"Cammi Granato" xiv

Preface xv

1
The Darlings of Nagano
"Red-White-and-Beautiful" 1

2
The United States National Team
"Play with Passion, Play with Pride" 17

3
The Olympic Hopefuls
"On the Bubble" 55

4
The Inner Circle
"For a Higher Purpose" 101

5
Team USA
"Games from the Heart" 135

6
Gold-Medal Contenders
"Surprise Me. Show Me Something Special" 187

Epilogue 217

Index 227

ACKNOWLEDGMENTS

This author has many friends and allies.

My dear friend Ben Smith entrusted me with the story of his beloved Olympic team. He then stewarded the project carefully and supported the author affectionately. Thank you, Ben, for your faith, honesty, and good humor.

I would like to thank David Halberstam for his generosity, Amanda Urban for her vision, Joëlle Delbourgo for her encouragement, and Gail Winston, my editor, for her talent, insight, and understanding. These four helped to manifest the original proposal as a book. I also appreciate the support of Amanda's associates Jenna Dimond, John Delaney, and Richard Abate, and Gail's associates Bridget Sweeney, Beth Neelman, and Trip Kirkpatrick.

For enthusiastically providing personal information and research materials, I am indebted to the members of the 1998 Women's U.S. Olympic Ice Hockey Team: Chris Bailey, Laurie Baker, Alana Blahoski, Lisa Brown-Miller, Karyn Bye, Colleen Coyne, Sara DeCosta, Tricia Dunn, Cammi Granato, Katie King, Shelley Looney, Sue Merz, A. J. Mleczko, Tara Mounsey, Vicki Movsessian, Angela Ruggiero, Jenny Schmidgall, Sarah Tueting, Gretchen Ulion, and Sandra Whyte. I am particularly grateful to Lisa Brown-Miller, Karyn Bye, Sara DeCosta, Cammi Granato, Tara Mounsey, and Sandra Whyte for allowing me to employ literary license to weave their personal experiences—at certain points during the national and Olympic team tours and the Olympic Games—into one story to relate the general experience of the entire Olympic team. Each of these six women was also kind to read and edit a draft of the chapter where she is the prominent voice.

I am also very grateful to the many parents, grandparents, spouses, siblings, and close friends of the twenty athletes who took the time to speak with me or send me materials. Special thanks to Natalie, Don, and Tony Granato and Sue and Mike Mounsey.

For candidly sharing the details of their adventure with the Olympic team I would like to thank team chairman Bob Allen, team leader Amie Hilles, sport psychology consultant Peter Haberl, assistant coach Tom Mutch, and equipment manager Bob Webster. For his special advice and assistance I am grateful to USA Hockey Senior Director of International Administration Art Berglund. In addition, for their cooperation and assistance before, during, or after the Olympic Games I would like to thank the following individuals at or affiliated with USA Hockey: Walter Bush, Ron DeGregorio, David Ogrean, Brian Petrovek, Kris Pleimann, Heather Ahearn, Darryl Seibel, Kim Folsom, Karen Lundgren, Kelly Dyer, and Tony Rossi. Thanks also to Tom Carlsen, M.D., and Sue Snouse for sharing information about the United States Olympic Committee's and International Olympic Committee's medical protocols. Bob O'Connor was a great help in sharing videotapes of the team's important games.

Four members of the U.S. men's Olympic team—Bryan Berard, Brett Hull, John LeClair, and Matt Schneider—took time to speak with me in Nagano. Thanks to them and to Veronica Richter (Mrs. Michael Richter) who also shared thoughts about the women's team.

My wonderful friend Nancy Moye was an expert transcriber and typist. Anne Tetreault was kind to serve as an additional transcriber. Dartmouth undergraduates Jennifer Karlen and Michelle Kraemer were enthusiastic research assistants.

The original proposal was written with advice from veteran sports writer and editor Jim Sarni. Jim also provided invaluable advice concerning the storyline. Thank you, Jim.

My sincere thanks also to an inspirational woman in her own right, pediatric cardiologist Lucy Wood Arnold, M.D., who helped to edit the original proposal.

Anita DeFrantz, Donna de Varona, Mike Eruzione, Billie Jean King, Jim Nantz, and Tara VanDerveer were extremely kind to read and comment on the manuscript.

I appreciate the countless ways in which Stefanie and Ted Leland, Marie Colacchio, and Janice and Joe O'Donnell advised and supported this project. I also appreciate the personal or professional support I received in various ways from all of the following people: Carol Adams, Tom Babson, Bud Beatty, Pam, Wally, and Bruce Berard, Kate Bowden, Len and Judy Cashman, John Collins, Roger and Christine

Demment, Phyllis Deutsch, Woody Eckels, Skip Freeman, Joanne Gurley, Mikki Hebl, Bob Higgins, Alex Huppe, Tom Lee, Joe Mehling, Sally Otos, Marcia Peraza, Holly and Mike Sateia, Sally Schwager, Tom Sherriffs, Sandy Smith, Tom and Anne Tetreault, Miguel Valladares, Geoff Vitt, Linda Wilson, J. P. and Dwight Ware, Erica Warrington, Bill Wright-Swadel, and dozens of colleagues at Dartmouth College.

My extended family—the Gardens and Murphys—have, as always, been wonderful.

Behind the production of every story is another story. Mine involves three terrific children and a remarkable husband. Thank you Mark, Scott, and Molly for alternatingly encouraging, teasing, and supporting me. I learned a lot from your passion for the game and joy in playing well. Thank you Jack for coaching me through the tough times, laughing with me during the funny ones, and always acting as my greatest ally.

Cammi Granato

When I invented me the, word went, what?
Women don't play hockey.
A place for me didn't even exist when I first came along.
Well, OK.
When the ice opens up in front of me,
wide and wild,
I don't feel like a first,
I just don't see anything in my way.
When a woman wins, victory is passed around like cake—
Everyone gets some
Wallflowers and followers and fierce ruling divas alike.

Play 'cause you love it.
Play 'cause you mean it.
And win
For a bigger world than the one you started in.

—EMILY XYZ
  NIKE INC. ADVERTISEMENT, WINTER 1998

PREFACE

Crashing the Net tells the story of the U.S. Women's Olympic Ice Hockey Team and its quest for a gold medal at the 1998 Winter Olympics in Nagano, Japan. The tale revolves around twenty high-achieving, beautiful, and defiant women athletes and their coach, Ben Smith, and is told through the personal experiences of six members of the team.

I wrote *Crashing the Net* to inspire young people, especially young women, to believe that dreams can be fulfilled. If you set goals and work hard, you can break barriers, smash stereotypes, rewrite traditions, and succeed. I hope that these girls, ordinary American women, will show you that women can do anything: fly space shuttles, build bridges, command armies, lead nations.

Mary Pipher, Ph.D., author of *Reviving Ophelia,* has called America "a girl-destroying place"—a place that fosters girls' low self-esteem, eating disorders, and self-loathing. But she also points out that many girls find protected places in which they can thrive, one of them being athletics. "Girls in sports," she explains, "are often emotionally healthy. They see their bodies as functional, not decorative. They have developed discipline in the pursuit of excellence. They have learned to win and lose, to cooperate, to handle stress and pressure. They are in a peer group that defines itself by athletic ability rather than popularity, drug or alcohol use, wealth or appearance." All of the women on the first U.S. Women's Olympic Ice Hockey Team found this protected space in athletics. From early childhood, each played and excelled in many sports including field hockey, basketball, soccer, lacrosse, and softball. Almost all of these athletic endeavors were on girls' teams, which was fine. But then they fell in love with another sport, one that many of them were told girls could not play: ice hockey. What happened next was quite remarkable.

With the support of loving parents, they cut or tied back their hair, adopted boys' nicknames, borrowed brothers' equipment, and set out to prove otherwise. Along the way some of these young athletes encountered closed-minded adults and children who didn't want girls on the ice. But they also encountered many adults and children who cheered them on and admired their spunk. In dealing with both naysayers and advocates, the girls became tenacious. They built their dreams around the sport they loved best, and then they refused to let anyone take their dreams away.

Despite the many advances in opportunities for women, the final decades of the twentieth century have offered few new and progressive role models for adolescents, particularly girls. My protagonists fill this void powerfully. Since childhood these athletes have demonstrated that girls can do the same physically and emotionally demanding activities as boys, and succeed. These ordinary American women set their first goals, as little girls, when they decided not only to join boys' teams but also to play the "boys' games" as well as, if not better than, their male teammates. As one athlete put it, "I decided that if I was going to be the first girl on the team, I sure as heck wasn't going to be the worst player." Having accomplished what was at the time unheard of, these girls set higher goals: to play for single-sex male high school teams and win state championships, to earn college acceptances with generous athletic scholarships and achieve academically, to play for a national team and defeat international opponents, and to join an Olympic team and win a gold medal for the United States.

I also wrote this book to show girls' natural allies—their parents, teachers, and coaches—how to be strong supporters. You will meet adult mentors in these pages who learned to open their hearts, minds, and wallets for girls in ways that were not customary twenty-five years ago. Many of these individuals had to question the sexist notions they were raised with, challenge prejudicial attitudes that are still rampant in this society, and confront the antigirl sentiment that permeates much of male athletics.

The idea for writing a book about women athletes, and particularly women hockey players, occurred to me in 1996 at the U.S. Girls' National Ice Hockey Championships in Bloomington, Minnesota. I accompanied my then thirteen-year-old daughter to Bloomington after her girls' state select team qualified for nationals in the New England regional tournament.*

Before arriving in Minnesota, my only experience with national tournaments had been with boys' hockey. My two sons' teams had qualified twice. The competition and excitement at the boys' national tournament were unforgettable. I wondered if the girls' tournament would be half as memorable.

What I discovered in Minnesota surprised me. There were talented girls' hockey teams from practically every region in the United States. The level of play was high. The games were extremely exciting. At the beginning of the tournament, the organizers held a meeting at which every team was present. Hundreds of girls listened as directors, hosts, and keynote speakers celebrated the girls' athletic accomplishments. Each team was introduced and congratulated. The atmosphere was electric. The ceremony mirrored the boys' version with its public recognition of achievement.

I started taking notes. Something interesting was happening. In the rinks in Bloomington, college scouts were watching. In the hallways, corporate sponsors were selling. In the locker rooms, hundreds of adolescent girls were braiding their hair, pasting decals on their helmets, and painting symbols on their faces. These healthy, happy girls talked a lot, joked a lot, and laughed out loud. During pregame preparation they donned shoulder pads and pelvis protectors over T-shirts and boxer shorts. The most popular T-shirt read DON'T TELL ME WHAT I CAN'T DO, Louisville Hockey's product motto for its women's athletic apparel. Instead of stockings, the girls wore shin pads. Instead of high heels, steel-bladed boots. Instead of white gloves, padded leather.

---

*Most of the girls at the nationals play as small children on local youth hockey teams in their hometowns and then move on to more competitive girls' teams in their age group in their state. If the state team in their age category excels, it earns the right to represent the state at the regionals. The top one or two teams in the region qualify for the national competition. The winning team at the nationals becomes the American champion. Many college coaches attend the nationals to watch the finest skaters in the country. USA Hockey representatives, including the women's national team coach, watch regional as well as national competitions to decide whom to invite to the National Junior Camps at the Olympic Training Center in Lake Placid. From these camps women are invited to try out for the Women's National and now Olympic teams.

Instead of bracelets, elbow pads. The girls' angelic faces slipped behind face masks. Their shapely figures disappeared beneath neck-to-
thigh jerseys. This was no fashion show. It was preparation for
competition. When the puck dropped at game time, the only thing
that mattered was performance. Being feminine—attractive and pre-
sentational—was irrelevant. Being competent—strong and skilled—
was everything.

Given my work as a women's studies professor at Dartmouth College, my notes and observations generated research questions: Are
these girl athletes transcending social roles without rejecting femininity? Are they succeeding at a "men's game" in men's equipment under men's rules without behaving in male-defined ways? Are these
girls redefining what is masculine and feminine? What can these girl
athletes teach us about how far we have come, in the post–Title IX[*]
era, in enabling women to achieve?

I knew the research questions were important. In a course I teach
about contemporary issues in American education, a burning topic
for both men and women is sex equity. People wonder how American
girls are doing in the postfeminist era, with its equal doses of enlight-
enment and backlash. Have the civil rights policies designed to eliminate sex discrimination helped women? Specifically, has Title IX
made a difference?

As a teacher concerned with finding ways to support girls' achievement, I began to think that a book about girls struggling with social
roles, told through the narratives of successful women athletes, might
inspire girls and help make the case that girls must be given more opportunities to play, and play whatever they choose. Regrettably, too
few high school and college women have thus far had that chance.
According to the Women's Sports Foundation, as of 1996, 53 percent
of college students but only 37 percent of National Collegiate Athletic Association (NCAA) athletes were women. These women athletes received 37 percent of their schools' athletic scholarship dollars,

---

[*]Title IX, a section of the 1972 Federal Education Amendments, requires that "no
person in the United States shall, on the basis of sex . . . be subjected to discrimination under any education program or activity receiving Federal financial assistance."
This statute affects virtually every school in the United States, therefore the ramifi-
cations for women's sports are vast. Sadly, schools' compliance and federal officials'
enforcement of the statute have been slow.

but this figure amounts to $142,622,803 less than male athletes received at the 767 schools reviewed. As of the same year, only 39.5 percent of high school varsity athletes were girls. This figure represents an enormous increase over the 17.8 percent in 1972, the year Title IX passed, but it indicates that opportunities remain unequal from high school through college.

As someone who has raised three children, two boys and a girl, I understand the importance of presenting children with equal educational and athletic opportunities. My sons have benefited enormously from consistent school-based academic encouragement as well as consistent school-sponsored athletic participation. I want my daughter to have similar opportunities. Reflecting on what I know and observe as a parent and educator, I can make the case that, while not all of the evidence about the impact of Title IX has been recorded, studied, and analyzed, many positive changes are happening for girls.

Ben Smith, a former Dartmouth colleague, agrees. One month after the Bloomington tournament, Ben, who was the men's Division I hockey coach at Northeastern University, announced his resignation. He had decided to leave men's hockey to coach the 1996 women's national team. He told me he was fascinated by the advances being made in women's athletics and was hoping for an opportunity to return to the Olympics. In 1988, Coach Dave Peterson had selected Ben to be assistant coach of the U.S. men's Olympic team in Calgary. We discussed my daughter's experience at the girls' nationals, the enthusiasm and excitement as well as the hundreds of talented athletes in the pipeline. Ben and I shared our curiosity about the historic, cultural, and social implications of women's new opportunities.

One year later Ben was named coach of the first women's Olympic team. When we spoke on several occasions after his selection, we discussed why this particular Olympic team presented a wonderful opportunity to learn about women athletes. Ben suggested I draft a proposal for a women's studies research project. After consulting with various experts, including Division I athletic directors, sports medicine experts, and 1996 Olympic women's basketball coach Tara VanDerveer, I suggested to Ben that I gather personal narratives from the players, their coaches, and staff during the Olympic odyssey to create a book that would inspire young women, whether or not the Americans won.

Ben liked the idea. He consulted with USA Hockey officials who were responsible for hiring him and funding the team, and told me to proceed. I was given direct access to the team, which enabled me to watch the players during their national team tour from September to December, during their showcase in San Jose in January, and during the Nagano Games in February. I invited all of them to complete a formal (although voluntary) research questionnaire, and some of them to participate in interviews. Some players also shared their personal journals, e-mail messages, and photographs. In Nagano I had the good fortune to meet many of the players' parents, siblings, and partners on an informal basis. I also had the opportunity to meet and interview members of the U.S. men's Olympic team and a few of their spouses and parents and hear their views on the evolution of both the men's and women's teams. Although most USA Hockey officials were terribly busy in Nagano, several—including Art Berglund, Walter Bush, Ron DeGregorio, Dave Ogrean, and Tony Rossi—were kind enough to speak with me. I was a fly on the wall during the games but had an opportunity to speak with the players, coaches, team leader, team chairman, sport psychology consultant, and equipment manager either during the pre-Olympic tour, immediately after the gold medal game in Japan, or following their return to the United States. The book contains details that no television camera or newspaper reporter was able to record.

Athletics, in the words of Mary Pipher, is a "cultural battleground where girls' hearts and minds are being fought for." The evidence of this cultural battlefield is everywhere—on playing fields, in courtrooms, in classrooms, in marketing campaigns and media coverage, and in families.

On the playing fields, in spite of delayed compliance with Title IX, the numbers of girl athletes are increasing dramatically. In 1971, according to the National Federation of High School Athletic Associations, 294,000 girls played high school sports. By 1996–97, according to the NCAA, the number grew to 2,472,043. Many girls are playing traditional sports, but some are playing the contact sports—football, baseball, wrestling, and ice hockey—on boys' teams. Joanne Gurley, a professor of legal studies at Lake Erie College, discovered that in 1995–96 in the state of California, 554 girls played football, 640 girls played baseball, and 542 wrestled on boys' teams. In Alaska, 44 girls played boys' ice hockey. In Wisconsin, 461 girls played boys' soccer and 123 girls played boys' golf. Some girls sued for the right to play. The presence of thousands of girls on boys' teams, millions of girls on traditional teams, and millions more girls in feeder programs in lower grades foretells the rapidly growing demand. Right now, for example, more than 200,000 girls under twelve play baseball, and love it. If barriers are removed, many of these girls will also play the national game in high school.

Young women also want the opportunity to compete, earn scholarships, and excel at the college level. They want first-rate coaches, facilities, and schedules. Regrettably, many college-age women athletes still must sue to play because the opposition to sex equity at this level has been and remains formidable. Even at outstanding institutions like Brown University, which cut two men's and two women's teams for budgetary reasons and was sued by women gymnasts and volleyball players as a result, reaching full compliance has been difficult. Before *Cohen v. Brown University*, which has become the landmark legal case concerning Title IX and women's athletic programs in higher education, the NCAA was already concerned. According to Title IX attorney Sally Otos, between 1991 and 1993 approximately thirty-four colleges and universities were sued, threatened with lawsuits, or cited for sex discrimination. The litigants and complainants won every case, but few schools took serious notice. In 1993 the NCAA charged a sixteen-member Gender Task Force to establish new guidelines for sex equity. In spite of the NCAA's initiative, Brown University decided to continue to fight gymnast Amy Cohen and her co-litigants.

Brown University officials didn't get it. They didn't understand that girls will fight for the opportunity to play and that the public supports them. Stanford's athletic director, Ted Leland, put it well. He said, "Title IX is one of the few times when the federal government took a stand and changed the values of the general public." Deborah Blake of the national Women's Law Center called *Cohen v. Brown University* "a clear wake-up call to higher education." She pointed out that Brown was willing to spend "$1 million defending itself and another $1 million paying the plaintiffs ... to save $60,000 by cutting women's sports." The Supreme Court wrote,

> Title IX has had dramatic and positive impact ... on
> women athletes, particularly in team sports ... more-
> over, the Supreme Court has repeatedly condemned
> gender-based discrimination based on archaic and
> overbroad generalization about women.

In the wake of *Cohen v. Brown University,* American high schools,
colleges, and universities have been alerted to reexamine their athletic
programs for sex equity or risk being targeted for litigation. The complainants will be girls, parents, lawyers, and social activists. The simple fact is that girls want to play sports and are prepared to exercise
their legal right to do so.

At the national level women also want to play. In 1972, there were
only 72 American women at the Summer Olympics. In 1996, there
were 280 American women. At the 1996 Summer Games a total of
4,000 women from around the world competed. American women
won 38 of 101 medals. But increasing the numbers of women athletes
and women's teams has been an uphill battle. The problem is at the
top. In 1995, only 7 of 106 International Olympic Committee members were women, and only one woman sat on the executive committee. In the United States, among the 39 sports federations (where
42 percent of the athletes are female), only 29 percent of the board
members are women.

Girls are pressing on the playing fields and in the courts, but in
classrooms, a key cultural battleground, girls may be losing. Myra
and David Sadker's *Failing at Fairness: How Our Schools Cheat Girls*
(Simon and Schuster, 1994), Peggy Orenstein's *School Girls* (Double-
day, 1994), Judy Mann's *The Difference: Growing Up Female in
America* (Warner Books, 1994), and the American Association of University Women and Wellesley College Center for Research on
Women's *How Schools Shortchange Girls* (Marlowe, 1995) docu-
ment the problems. The Sadkers, for example, fault schools for their
complicity in sustaining patriarchal systems that can undermine girls.
Some of the research suggests that girls underachieve in what are often hostile or nonsupportive school environments. Many girls are
given very few female role models, academic or otherwise. As an example, during the mid-1990s, young girls had two-thirds fewer female
role models in literature about sports than boys did. Thus, when girls

nine to thirteen years old were asked to name three sports heroes, 83 percent of the girls named three men.

While many schools may not be concerned about the hearts and minds of girls with regard to athletics or other areas, most marketing and media executives are. *USA Today* reported in late 1997 that "marketers aren't just accepting women's sports: They're shaking the rafters to get in." Corporate sponsors for women's sports spent $600 million in 1997, double what they spent in 1992, to attract females to buy their products. Realizing that girls and women are "flocking into sports" and that they "control or influence about $2 trillion of the $3 trillion consumers spend annually in the United States," marketers and media executives are salivating. This attention could be positive overall if it helps to promote women's achievement, good health, and well-being. The attention could be negative, however, if it promotes products that exploit and undermine women or turns legitimate female role models—for example, premier athletes—into standard glamour girls who send the wrong message.

The attention on women athletes has been fueled by recent Olympic Games. The 1994 Winter Olympics women's figure skating final on CBS was the fourth-most-watched event in U.S. television history. In analyzing this phenomenon for *Financial World,* Brooke Grabarek wrote, "Where this kind of audience—read younger women—goes advertisers, marketers, and broadcast executives follow." Grabarek correctly predicted "softer" sports television coverage. During NBC's coverage of the 1996 Summer Olympic Games, player profiles often preempted live events.

Big-name corporations sponsored women's teams at the 1998 Olympic Games. Visa and Nike were among the sponsors of the U.S. Women's Olympic Ice Hockey Team. One of Visa's print ads read, "Wicked slapshots, dazzling puck handling and diving saves. Girls will be girls." Reebok, an official sponsor of both the Women's National Basketball Association and the American Basketball Association, understands the dynamic. As Kathy O'Connell, Reebok's women's-sports executive, said, "Instead of models walking down a runway, girls can now see women athletes as role models."

The cultural battle for the hearts and minds of girls rages on amid parents, coaches, teachers, lawyers, businessmen, media executives, physicians, and academics like myself. Meanwhile, more girls with more dreams join more teams. Who is winning the battle and why? *Crashing the Net* addresses some of these pertinent questions, not from the perspective of cultural commentators, as many other books have done, but through the experiences of women athletes to whom young girls and their allies can look for hope and inspiration.

I have chosen six women on the team who reflect the quality and diversity of the group to tell the story of their shared and individual struggles and success. These women include Cammi Granato, the forceful and beautiful team captain. When asked by *Good Morning America*'s Jeff MacGregor why she played "a man's sport," Cammi responded that she "loved the action" and believed that women's hockey, in comparison to men's, is "a finesse-style sport." She was the spiritual leader and voice of the team. In her compassion and caring for her teammates she represents the gentler side of a highly physical game. The darling of the press, she constantly sacrificed her time and energy to be the ambassador for her team and her sport.

Karyn Bye was the energetic organizer of the team and its assistant captain. An all-world athlete, she was one of the strongest and most skilled players. She loved to make people laugh, play the game, and win. Karyn, a consummate dreamer and enthusiast, was a powerful agent for change. As a twelve-year-old she petitioned the U.S. Olympic Committee for a women's ice hockey team; as a twenty-six-year-old she was delighted to be playing on the first one. Karyn, like several of the older women on the team, represents the generations of women pioneers who paved the way for Olympic victory. She was always mindful of the past and attentive to the future.

Lisa Brown-Miller, one of the bona fide pioneers of the sport in the United States, was at thirty-one the team's oldest member and the only married player. Lisa was the heart of the team, a "coach's player" who demonstrated to teammates and opponents alike, in every shift of every practice and every game, how proud she was to have the opportunity to wear a USA uniform. The symbol of dedication and hard work, Lisa sacrificed for many years to be a part of the Olympics. She shared many of those sacrifices with an unselfish and loving husband who understood and valued her motivation.

Sandra Whyte is the symbol of the team's shared tenacity and determination. Sandra was committed to winning the gold medal for the higher purpose of achieving something extraordinary for the women who will follow. Like Lisa, Karyn, and Cammi, Sandra is a veteran. A 1992 Harvard graduate, she deferred career and personal relationships to reach her goals. When the pressure of international competition became intense, she was the model of inner strength and personal courage. Under the most intense public scrutiny, Sandra had the greatest game of her life and led the United States to the gold.

Tara Mounsey represents the many young superstars on the team. One of the finest all-around woman amateur athletes in the country, Tara played high school hockey on the boys' team, excelling among her male peers in spite of serious injuries. She was the model of perseverance and self-sacrifice. She worried that her injuries would impair her and that her coaches, concerned about her physical challenges, would not select her for the Olympic team. Yet she played all-out in every game before and during the Olympics. Tara wanted to be on the ice for every power play, penalty kill, and final-period countdown. She became a "go-to girl" in the most important moments of each game in spite of her limitations, proving that a lot of heart and a fair amount of guts can help an athlete overcome physical boundaries.

I chose Sara DeCosta to represent the rookies of Team USA. On a squad filled with unselfish role players, she exemplified the group's remarkable team spirit. Asked to be backup goalie in the gold medal game, she told her coach she would happily do whatever was best for the team. Like Tara and some of her other young teammates, Sara played hockey on a high school boys' team and earned respect the hard way. One of her high school opponents, Bryan Berard, a member of the U.S. men's Olympic team, waited for her at the end of the gold medal game to extend his congratulations. Sara was the girl next door, the kid who worked really hard as an amateur athlete to make it to the Olympics, win a gold medal, and make Americans proud.

In *Crashing the Net* these six players' voices are more prominent than the others, but all of the women's stories emerge to describe the sacrifice, pathos, humor, and joy that accompanied their struggle.

No voice is more prominent in describing these phenomena than that of their coach, Ben Smith. A mythical character in men's ice hockey, Ben brings an uncanny appreciation for what is precious not only about the sport but also about this team's moment in the spotlight. He understands what makes the game joyful, almost spiritual, and how the men's game is losing that quality. He knows why men who are the fathers of daughters, love coaching women and girls. He knows why increasing athletic opportunities for girls have opened new possibilities for father-daughter relationships. Why the pleasure of having fun today eclipses all promise of financial gain tomorrow. Ben knows why men's coaches at the college level today dread some aspects of coaching: athletes' "squeeze plays" for admission (playing one interested school off another), financial aid "negotiations" (forcing increased and not necessarily more deserved assistance), and threats to leave their college team for the money available in the pros. He remembers what it meant to be a scholar-athlete, a principled coach, and a civilized fan. Ben retains a sense of what is wonderful about amateur athletics and believes that women and girls should have the fun and opportunity that men and boys have always had.

"Crashing the net," a hockey term that is often used in other sports, refers to the action of directly attacking the goal in a forceful way, usually with the support of one or several teammates. The point of the action is to score with power, conviction, and determination. In the game of ice hockey the player who assists is as important as the player who scores the goal. It is a game that values joint effort for a common purpose. Crashing is what a team does when it is going all-out and will stop at nothing, within the rules, to win. In exercising its talent and tenacity to reach a higher level, it is forcing its opponent to pay serious attention. It is asking the other team to play a better game. Only one team will win, but it is possible for both teams to be ennobled by the struggle.

One can easily apply my phrase "crashing the net," or Mizue Yamada's "breaking the ice," or Emily XYZ's "winning for a bigger world" to the achievements of the women on the 1998 U.S. Olympic ice hockey team. Through their persistence and passion, they eliminated some of the discrimination that women face in athletics by opening up one sport to thousands of young women who will now have an opportunity to play. Some writers have argued that in these women athletes' commitment to excellence as pure amateur athletes, and in their unwavering tenacity in the pursuit of the right to play the game they loved, even more was accomplished. In the *International Herald Tribune,* Helene Elliott wrote,

This was a triumph for anyone, male or female, whose dream has ever been ridiculed. It was a victory for whatever innocence remains in sports, for everyone who competes for the love of a sport and not financial rewards.

And so it was no surprise that, when "The Star-Spangled Banner" played during the gold medal award ceremony for the women ice hockey players, most of the people in Nagano's Big Hat Arena were in tears. As the music ended they watched Cammi Granato skate to the glass and press her gold medal against the palm of her mother's outstretched hand on the other side. Ten feet away, Shelley Looney, who had scored the game-winning goal, pressed her lips on the glass as her mother, also on the other side, kissed back. One of my favorite memories is of petite Lisa Brown-Miller climbing the boards, scaling the bench, standing tiptoe on skates, and then reaching up to kiss her husband, John, who was leaning over the glass. Michael Wilbon of the *Washington Post,* writing in the press box, captured the feeling best. He wrote,

> I've watched a lot of people win championships and medals before; I've never seen so many hard-boiled eggs have to reach for a tissue until this. Corny as it sounds, I guess this is why you come to the Olympics, hoping to stumble upon something that makes you feel better than you thought you could feel, to connect to someone or some team. The more unexpected, the more unbridled the joy.

The 1998 U.S. Women's Olympic Ice Hockey Team was truly, as their coaches liked to say, "something special." In their story I hope you will find the inspiration to crash your own net, break some ice, and win your gold.

—MARY TURCO

THE DARLINGS OF NAGANO

"Red-White-and-Beautiful"

NAGANO, JAPAN ~ FEBRUARY 17, 1998

Karyn Bye grabbed Cammi Granato's arm and pointed down the runway to the open gate leading to the rink where their game had ended ten minutes earlier. Beyond the gate, Nagano's Big Hat Arena sparkled with the flashes of what seemed to be thousands of cameras. Cammi's dark eyes reflected the sparkling lights as Karyn asked, "Are you ready for this?"

Cammi smiled broadly and responded, "Are you kidding, K.L.? I've dreamed of this ceremony a thousand times and, honest to God, I don't think I can wait another second for it to begin." As she spoke, Amie Hilles, the team's leader, signaled to her and Karyn that the medal ceremony was about to start and that they should lead their teammates back onto the ice. Karyn and Cammi turned to the women standing behind them in the hallway and passed the happy word. Then, taking a very deep breath, Karyn Lynn Bye and Catherine Michelle Granato led eighteen excited teammates down the runway, through the gate, and into the sparkle.

The locker room Karyn and Cammi emerged from had been absolute pandemonium just five minutes earlier. After the victory, Olympic officials had interrupted the players while they were rejoicing on the ice and asked them to return to their locker room so they could arrange for the medal ceremony to take place. The excited players pranced down the hallway to their locker room hugging everyone in their path including the members of the U.S. men's hockey team, who were waiting to congratulate them. Pat LaFontaine, Mike Richter, and Ron Wilson gave high-fives and handshakes, while Bryan Berard gave Sara DeCosta a hug. Two years earlier Bryan and Sara had played against each other in high school in Rhode Island. Now both were Olympians and one had won a gold medal.

Moments later, when they were safely behind the locker-room walls and free from the scrutiny of the media, the American women went wild. Some hugged teammates and kissed their favorite staff person. Others hooted and hollered while stripping off their shoulder pads and throwing them in the equipment bags. They jumped around on their skate blades shaking hands, slapping backs, and spilling champagne. The mayhem quieted down slightly while they toasted their remarkable accomplishment.

When the toast was over, many players grabbed cameras and started taking pictures. Others pulled out cell phones hidden in their duffel bags and called loved ones in the United States. A few, like Karyn, retired to their stalls to try to regain their composure.

After the euphoria of beating Team Canada, Karyn needed a breather. Although she was the most high-spirited woman on the team, she felt exhausted. The game had been draining both physically and emotionally.

Since the start of the day, Karyn had concentrated on placing herself physically and emotionally "in the moment," which, as the team's sports psychology consultant, Peter Haberl, had taught her, meant being totally present in time and in space, totally focused on reaching her goal. Haberl believed that being in the moment meant practicing "focused fun." He told her that, in order to play her best, she had to think of herself as a child immersed in an activity, completely oblivious to everything around her. Peter said, "Stop evaluating yourself and just skate. Very few people have the chance to be an Olympian. Play well and enjoy it."

Karyn remembered that Haberl had told her about the great Olympic swimmer Sumner Summers, who, after winning a gold medal, said that she had just wanted her race to be over; it was too much pressure and too little fun. Haberl and Coach Ben Smith wanted the players to avoid this mind-set, for they believed that athletes perform at their highest level when they are having fun.

And Karyn loved to have fun. She had started playing hockey at age seven when her dad, Chuck, suggested that, as a practical joke, she substitute for her sick older brother Chris at a youth hockey practice. Karyn and her father succeeded in fooling the coaches and players into thinking Karyn was Chris for a very short time, but the impact of that experience was lasting. Karyn loved practicing the game and wanted to play. A naturally "wired" child bursting with energy, Karyn became a regular player. At every game she skated hard, led cheers from the bench, pulled pranks (like her dad), and teased her coaches. When she was nine years old she watched the 1980 U.S. men's team win a gold medal in Lake Placid and decided Bill Baker was her hero. I can do that, she thought. She adopted Baker's number, 6. When she turned ten her aunt gave her a plaque that read GIRLS CAN DO ANYTHING. Karyn made the motto her creed and a strong work ethic her method. At twelve she decided that she too would be an Olympian. She wrote a letter to the U.S. Olympic Committee petitioning for a women's ice hockey team. When the committee sent back a form letter thanking her for her interest in field hockey, she was irritated but undaunted. In her juvenile mind she believed that someday it would happen.

Inspired by an Olympic dream and fortified with french toast from her mom, Dotty, Karyn grew fast and strong playing hockey with her brother and nineteen other boys during four years of high school. To minimize negative reactions from opponents, she adopted the nickname "K.L." Most of the guys she played with and against respected her ability. Those who didn't had to deal with her protective teammates. Karyn also excelled at tennis and softball in high school, but the more she played hockey, the more it became her favorite.

When the time came to go to college, Karyn picked the University of New Hampshire, a powerhouse in women's ice hockey. She scored one hundred goals in eighty-seven games at UNH, became an Eastern Collegiate Athletic Conference All-Star, and earned a place on five U.S. national teams. By 1997, Karyn was considered one of the finest players in the world. She set her sites on making the Olympic team and happily started acting as the national team's archivist. On a daily basis she typed journal entries into her computer and saved precious team memorabilia. The truth was that Karyn had extraordinary energy, and all of it was positive.

Karyn followed Peter Haberl's advice, practicing focused fun and performing skillfully throughout the Olympic Games. The entire experience had been upbeat and now she felt wonderful. She was exhausted but she was experiencing the genuine thrill of victory.

The thrill felt strangely familiar. Like Cammi, Karyn had rehearsed winning the gold medal in her dreams. She had choreographed special scenes and replayed them in her head a million times. There was always one prop in the picture, an American flag.

When Karyn had packed her bags in River Falls, Wisconsin, in January, she had removed the large American flag from her bedroom wall and placed it in her suitcase. Win or lose, she knew it was going to be important to her. One month later in Osaka, Japan, when forty pieces of Olympic gear were issued to each athlete, Karyn added Old Glory to the inventory. Between the second and third periods of the gold medal game, she asked Bob Webster, the equipment manager, if he would bring her flag to the bench. Although the coaches' rule was that nothing extra could be placed on the bench, Bob knew how much the flag meant to her. "Relax, K.L.," he said quietly, "I've got it taken care of."

When the final buzzer sounded, Karyn rushed to the bench. Bob handed her Old Glory, which she kissed before unfurling. She draped the flag quickly over her shoulders and then, like a whirling dervish, swirled to the center of the ice. Her teammates were getting up from a gigantic mid-ice pigpile, their helmets, gloves, and sticks littered all around them. Karyn handed her flag to Cammi, who lifted it proudly above her head. When Cammi returned the flag, Karyn fell to her knees, overcome with emotion. Lisa Brown-Miller knelt down beside Karyn and asked if she was all right. "Brownie, I just can't stop crying," Karyn said.

Lisa wrapped herself inside the flag with her friend and said, "You just won a gold medal, K.L., you can do anything you want." Then, literally swaddled in the stars and stripes, the two veteran players and former roommates laughed and then cried together convulsively. Their shoulders heaved beneath the cloth as they tried to keep one another from collapsing.

The convulsing Olympians affected the entire audience. Spectators, reporters, and security guards, not expecting such a spectacle, became teary-eyed. It was terribly moving to see these young amateurs who had dared to dream and then proven that dreams really can come true. Tomboys and rebels, but extremely feminine and likable, these women had shattered stereotypes since childhood. The audience knew them well. Each of them was "the girl next door," the one who baby-sat their kids, checked out their groceries, and waited on their tables. And now there she was melting the ice with her tears.

Steve Rosenbloom of the *Chicago Tribune* called the American women hockey players who became so emotional after their gold medal victory "red-white-and-beautiful." And they were. When Cammi lifted the flag and Karyn and Lisa fell to their knees, the emotional response was as much about patriotism as about sacrifice. Karyn had packed her precious banner because she was a proud American athlete. She wanted her country to know that Team USA's victory would not only be a giant step forward for women but also a shared national achievement. The pride and patriotism were not lost on the adoring audience.

Later, in the locker room, leaning over her stall with her beloved flag still wrapped around her, Karyn reflected on what had just happened. She had lived the first scene in her dream, the victory, and the second, the ceremony, was about to begin. Sweat poured off her face. She removed the flag from her shoulders, folded it carefully, and stored it safely in her duffel bag. It was now a family heirloom, a relic always to be cherished. On top of it she placed a telegram she had received before the game from Dr. Bill Baker, her Olympic inspiration.

Karyn removed the new hat that had been handed to her on the ice by a teammate. The insignia read OLYMPIC GOLD MEDALIST, NAGANO 1998. A crimson USA was embroidered above the five Olympic rings. Karyn pulled her hockey jersey over her head and temporarily set it aside. Next she slid her elbow pads off each arm and threw them into her equipment bag. She released the straps on her shoulder pads and lifted the steamy fabric over her head. Her head, neck, and body were drenched. No matter. Karyn threw the shoulder pads in the bag and wiped the sweat with her towel. Then she threw the towel on the floor, turned her jersey right side out, and pulled it back over her head. She swept her short brown hair back with her fingers, looked down at her skates, and tried to catch her breath.

All around her people were emotional. She could hear giggling, laughing, sniffling, and crying. Many players were desperately trying to reach friends and loved ones in the United States on cell phones. CBS was showing the game on its morning news program with a delay, so at home few knew the outcome yet. She could hear A.J. Mleczko calling her Harvard College teammates, who had gathered at their coach's home to watch the game. Harvard coach Katie Stone had put her Canadian players in one room and her American players in another to keep things from getting too wild. To A.J.'s dismay, no one in either room was answering the phone during the broadcast!

Karyn could hear Sandra Whyte standing at the trainer's table leaving a tearful, happy message on her father's answering machine in Saugus, Massachusetts. "We did it! We did it, Dad!" she cried, wishing that her father or brother would pick up the phone. Like many other people anxious about the game, Sandra's father had turned on his answering machine so he could listen and watch without interruptions.

Karyn could hear Angela Ruggiero reacting to the sound of her father's voice in Michigan. "Dad, we did it!" Angela screamed. "We beat the Canadians!" Karyn tried to picture Angela's father's face on the other end of the line as the rookie yelled, "At the end of the game some guy handed me a flag, Dad, and I skated around waving it like a crazy woman. I wish you, Pam, and Billy were here. Mom's having a great time. She's covered with face paint and she made a great poster that says 'Rugger.'"

Just beyond Angela, Alana Blahoski was waiting for her younger brother Petr to pick up the phone in Minnesota. Alana started bawling when Petr said hello. "What are you doing?" she asked. When her brother responded that he was watching the game, she exclaimed, "I hate to spoil it for you, Petr, but WE WON!" Then Alana cried uncontrollably while her brother reacted to her news.

Karyn saw Cammi start to cry as she picked up a call from her brother Tony in San Jose, and she decided to tune out all of the telephone conversations. Regrettably, a lot of the parents and siblings were missing. She wished that all of them were present to share this remarkable moment.

Many of the family members who had come to Japan had struggled to find $5,000 for one economy airfare to Tokyo, a modest hotel room on the outskirts of Nagano, and local transportation for seven days. The National Hockey League Players Association had negotiated for each NHL player selected for an Olympic team—American or otherwise—to receive one extra first-class round-trip air ticket to Japan and a resort-quality hotel room so that a parent, spouse, or friend could attend the Olympic Games. The women, of course, had no such arrangements. Some women's families received donations from wellwishers who wanted to help parents see their children compete in Nagano. There were fund-raising dances held in New Hampshire, auctions in Rhode Island, banquets in Michigan, and parties in Massachusetts. Friends of Vicki Movsessian's deceased father, Lawrence, had organized a fund-raiser for her mother in Lexington, Massachusetts. Hundreds of people attended. And thousands of strangers contributed generously when the women's parents sold T-shirts at national team contests around the country during the pre-Olympic tour. Colleen Coyne's father, Dennis, sold over a thousand T-shirts to help pay for Colleen's mother's ticket to Nagano. When the Coyne family lost their home in a tragic house fire before the Olympics, Oprah Winfrey helped publicize their plight and AT&T helped finance tickets to Nagano for Colleen's three siblings.

Caring friends and supporters were extremely generous to the players' families, but donations, shirt sales, and discretionary incomes fell short of the amount needed to provide every family member with a ticket. So some parents and siblings stayed home. Others, of course, chose not to travel for personal reasons. But most would have come to Nagano if it had been possible financially. Karyn couldn't imagine not having her loved ones present. She thought of her parents, brother, and sister in the stands and couldn't wait to find them after the ceremony.

Karyn looked at Lisa, who was removing her shoulder pads four stalls away. Lisa was still weeping softly. Karyn knew that Lisa couldn't wait to see her husband, John, who was also in the stands.

John would understand all the tears, shed not only for themselves but also for the many women who were not present who had helped to build the women's program.

Karyn and Lisa were happy for the other veterans who had made the Olympic team—Sandra Whyte and Cammi Granato—but they were also thinking of the many pioneers and veterans, either back in the States or perhaps somewhere in the stands, who hadn't. They thought of the women who had just missed making the team—Barbara Gordon, Kelly O'Leary, Stephanie O'Sullivan, Jeanine Sobek, and Erin Whitten—all of whom were outstanding athletes. They also thought of the hundreds of older players who had willed the Olympic medal for women into reality. They thought of remarkable athletes like Julie Andeberhan, Cindy Curley, and Kelly Dyer, who believed girls could do anything long before it became a slogan. These women glowed before advertisers glamorized sweat.

When the ten-minute time-out was almost over, Karyn stood up, placed her new hat in her stall, and walked over to Bob Webster. "You're the best, Webby," she said. "We couldn't have won without you. Thanks for bringing my flag to the bench."

Bob smiled self-consciously and responded, "It was my pleasure, K.L. You guys played a great hockey game. You deserved to win this medal."

Then Coach Ben Smith entered the locker room to deliver his final instructions. Karyn could tell he was frazzled from trying to fend off reporters. In seven days Smith's team of unknowns had captured everyone's imagination. Their Japanese hosts adored them. The international press pursued them. His twenty all-American girls were now the darlings of Nagano.

The women greeted their mentor with cheers as he shuffled to the center of the room. Smith shook a few hands, looked around, and thought, This is a happy, tired bunch. I better be careful what I say. I don't want everyone to go crazy at this point. He hadn't spoken to his players since the game ended and there was so much he wanted to say, but this was not the time or place.

Smith could sense the suppressed pandemonium in the room and it made him a little bit nervous. He swept back his bangs and rubbed his neck. This would be his last locker-room speech. How could he put into words how much he admired these women? They had just won an Olympic gold medal!

The players hung up their cell phones and settled down to listen. Smith spoke slowly and succinctly. His voice quavered: "Great goin', folks. I couldn't be more proud."

The team clapped and chanted, "Coach! Coach! Coach!"

Smith smiled and signaled them to stop. He continued, "Okay, gang, let's settle down. We've got a lot left to do here. First, I think we should take a minute to recognize the people at USA Hockey who made this whole thing possible. Let's hear it for Bob Allen, Art Berglund, Walter Bush, Dave Ogrean, and Ron DeGregorio! What a super job you guys did. Thanks a million!"

The women cheered for the USA Hockey officials who stood in the doorway with tears in their eyes. Karyn laughed, knowing the older men always hesitated to come into a locker room filled with women.

Smith continued, "And thanks so much to all the staff. Amie, our team leader, you've been terrific. Jeanna, thanks for being a great trainer. Sandra, you've been a super doc. Peter's not here, he's upstairs, but thanks for keeping us focused on the fun. Kris, thanks for a fine job with the press. Webby, old buddy, you're the world's greatest equipment manager. And Tom, thanks for being my assistant; as everybody knows, you're something special. How about those power plays and face-offs, Tommy? I think Tommy will agree the players made their coaches look like geniuses. To a person, you've been an outstanding staff. We appreciate all of you!"

Smith's remarks were followed by more applause and backslapping.

Again Smith swept back his bangs. He knew time was running out and he had one more very important thing to say. He called the group to order. "Okay now, listen up. Very important. Let's do this thing right. Remember, when you go out on the ice, to be respectful of the two teams waiting there. Canada is getting a silver medal when their coach promised the country a gold. That hurts. Finland is getting bronze when they hoped to unseat one of us for silver.

"The Canadians are a wonderful hockey team. They played great today, but they lost. They have nothing to be ashamed of; they've been absolutely super opponents. I'm proud of our rivalry. It has elevated our sport. This is a great moment for all of you and a historic moment for hockey. So let's show the Canadian and Finnish teams that we truly respect and appreciate them. These are the women with whom you're going down in history.

"Okay, Team USA, let's finish this thing up. When Amie sends the signal, get out on the ice and collect your hardware!"

The women cheered once more. Smith looked at their faces. They were radiant. Walking out of the room he thought, The faces tell the story. What a team. What a finish. Smith felt tremendous satisfaction. He had done exactly what he set out to do. Win or lose, he wanted the Olympic experience to be joyful.

Coach Smith exited the locker room with Tom Mutch and Bob Webster, who walked down the hallway and runway and slid onto the bench. Amie Hilles, Kris Pleimann, Jeanna Schepman, and Dr. Sandra Glasson filed in behind them. The USA Hockey officials gathered on the runway to watch from the wings.

As Team USA exited the locker room, a gauntlet of photographers respectfully cleared a path. The procession moved past the security guards and onto the runway to wait for Amie's signal. When it came, Cammi and Karyn led the team through the open gate and into a glittering stadium. The skaters glided to a brilliant blue carpet placed in the center of the ice.

As the American athletes stepped one by one up to the carpet, the sparkle increased dramatically. Horns blew, bells rang, and hands clapped. Hundreds of American flags fluttered in the stands and the audience chanted, *"U-S-A! U-S-A! U-S-A!"* Little Japanese girls, wearing Minnie Mouse earmuffs and waving tiny Olympic flags, joined the chorus, *"U-S-A! U-S-A! U-S-A!"* Their brothers stood on their seats making faces for cameramen while their parents lifted babies onto their shoulders for a better view.

As Karyn took her place between Cammi and Lisa, she noticed U.S. speed skaters, skiers, and bobsled racers, dressed in their special Olympic jackets, climbing up the boards and hanging over the glass. The Olympians screamed to the teammates they had trained with in Lake Placid. "Way to go, Team USA! We love you! Great job! You're the best!"

Above the screams Karyn could hear the cheers of players' friends and families. She looked for her family. Her mother, father, sister, and brother were waving madly. The entire audience was now on its feet, every eye focused on the U.S. Women's Olympic Ice Hockey Team. Big Hat Arena was electric. History was unfolding.

Team USA lined up facing the international dignitaries gathered in the center stands. On the ice to the Americans' right stood the women of Team Canada, agony written on their faces. On the left stood the women of Team Finland.

A ten-man uniformed color guard appeared behind the line of Canadians. The guardsmen, dressed in khaki-colored outfits, marched into position and intercepted three horizontal flagpoles lowered from the rafters. They attached three national banners and secured them. Then the guardsmen took a step back from the poles and awaited their cue.

Karyn reached for Cammi's and Lisa's hands and pulled her dear friends closer. She said, "Hang on tight. Here comes something special." Lisa took Alana Blahoski's hand. Alana found Colleen Coyne's and Colleen grabbed Angela Ruggiero's. At the other end of the line Sarah Tueting slipped her right hand into Katie King's as Katie spontaneously reached for Tara Mounsey's. Tara took Tricia Dunn's hand as Chris Bailey, Gretchen Ulion, Sandra Whyte, A.J. Mleczko, Sara DeCosta, Vicki Movsessian, Laurie Baker, Shelley Looney, Sue Merz, and Jenny Schmidgall did likewise. Within a matter of moments, the twenty women athletes were linked physically and emotionally. In their interconnected hands they held tightly twenty tiny American flags.

Three public-address announcers introduced the ceremony, the first in French, the second in English, and the third in Japanese. The boisterous crowd promptly quieted. "Ladies and gentlemen. The officials who will present the medals and flowers now enter."

A grand flourish of orchestral music joined a formal chorus of voices as the parade of presenters appeared. A beautiful Japanese girl, dressed in a red-and-gold kimono, led the procession. She passed through an opening in the boards and stepped safely onto the blue carpet. Behind her walked the three sets of dignitaries specifically chosen to present the Olympic medals. Each pair of presenters was accompanied by four Japanese girls, also dressed in elegant kimonos. One led the procession, two carried wooden boxes containing a set of the medals, and one guided a black metal pushcart bursting with bouquets of flowers. The medal-bearers used both hands to hold the heavy boxes above the waistbands of their kimonos. All of the Japanese girls wore their hair pulled back in a formal fashion and walked in traditional open sandals. The formality of their dress reflected the honor of their responsibility.

The chorus sang solemnly in the background while the announcers delivered further proclamations. Karyn heard only the first. The announcer said, "The gold medal will be presented by Miss Anita De-Franz, International Olympic Committee member from the United States and vice president of the International Olympic Committee."

When the silver- and bronze-medal presenters had been introduced, the parade stopped and the presenters took their places before the captain of each team. The chorus finished its song and the formal music ended. There was complete silence.

Karyn's heart pounded. Immediately to her right, directly in front of Cammi, was Anita DeFranz. DeFranz stood eye-to-eye with Cammi, who stood five feet, ten inches tall in her skates. This impressive African-American woman, the granddaughter of slaves, had earned a college education, a law degree, and a place on the 1980 U.S. Women's Olympic Rowing Team. The U.S. boycott of the 1980 Olympics in Moscow ended DeFranz's Olympic career, but she remained involved with the Olympics as both visionary and advocate. DeFranz had supported the addition of women's events to the Winter and Summer Games, including this first-ever competition in ice hockey. Every woman on the ice knew she would not be standing there but for Anita.

The announcers broke the silence. They spoke slowly and formally, enunciating every syllable. Their tone was serious. Karyn listened breathlessly. The English speaker said, "Presenting the Olympic champions and the gold-medal winner, the United States of America."

Suddenly, as the building erupted with cheering and screaming, a most remarkable music filled the arena. It was ethereal and hauntingly beautiful. Karyn watched Anita DeFranz turn to her left and remove from the velvet-lined box held by her escorts a light blue satin ribbon attached to a glistening golden ornament. Karyn gasped. The medal was stunning. It bore the symbol of the Nagano Olympics, and images of athletes as the petals of a multicolored flower. The medal was larger and more elegant than Karyn would ever have expected. Japanese artisans had spent one entire day creating each medal.

Anita motioned to Cammi, who looked straight into her eyes. Cammi bowed her head slightly, and then, with the motion of a queen crowning a most beloved princess, Anita placed the precious object over Cammi's head and onto her shoulders. The jumbo electronic screens on both sides of the arena carried a close-up of the coronation.

Cammi let go of Karyn's hand, looked down at her gold medal, and shook Anita's outstretched hand with both of her own. She then clenched her fists and threw both of her arms straight up in the air. Blinking back tears, she turned toward her family in the stands. Cammi could no longer control herself. The American captain put her face in her hands, bent over at the waist, and cried. When she finally raised her head, she was handed a rainbow of daisies and alstrumeria, tied in a pretty purple ribbon. Cammi bowed in thanks to Anita and the flower girl and then turned and waved her flowers to the audience. The crowd's roar lauded the importance of the moment. Cammi's prize was the first gold medal awarded in women's ice hockey. One more barrier broken. One more milestone for women. One more chapter in Olympic history.

The music moved to a crescendo. Karyn's emotions washed over and engulfed her. In the music and in the moment was a profound sense of personal contentment. At this dramatic instant, when her long-deferred dream was coming true, absolutely everything was triumphant. The haunting and beautiful melody punctuated her emotions gloriously.

Anita DeFranz stepped toward Karyn and greeted her. With every nerve in her body exposed, Karyn bowed and received her gold medal. She could barely speak. She could hardly breathe. She thanked Anita, accepted her bouquet, and smiled at the beaming flower girl. Then, with profound joy, she watched Anita DeFranz smile at Lisa and place a blue satin ribbon with a glistening gold medal over her shoulders. Lisa's fresh, warm tears flowed slowly down her cheek and dropped onto the ribbon. Anita caressed Lisa's hands and sincerely congratulated her.

The three veterans couldn't hold back. While Anita turned to Alana, they embraced and examined their medals. Cammi cried, "Oh, my God, they're so beautiful! They're absolutely beautiful!" Karyn said, "And they're ours! They're all ours!" The three women laughed and turned to embrace Alana. And then Colleen, Angela, and Jenny. As Anita continued her duties, they again held hands and watched their joy ripple down the human chain.

Twelve medals and bouquets later, Anita DeFranz stood before Sarah Tueting, the final American athlete awaiting a medal. "Last but not least," she said as Sarah bowed her head. Cammi, Karyn, Lisa, and their teammates watched attentively as Anita prepared to make the last piece of a shared dream come true. Sarah's face was beaming. She had had the pleasure of seeing every one of her teammates receive her medal. Now they all watched together as Sarah received hers. Sarah's rosy cheeks exploded into color as the ribbon and gold medal were placed around her neck. When she received her bouquet, she lifted it above her head. Her teammates followed suit. Team USA, glistening in gold, proud and patriotic, raised their American flags and bouquets of flowers and saluted the audience. The crowd exploded in applause and roared its approval. As they roared, the beautiful melody which had punctuated the presentation ceremony faded and was gone.

The announcers interrupted the chanting. Once again they spoke in French, English, and Japanese: "And now, the playing of the national anthem of the United States of America."

Karyn gulped as all eyes turned to the color guard, who stepped forward and released the national banners. On the center rod, between the red maple leaf of Canada and the blue cross of Finland, the stars and stripes began to ascend. Karyn looked quickly at the bench. The coaches and staff stood shoulder-to-shoulder against the glass. Several placed their hands on their hearts.

When the first notes of "The Star-Spangled Banner" emerged from the sound system, the 1998 U.S. Women's Olympic Ice Hockey Team placed their tired arms around each other's shoulders, focused their swollen eyes on Old Glory, and began to sing out of key, but clearly and passionately, with every ounce of their being. "Oh, say, can you see by the dawn's early light, what so proudly we hailed at the twilight's last gleaming? Whose broad stripes and bright stars, through the perilous fight . . . "

They sang because they were happy. They sang because they were proud. All the hard times were forgotten. They had risen above ridicule and prevailed. They had competed in innocence and been glorified. They had collectively and individually dared to dream and succeeded. "Gave proof through the night that our flag was still there. . . ."

The sparkle that had glittered around them since they first stepped out of the locker room now overwhelmed Karyn and Cammi. Chills ran down their spines. Tears flowed over their smiles. As they sang the final phrase of the national anthem, "O say does that star spangled banner yet wave o'er the land of the free and the home of the brave," the arena exploded with cheering. They had done it. These twenty unknown women had made an impossible dream come true. The audience was thrilled for them. Many eyes in the audience were full of tears. Spectators knew they had just witnessed something historic and admirable.

While the players rejoiced, their coaches and staff slid across the ice to congratulate them. Bob Webster brought Karyn's flag. Ben Smith helped a photographer in street shoes walk on the slippery surface. When Smith reached his euphoric players and staff he asked them to come together for the gold-medal photograph. The two goalies dropped to the ice, placing their heads close to each other and creating a frame with their pads. Their teammates and entourage filled in behind them. Standing in the back row, leaning over his excited players, Smith proudly said, "Okay, Team USA, this one's for the history books." As he spoke, Karyn and her teammates leaned on one another, lifted their Olympic medals, and smiled. When they did so the lights once again sparkled and twenty remarkable American women passed with unconditional joy into the annals of Olympic history.

2

THE UNITED STATES NATIONAL TEAM

"Play with Passion, Play with Pride"

BURLINGTON, VERMONT ~ DECEMBER 17, 1997

Ceremonially, Tara Mounsey folded her red, white, and blue bandanna into a perfect triangle: white stars on a blue field on one side, red and white stripes on the other. Wrapping the bandanna around her head, she pushed her brownish-blond hair under the soft and faded cloth so that stars adorned her temple. She brought two corners of the triangle together at her neck and tied a simple knot. Okay, that's good, she thought. At least my head feels ready.

She could not say the same for the rest of her body. As always, the condition of her knee was questionable. The trainer had attended to Tara's knee to help her through tonight's game, but her neck was stiff and her shoulder muscles were tense. Even her stomach felt queasy. Tara had arrived in the locker room thirty minutes early to prepare for her team's showdown with Team Canada. The United States and Canada were the two best women's ice hockey teams in the world. Tonight's winner in Burlington, Vermont, would have a psychological edge going into the final game of their last international tournament before the Winter Olympics in Nagano. The teams would have another showdown in January, but the countdown to the Olympic Games had started.

Tara not only needed extra time to get ready mentally for this stressful game, but she didn't want to miss one moment of the pregame banter. She loved to listen to the funny stories her teammates told about their families and friends, their tales of crazy adventures, and the tidbits of silly gossip. Sometimes the talk was about a practical joke played on a teammate or a comical remark made by a coach. Other times it was about important events in the news. And more often than not, the players discussed the latest *Oprah* show.

Tonight the mood was different. Tara silently watched all of her teammates complete their own pregame rituals. The Burlington locker room was uncharacteristically quiet as players adjusted straps and tightened laces. Everyone knew this game might be the last time their team would play together. The thought was depressing. Not only might their four-month adventure as a national team end, but the final lineup for what would become the Olympic team was about to be determined. Three players had to be cut by Saturday, leaving the chosen twenty who would meet in Colorado Springs in January to prepare for Nagano. Tara wrapped plastic tape around her shin pads, ripped off the excess, and threw the roll into her locker. Who would be cut? she wondered. So many great friendships had been established. The players shared each other's dreams, respected each other's abilities, and felt almost like sisters. How will I possibly celebrate my own success if my friends' hopes are shattered? she thought. How will I deal with my own disappointment if my friends' dreams come true?

As she sat in her stall dreading the inevitable, Tara's thoughts wandered to a joyful event in October, at the beginning of the national team's 1997 tour. Ben Smith, the team's coach, had intentionally scheduled the national team's first game in the United States in Tara's hometown, Concord, New Hampshire. The members of the American team had been named in late August in Lake Placid. During September the team played games in Sweden and Finland and, of course, their home base, Lake Placid, bonding with each other and their coaches. The Scandinavian trip helped the players gain confidence. But it was the Concord game that introduced the team to the nation.

Tara closed her blue eyes and pictured herself in that distant locker room. Everett Arena was a typical dingy, hangarlike facility with a snack bar at one end and a skate shop at the other. Championship banners hung from the rafters. The aroma of sweaty equipment blended with cinnamon on fried dough. How she had loved that place!

It was in that worn-down building that Tara had played hockey hundreds of times—as a mite, squirt, peewee, bantam, and midget—for the Concord youth hockey program. Her Capitals uniform was red, white, and blue. She had loved the bright red pants with the blue satin seams and white stars. Tara recalled how she had worn the tattered outfit proudly into the ninth grade before she tried out for the Concord High boys' team.

Back then she thought that trying out for the boys' team was almost impossible. It meant smashing barriers, fighting systems, and possibly losing friends. As a fourteen-year-old girl, she wondered how she could possibly play with the older boys. Most of the younger boys who were trying out had been her teammates on the Capitals, and she certainly wasn't intimidated by them. But the older boys—they were formidable.

It was a scary time. Her ninth-grade friends cared more about boyfriends than slap shots. She worried about failing and about what people would say. As she told her father, "I just don't want to try out, Dad, I'm only a freshman. I'm not going to make it."

Mike Mounsey listened carefully and then responded, "You know, Tara, you've got nothing to lose. Why not try it? I think you have a shot."

Tara considered her father's words seriously for several days and then set a personal goal. She would be the first girl to make the varsity boys team, if not during her first year, then in her second.

During the three days of high school tryouts, Tara went out on the ice and gave it her best. Most of the guys were bigger and faster but not necessarily more skilled. On the last day of the tryouts, she listened carefully as Coach Duncan Walsh read the names of the players he had selected. She was euphoric when he said, "There'll be two ninth-graders, one forward and one defenseman, Tara Mounsey."

Six years later, coming back to Concord with the national team, Tara felt incredibly proud. She knew that somewhere in the building her high school teammates would be watching. She cherished the fact that they had voted her team captain in her senior year. She thought about how much she owed those guys who had been so good to her. Being part of that team had made her a better player. It had brought her to the next level. Tara had not realized it during high school, but she knew now that playing with boys had taught her to ignore sexist behavior and stick to her objectives. She discovered that hard work can overcome prejudice and good people can offset bad.

As she sat with her eyes closed, waiting to play Team Canada, Tara realized that the Concord debut two months earlier had been her happiest time with the national team. Coach Smith had given her favorite pep talk that day. As he started, the Everett Arena sound system blasted Aretha Franklin's "Respect": "R-E-S-P-E-C-T . . . Find out what it means to me."

Smith spoke above the racket outside the locker-room door. He reminded them that it would be the first time a U.S. audience would see the 1997 U.S. women's national team—as if they needed reminding. And he went on to say that the situation made him think of one of his favorite Joe DiMaggio stories.

"DiMaggio was an aging athlete late in his career," Smith began. "He was wracked with injuries and pain. A sportswriter was watching him in a game late in September in Yankee Stadium and was impressed by the way he hustled to first base after a seemingly meaningless one-hopper to third. After the game the reporter asked DiMaggio, 'Joe, why are you playing your ass off in a game that doesn't really matter?' DiMaggio answered, 'I'm afraid there may be a youngster out there who hasn't seen me play before and I want to make sure he has the right impression of me.'"

Turning to the young women sitting in rapt attention before him, Coach Smith continued, "Okay, that's the point. It's really important that you play your hearts out. For some of you this is the hometown crowd. For others, it's not. But you're all great athletes and you've all got a lot of pride. And so does this country. In a minute you are going to realize for the first time what it means to be America's team. So go get 'em. Show them you're a great team. And, hey, win one for Joe."

Coach Smith had realized that the opening game was special for everyone, not just Tara and the other players from New Hampshire, Tricia Dunn of Derry and Katie King of Salem. He wanted everyone to excel.

As the team hit the Concord ice, Tara remembered thinking that the scene was surreal. The enormous crowd stood up to cheer. American flags waved in the stands. The loudspeakers blared KISS's "Rock and Roll All Nite." Above the din, she could hear children screaming her name.

The game was a sellout. Fifteen hundred tickets had been sold in ninety minutes. Several players' relatives and friends had lost out in the rush. Arena officials knew they could have sold ten thousand tickets if they'd had the space. The first game was, after all, not simply a national debut for the team but also, as Mark Labore of the *New Hampshire Sunday News* reported, "an emotional New England coming-out party," a reflection of "the love affair between the city of Concord and its favorite daughter." Tara had become a legend.

The crowd applauded energetically as the teams were introduced: first the women of the Eastern Collegiate Athletic Conference All-Stars, and then the U.S. national team. The public-address announcer read the names of the Americans in descending numerical order. Freckle-faced redheaded girls in hockey jerseys bit their fingernails. Relatives held their breath. One name was left. The announcer paused, then shouted at the top of his voice, "Number two, from Concord, New Hampshire, Tara Mounsey!"

The rickety old building shook as Tara skated forward, raised her stick in greeting, and then returned to the blue line. She bowed her head and the crowd cheered louder, acknowledging her achievements with special affection. Fans blinked back tears. Here was an accomplishment unimaginable a generation earlier—a local woman one step away from playing on an Olympic ice hockey team. A woman! Many had known her since she was a kid. Most folks weren't astonished, though, just proud. Tara's historic achievement may have reminded them of another Concord heroine, Christa McAuliffe, America's first teacher-astronaut.

When the Concord game ended, Tara remembered feeling embarrassed by both the attention and the 10–1 national team victory. In the long run, however, the score didn't matter. What did matter was that in every section of the bleachers there were young girls wearing their hockey jerseys. Whereas Tara had had to play on boys' teams, many of these girls now played on girls' teams. The young girls hung over handrails to watch the women players. With "virtual pets" on keychains hanging from their belt loops, they grasped programs for postgame autographs. When the national team entered and exited the locker room, the little girls and their brothers crowded the entryways and touched the players' sleeves. Between periods the girls tracked down injured or resting athletes, dressed alike in Team USA navy blue-and-white warm-ups, and politely gathered signatures and handshakes. Goalie Sara DeCosta, forward Jeanine Sobek, and three other teammates happily complied. At the postgame press conference, Tara noticed adolescent girls with twisted ponytails conducting and videotaping interviews for local cable stations. She asked the girls to send copies to her mother.

Tara's embarrassment faded in the enthusiasm of these children. She reflected with her teammates at the end of the night in Concord, after they had all signed hundreds of autographs, that somehow they had suddenly become role models for these little girls and boys. They had filled a void and become tangible, accessible examples of successful women athletes.

Tara reflected on the growing excitement among young fans—girls and boys—throughout the team's national tour, but particularly tonight as she had entered the Burlington rink through the players' designated entrance. As she walked into the building she noticed flocks of children gathered in the hallways, girls and boys with face paint and hand-drawn signs. They called to the American players by name and wished them luck against the Canadians. Tara never ceased being surprised that girls and boys in different cities around the country actually knew her name.

Tara's thoughts of the children's hero worship at the Concord homecoming and throughout the national tour ended abruptly as Coach Smith noisily entered the Burlington locker room for his pregame soliloquy. Tara opened her eyes. It was time to focus on the present—the fearful, immediate present—which included a major contest and the impending Olympic team selection process.

Smith's simple navy sport coat, checked tie, and hand-painted black sneakers were by now very familiar. The players had suggested he wear dark shoes when he dressed up because his white sneakers, although safer on ice than street shoes, looked goofy. A practical guy who appreciated their advice, he let forward Shelley Looney paint his sneakers black.

The coach cleared his throat. The forwards, who had dressed in an adjacent room, joined the defensemen and goalies in the overcrowded space. Every player sat down and waited. The room fell silent. Many women dropped their gaze. They knew they should look at the coach, but they just couldn't. To catch his eye might be to catch an unwanted signal about the impending cuts.

Tara looked at Smith briefly and then lowered her eyes also. I may have only two hours or, at the most, two days left to enjoy his company, she thought. By morning, I might despise and resent Coach Smith even though he's been wonderful to me. I hope I can handle the disappointment, the bitterness. I hope I can remember the best times and move on.

Smith stood in the middle of the room and spoke in soft tones. "Big game tonight, folks. We've got a super crowd outside. Lots of little kids and millions more watching in TV-land. In a few minutes they're going to meet their U.S. national team. Let's show them what a great team you are.

"So let's get out there and skate hard and shoot straight. Or is it skate straight and shoot hard? Well, you know what I mean. Let's play well and have fun."

Tara listened and thought, That's perfect. No pressure. Short and sweet. She wasn't in the mood for an intense locker-room pep talk.

The room came alive as the players set aside their fears momentarily and grabbed their gear. Tara picked up her white helmet and looked around the locker room. Coach is right, she thought. We are a great team—historic, gifted, proud. Every one of us deserves to go to Nagano. I'm glad I'm one of the youngest. If not this time, next time.

Tara could no longer contemplate disappointment. She grabbed her mouth guard and marched confidently to the locker-room exit. She was one of six American starters who would be introduced on-camera. Remembering the camera close-up, she decided to remove her bandanna. She tossed it in her stall as she lined up behind the starting goalie, Erin Whitten. It felt great to stretch her muscles and work out some of the tension. She smiled at Erin and tapped her on the shoulder. "We can do it, Whitty. You go, girl. Let's beat Canada."

Erin smiled back and quietly wished Tara good luck. Like many goalies, she was reserved. Erin was preparing mentally for the upcoming contest. She was in a state of mind her teammate and fellow goalie Sarah Tueting referred to as "goalie world."

The audience saw Team Canada appear in the hallway. The Canadian skaters, who were to be introduced first, were chanting and yelling, mostly patriotic slogans. Tara wondered why the Canadians were always so noisy. Their boisterous pregame rituals annoyed her. She tuned them out and listened to the audience. The music was blaring and the crowd was roaring. The scoreboard flashed, LET'S MAKE SOME NOISE, and the audience complied. One section of the arena chanted, *"U-S-A! U-S-A!"* Another screamed, *"Can-a-da! Can-a-da!"* Each side tried to outdo the other.

Ben Smith was well aware that Burlington would attract a lively audience when he scheduled the historic first national broadcast of a woman's ice hockey game in Gutterson Fieldhouse on the campus of the University of Vermont. And, of course, he wasn't disappointed. As he waited by the locker room with his team, Gutterson felt exactly the way he wanted it to, pulsating and happy. Kids screamed and whistles blew in every corner of the building as the six starters for Team Canada received their cue and stepped forward to be introduced.

Mike Emrick, the announcer for the special Lifetime Television broadcast, did the honors for the television audience as well as the noisemakers in Gutterson. "Ladies and gentlemen," he announced, "Here are tonight's starting lineups.

"First, for Team Canada, in goal, from Charlesbourg, Quebec, number thirty-three, Manon Rhéaume."

With her glistening red helmet already in place and hiding her beautiful face, the first woman to play goalie in a sixty-minute game of professional men's hockey stepped onto the ice and skated to her team's blue line. Most fans were already on their feet; those who were not stood in homage to this respected pioneer in women's athletics.

As the applause gradually subsided, Mike Emrick continued. "At defense, from Edam, Saskatchewan, number nine, Fiona Smith."

The quick-thinking, agile skater and all-around defenseman for the Canadians, wearing her helmet like Manon, skated to the blue line.

"At defense, from Frederickton, New Brunswick, number six, Therese Brisson."

Canada's bravest and most mobile defender took her place.

"At left wing, also from Frederickton, New Brunswick, number fourteen, Kathy McCormack."

Listening carefully to learn which players Canada was starting, Tara thought, Kathy is a prototype power forward and a defender's constant challenge.

Emrick hesitated briefly and then continued, "At right wing, from Kingston, Ontario, number sixteen, Jayna Hefford."

The crowd applauded loudly. Jayna was an opportunistic forward, a top offensive weapon.

"And, at center, from Calgary, Alberta, number twenty-two, Hayley Wickenheiser."

The crowd erupted as Canada's most threatening forward, considered by some to be the best woman player in the world, jumped on the ice. The remaining fourteen Team Canada players skated behind her to their blue line.

Here was arguably the best women's hockey team in the world. Prior to the December 1997 Three Nations Cup tournament, Team Canada had met the American team in international competition on eleven occasions over seven years and had beaten them nine times—four for world championship titles. The Canadians were polished and cocky; after all, they believed they owned the game they called "hockey sur glace." It was their national pastime, their passion and point of pride. Their chic red-and-white uniforms symbolized Canada's tradition of excellence in the sport. To Team Canada, the American women, like the American men, were a bunch of wannabes, a pack of pretenders. Over the border, approximately one hundred miles north of Burlington, millions of souls confidently charted Team Canada's progress toward the Olympic gold medal, exactly two months hence. In the minds of Canadian fans, the first Olympic medals for women's ice hockey were destined to hang on these women. Canada was a team of destiny and these women were the anointed.

When the Canadian team had assembled in order on their blue line, Emrick introduced their opponents. "And now, the starting lineup for Team USA."

The Burlington fans went wild. Unlike their rivals, the American players wore no helmets and the cameras and audience could see their faces clearly.

"In goal, from Glens Falls, New York, number thirty-four, Erin Whitten."

The audience applauded excitedly. The first woman goalie to win a professional men's hockey game looked poised. She too was a remarkable pioneer. Erin wore her golden-blond hair in an all-American ponytail, which bounced as she walked in her heavy pads and equipment up to the camera through a canopy of banners.

Erin's dream was to play in the gold-medal game in Nagano and defeat the Canadians in a shutout. To get there she would have to demonstrate greater skill than the two younger goaltenders still on the American roster. Coach Smith had arranged the goalie assignments so that Erin, Sara DeCosta, and Sarah Tueting would face Team Canada three times each. This plan would simplify the selection process. Tonight was Erin's biggest challenge. Her record thus far was 0 and 2 versus Canada. The two younger goaltenders had better records. Erin told Lifetime Television's interviewer that she was hoping to prove herself in Burlington and earn a place on the Olympic squad. It was a phenomenal opportunity. She could secure a spot on the first U.S. Women's Olympic Ice Hockey Team by winning the first nationally broadcast women's contest. Millions of viewers rooted for her as she bounced onto the ice and bobbed toward the opposite blue line.

The camera turned to Tara next and caught her doe-in-the-headlights expression—bright-eyed, alert, and focused. Mike Emrick introduced her: "At defense, from Concord, New Hampshire, number two, Tara Mounsey."

The Burlington audience, like the one in Concord, cheered loudly. Tara was becoming well known nationally. Many New Englanders knew her because she had been voted the 1997 Eastern Collegiate Athletic Conference and Ivy League Rookie of the Year during her first year at Brown. Her defensive prowess and exceptional slap shot drew raves from reporters. Photographers liked her beautiful smile. As she skated toward Erin, waiting alone on the blue line, Tara caught a glimpse of a sign that read TARA ROCKS. She recognized the phrase and knew immediately that her University of Vermont friends had gotten tickets. She glided to the blue line tipping her head to her friends, who went crazy.

Chris Bailey, Tara's partner on defense, stepped forward.

"At defense, from Marietta, New York, number twenty-four, Chris Bailey."

Chris's adorable face, round and rosy-cheeked, appeared framed in the blue field of white stars on her uniform's bandanna. The blue cloth accentuated her bright blue eyes. Chris peeked quickly at the camera and jumped onto the ice.

A veteran defenseman, Christina Bailey, fondly known as "Bails," was proud to be starting. She loved playing hockey, craved competition, and enjoyed facing the Canadians. Chris had made her national team debut in 1994, after an outstanding career at Providence College. She had since proven that she was extremely competent in the big games when everything mattered. A powerful skater, she could go stride for stride with the fastest forwards. Few could get around or by her. She was a stopper. Chris would do anything necessary to break up a power play, confound a two-on-one, or protect her goalie. She was ferocious.

But Chris Bailey's off-ice personality was quite different. She was full of fun and very much the sentimentalist. Chris had lost her beloved father when she was thirteen years old. After Albert Bailey's death, Chris became extremely close to her mother, Barbara, who raised her and her younger sister, Danyel, as a single parent. Chris carried a stuffed bunny in her duffel bag and dreamed about celebrating her twenty-sixth birthday in Nagano on February fifth. She knew that the coach had seven defenders on the roster, however, and that every one of them was excellent. She doubted that he would take seven to Japan. After all, some of the forwards could also play defense, and not every defender was strong on offense. Like Erin and Tara, Chris was worried. Tonight was a big game for her, too. She had to play great defense.

The first of the Americans' starting forwards entered the spotlight.

Emrick announced, "At left wing, from Dorchester, Massachusetts, number nineteen, Stephanie O'Sullivan."

Stephanie was ready to go. Like so many of her teammates, she had "freon in her veins" and was always ready to play. Stephanie grew up with seven brothers and three sisters in Dorchester, Massachusetts, a working-class suburb of Boston. Her father and five older brothers taught her to love hockey. When she was old enough, her dad brought his skinny little daughter to the local youth hockey registration session but was told she couldn't register. Twenty-four hours later he brought short-haired "Stephen" to the sign-up and enrolled "him." What was one more O'Sullivan brother when the program had already enrolled five ahead of him? It turned out that "Stephen" was a natural.

For the next twelve years Stephanie's mother and father enjoyed watching their talented daughter play this "boys' game" as well as many boys. Like Tara, she was a mainstay on her high school's boys' team, and mighty Matignon High School in Cambridge, Massachusetts, was a hockey powerhouse. From Matignon, Stephanie entered Providence College and became a record-setting Lady Friar. Unfortunately, Stephanie's dad, John, a linesman for the Boston Edison Company, never had the chance to see her win four national championships at Providence and make the U.S. National Team. He died of cancer in 1990, two years before Stephanie's mother, Ann, lost her own battle with brain cancer. In the wake of these tragedies, the eleven O'Sullivan children grew closer together. The older kids bought their parents' house, took custody of their younger siblings, and established the O'Sullivan Hockey Academy Foundation. Each year Stephanie and her siblings, including younger brother Chris, a National Hockey League player, awarded scholarships to needy children in greater Boston.

Earning a gold medal was Stephanie's special dream. She couldn't wait to get to Nagano, walk in the Opening Ceremonies, and get started. Like everyone else, she thought about the cuts. But she wouldn't let them get her down. She put her blade on the ice and hustled to her blue line.

Stephanie's winger on the starting line moved forward. Emrick continued, "At right wing, from Saugus, Massachusetts, number nine, Sandra Whyte."

Sandra looked straight into the camera with her dark brown eyes and conveyed a simple message: *We are on a mission.* At twenty-seven, Sandra was one of the sages on the American squad. She had skated in organized hockey for almost twenty-two years, seven of them as the only girl on the roster. She learned to skate with the Saugus "Rinky Dinks" at age five and moved up on recreational teams into secondary school. Like many of her teammates, she did not play on the local public high school's boys' team and instead persevered outside school on competitive coed and girls' teams in Saugus and neighboring Stoneham. While doing so, Sandra excelled in the classroom, earning entrance to and, in 1992, a degree from Harvard College. A three-sport athlete, Ivy Leaguer, and veteran of numerous unsuccessful world championship finals against the Canadians, Sandra had a singular objective: to beat Canada for the gold medal. She was determined to discover the Canadian team's weaknesses and exploit them. She would outsmart or outmuscle them, but eventually she would help Team USA beat them. She knew it was doable.

Sandra's passion was deep-seated. She was a scholar-athlete who had set aside personal plans to play for her country. She had prepared specifically for the Olympics for five years as an amateur, living with her parents and deferring decisions about her relationships and career. Sandra's three college roommates were now professionals: two were doctors, one was a lawyer. She admired their successes and wanted to join them in opening doors for younger girls. For Sandra Whyte, winning the first gold medal in ice hockey would serve this higher purpose. She believed that the women of Team USA, and the coaches who guided them, had something important to prove. They would make their point boldly, under the white-hot spotlight of the world's most cherished international event, the Olympics. Sandra wasn't fooling around. For her, this was a historic venture. She jumped onto the ice and skated quickly to her blue line.

Mike Emrick introduced the last American starter, Team USA's captain: "And, at center, from Downers Grove, Illinois, number twenty-one, Cammi Granato."

The applause for the American captain was deafening. A brown-eyed brunette, Catherine Michelle Granato was the poster girl of the American team and, more important, its leader. She looked into the camera with resolve. This was her team and she was proud of it. Feminine and forceful, Cammi was one of three players to earn a place on every national team since its inception in 1990. In 1996, USA Hockey had named her its Woman Player of the Year.

Cammi learned to play hockey and lots of other sports with her brothers in their basement, backyard, and living room. She had the most fun with her brother Robby, who was close in age and equally daring. She and Robby would run, throw, catch, skate, and shoot untiringly, often competing with older siblings Don and Tony, who would show no mercy. Little Sister earned the nickname "Cammi the Kamikazi" for her derring-do and outright tenacity. She was a beauty and a fighter, Mona Lisa in shoulder pads.

Cammi's parents, Natalie and Don, unlike the other national team parents, knew Coach Smith and the drill that would follow if their child became an Olympian. Their son Tony, a standout with the National Hockey League's San Jose Sharks, had been coached by Smith and the legendary Dave Peterson during the 1988 Olympic Games in Calgary, Alberta. The Granato family, including older sister Christina and younger brother Joey, were excited that Cammi's commitment to her goal—advancing women's ice hockey—was paying off. Cammi had petitioned for a women's Olympic team in the early 1990s, knowing the excitement and opportunity the Olympics had brought her older brother. She traveled with her family to see Tony compete in Calgary 1988 and found it thrilling. If American men could win a medal in hockey, she thought, then American women should be able to do so also. Cammi was elated in 1992 when the International Olympic Committee announced that women could compete in 1998.

In February 1998, the American poster girl was expected to lead the historic U.S. Olympic Team to Nagano. But Cammi wasn't looking that far ahead. Tonight she wanted the first televised Team USA–Team Canada showdown to be a victory, an omen for the future. She was tired of coming in second, of wearing silver, of hearing "O Canada" instead of "The Star-Spangled Banner" sung at world championships. Cammi wanted to beat Canada tonight, win the Three Nations Cup tournament on Saturday afternoon, and make the U.S. Olympic team on Saturday night—without fail and in that order.

As the captain of Team USA skated to her place on the blue line, her unannounced teammates poured onto the ice surface around her in a blaze of red, white, and blue. Behind them both teams' coaches, trainers, and equipment managers slid carefully in painted sneakers and street shoes to their benches. Then forty-three women, representing the finest women athletes of two nations, stood at attention while the first woman president of the University of Vermont, Judith Ramaley, welcomed the live television audience to the historic contest about to unfold.

Waiting impatiently for President Ramaley to finish, the twenty Canadian players held a significant psychological advantage over the twenty-three Americans facing them. Each Canadian already knew she was an Olympian. The Canadian coach, Shannon Miller, had made her selections and announced the team roster early in December, before the Three Nations Cup tournament started in Lake Placid on December thirteenth. Miller caught flak from some pundits for naming the team that early, but the strategy seemed to be working. Team Canada was relaxed and excited. Their Olympic gear, already a fashion statement across Canada, was being sized and prepared for their adventure in Nagano. No Canadian was wasting psychic energy worrying about being released from the team.

The Burlington game was part of the Three Nations Cup tournament round-robin. Each team had to play four games in six nights in three cities, and, if successful, a championship game on Saturday, December 20. The tournament had begun and would end in Lake Placid. The other games were played in Burlington, Vermont; Saratoga Springs, New York; and two cities in Canada. The Burlington contest was the fourth game for the Americans and their second meeting with Canada, who had won the first match.

Ben Smith had very intentionally not named his team before this tournament. He wanted to watch the three goalies, seven defenders, and thirteen forwards left on his roster perform against Finland and Canada, the likely medal contenders in Nagano. Why not evaluate each prospect in action against the world's best? He felt the cuts were going to be rotten Christmas presents for everyone anyway, so why not be sure the final three calls were the right ones?

The selection process was Smith's most dreaded responsibility. He hated making and delivering the decisions. It was a sad and serious business and, even though he understood that it was important to do it right, there was no perfect method. Someone was always heartbroken and more than a few got angry. Smith had learned a lot about the process in thirty years of high school and college coaching, but it didn't get any easier with time.

Smith dreaded making Olympic selections more than others. In August he had released twenty-nine Olympic hopefuls who had been invited to the tryout camp in Lake Placid. Players and parents had been devastated. Some publicly expressed their disappointment to Smith in the lobby of the Olympic Training Center. Given that the national team could carry only twenty-five skaters, twenty-nine outstanding women athletes had received one of the worst disappointments of their lives, then packed their bags and gone home to deal with it.

In some ways, the initial selection process in August had been the more difficult. There had been a limited amount of time in which to observe and evaluate a large group of talented athletes. Smith had become concerned about misjudging a player's ability if someone wasn't feeling well or was having a few bad days on the ice. He had agonized over every decision, knowing there would be no second chance for the athletes he released. It was a different situation for the players who survived the first cut. Once an athlete made the national team, she had four months to prove herself and impress the coach. If she showed up in practice every day and had numerous great games against Canada and Finland throughout the fall, she could win his approval. Smith knew that he would have ample time to assess the skills of the twenty-five national team players in comparison to each other and the world's best competition.

Having a longer assessment period for the players who made the 1997 U.S. national team did not make the final selection process any less gut-wrenching. On December 7, Pearl Harbor Day, Smith had notified two of the original twenty-five national players, Californian Barbara Gordon and Minnesotan Jeanine Sobek, that they would not be advancing. He delivered the news in a New Jersey hotel after a long bus ride from LaGuardia Airport. The team had flown into New York from Minneapolis after a game in Winnipeg, Manitoba. Two nights earlier they had played in Minneapolis and enjoyed a nice dinner and sendoff from the Minnesota girls' teams' regional district. The three Minnesota natives on the national team—Jeanine of Coon Rapids, Jenny Schmidgall of Edina, and Alana Blahoski of St. Paul—were honored at the dinner.

When the team got off the bus in New Jersey forty-eight hours later, Smith gave a directive: "Put your luggage in your rooms and join me in the conference room in five minutes. Don't be late."

The players were concerned and suspicious. They figured either he was laying down more ground rules or something important was about to happen.

When the players entered the hotel meeting room, most of the Team USA staffers were present. They saw team leader Amie Hilles, athletic trainer Jeanna Schepman, equipment manager Bob Webster, and public-relations manager Kris Pleimann waiting quietly. No one knew why Smith had called them together.

Smith took attendance, walked to the front of the room, and asked for silence. Then he began. "I know people here understand the difficulties of the decisions that are approaching. Everybody must realize that good players are going to be left behind.

"I want the team present because we have done everything as a team. The twenty players who go all the way will be going as twenty-five in spirit. I feel that and I know that to be true. I also know that the players left behind will continue to pull for their team because it is their team. Nobody should leave in a negative way.

"For the members who are left behind, it is not because they failed. This process is very, very, very subjective. And I know, and I want you to know, that ultimately the decisions are mine. I've done everything I can to be fair. God knows, I don't expect you to agree. But know that I have done my best."

Smith looked down at the floor, took a deep breath, and then raised his eyes and looked directly at Jeanine and Barbara. "At this point in time, I have decided to release Jeanine Sobek and Barbara Gordon. I wanted to do this here so that these players could be with their teammates and friends."

Smith walked over to the two stunned athletes, shook their hands, and thanked them publicly for their outstanding contributions to USA Hockey generally and the women's program specifically. While everyone in the room tried to grasp what was happening, he added, "Jeanine and Barb, if either of you have any questions, my room number is 647. Amie Hilles will assist you with travel arrangements and Bob Webster will help you with your equipment." Then the coach abruptly left the room.

Smith knew Barb's and Jeanine's release would devastate them individually and scare their teammates. That was an inevitable part of the dynamic. He also knew that each individual would handle the disappointment differently.

Barb handled the situation stoically. The former Colby College star said to her friends, "What can I say, guys? It's been great. I wish you luck." Then she packed her bags, said good-bye to her teammates, and went up to the coach's room to thank him personally for the opportunities he had provided. Her teammates knew Barb was a trouper and would be okay. As one team member said, "Barb always has stuff in perspective, and she's always pullin' for everyone—not just herself."

This teammate was correct; Barb was rooting for everyone. Several weeks later, when Smith announced the Olympians, she sent a letter of best wishes to the entire team.

Jeanine's release was as upsetting to two of her teammates as it was to her personally. Shelley Looney considered "Sobie" her mentor, role model, and inspiration. At Northeastern University, where Jeanine had had a remarkable hockey career, Shelley looked up to her as a leader, an older and wiser peer. Sue Merz considered Sobie a soul mate. Sue grew up in Greenwich, Connecticut, and attended the University of New Hampshire, a rival of Northeastern. She and Jeanine were intercollegiate opponents, but had become good friends serving on five national teams where they weathered the ups and downs of international competition. Shelley, Sue, and Sobie formed a tight trio. It was Jeanine who made absurdities seem funny. It was Jeanine who helped people feel good about themselves. And she was a terrific player! "How could Coach cut you?" Shelley and Sue asked.

Shelley and Sue cried while their friend gathered her belongings. Jeanine had to travel back alone to the city that had just feted her. All three women went into mourning. After sharing so much time together reaching for a dream, they had to accept the painful reality that for one the dream had ended.

After Barb and Jeanine departed, Smith felt the team's anxiety intensify. His conversations with individual players became brief and uncomfortable. All of them seemed to be thinking, What is Coach looking for? What are his criteria? Am I, is everybody, on the bubble?

In point of fact, in Ben Smith's mind, just about everybody was "on the bubble" and knew it, or should have. He had told all of the players named to the national team that the final selections for the Olympics would be made sometime in December. He did not specify a time or place. He said there would be no appeals or reconsiderations. His decisions would be final.

Smith had a great deal of experience releasing players, but he also received a lot of advice from colleagues. Some former Olympic coaches worried that Ben's good nature would impair him. Lou Vairo, who had the unenviable task of coaching the 1984 U.S. Men's

Olympic Ice Hockey Team following the gold medal "miracle on ice" performance by the 1980 team, expressed his concerns. "I'm really worried about you, Ben," Vairo said. "I don't know if you're selfish enough to do this thing right. You've got to do what's best for the team, and what's best for the team will be best for the coach."

Smith listened carefully to Vairo and other coaches who shared their wisdom. Smith knew that cutting Olympic hopefuls was a brutal exercise, but that selecting the right team was imperative. He had to believe he had the best players, young and inexperienced or older and wiser, but in any case, the best. When all was said and done, Smith had to believe that he was getting off the bus in Nagano with the best team. That meant making many tough decisions and a few lifelong enemies. While there was a selection committee made up of several college coaches and USA Hockey officials, the deciding vote on each player would most likely rest with Smith. He had watched the women on the roster in Burlington play in as many as nineteen games during the team's national tour. Some had also played during a tour in Scandinavia in September. Ben Smith knew that tonight in Burlington, or sometime in the next three days, he had to make and communicate the final selections.

When the president of the University of Vermont finished her remarks and handed ceremonial game pucks to the rival captains, Stacy Wilson and Cammi Granato, the Burlington game finally got under way. Mike Emrick explained that no national anthems would be played. Instead, as an incentive during the tournament and to mirror the Olympic medal ceremony, it had been decided that only the winner's anthem would be played at the end of the game.

Three female American referees, all of whom had been selected to officiate at the Olympic Games, took their positions: Vicki Kale of Jackson, Michigan; Evonne Young of Roseville, Minnesota; and Deb Parece of Medway, Massachusetts. They, like the players and coaches, would be stepping into Olympic history in February.

The referee whistled the starters to center ice. Huddled around their goalies at opposite ends of the rink, the Canadian and American players were listening to their captains' final remarks. Tara watched Cammi's face as she spoke. Cammi looked at every player intently. She was an exceptional leader who had earned the respect of all of her teammates. When Cammi finished speaking, the huddle exploded with a resounding *"USA!"* Skating away, each player tapped Erin Whitten's goalie pads with her stick. Erin didn't notice. Behind her red-white-and-blue mask she was deep in goalie world.

Tara took her place on the ice and prepared for the opening face-off. She bent her knees, positioned her stick, and stared at the ref's right hand. She felt perspiration on her brow and regretted having removed her bandanna. The opposing centers, Cammi and Hayley, readied themselves in the face-off circle. Watching them place their sticks on the ice, Tara said three short prayers: one for her teammates, one for Coach Smith, and one for herself.

"Get Ready for This," 2 Unlimited's rock anthem, blared on the public-address system and Tara's heart started to pound. The rhythm of the music rattled the rafters. The cheers of the crowd rattled her bones. Tara bit her lip and resolved to play her best game ever. *You know, Tara,* she said to herself, *you've got nothing to lose. Why not go for it? I think you've got a shot.* The official threw down the puck. Cammi slapped it first and Stephanie took possession for the Americans.

Was this a good omen? It was too early to tell. As always, Team Canada came out busting. Miller rotated her lines: 1, 2, 3, and 4; 1, 2, 3, and 4. Every player pressed. Every skater forechecked.

Team USA looked a little shaky. Their arrival in Burlington at two o'clock in the morning, after a 6–2 win against Finland in Saratoga Springs, hadn't helped. The Canadians, who had had the night off, looked crisper and faster. The Americans seemed tentative. No one wanted to make a mistake.

Lisa Brown-Miller checked a Canadian player and was sent to the penalty box. On the broadcast platform, Mike Emrick and guest commentator Margaret Degidio "Digit" Murphy, the Brown University women's ice hockey coach, expanded on the theme that "the road to Nagano goes through Burlington." They noted that the trip had been filled with many sacrifices for the American players, especially the older ones who were the pioneers in their sport. Emrick and Murphy offered thirty-one-year-old Lisa Brown-Miller as an example.

Five-foot-one-inch Lisa, a fleet-footed forward from Michigan, didn't think of herself as a pioneer, but simply someone who loved to play the game. Her parents, friends, and coaches knew better. Lisa was not simply a pioneer in women's athletics, she was also tenacity personified. In 1972, when Lisa first asked her mother and father to sign her up for the Waterford, Michigan, youth hockey program, she didn't know or care that hockey was considered a "boys' thing." Lisa was simply a determined child.

At that time, twenty-six years earlier, while Lisa laced up her skates as the only girl on a boys' hockey team, civil rights activists were introducing Title IX legislation into Congress. Lisa was symbolic of all of the little girls whose educational opportunities the legislators wished to codify. Advocates argued that she should have equal opportunity in all programs associated with her education, including athletic programs. Lisa, of course, knew nothing about Title IX. She was simply a child who instinctively expected that girls and boys would have equal rights. Her parents—out of love, admiration, and appreciation for her tenacity—supported her.

The support was at first apprehensive. Lisa's father, Bob, imagined kids dropping their gloves and fighting like the gladiators in the National Hockey League. "What, my little girl?" he asked. But when Bob Brown saw that the hockey program's "atoms" and "mites" could neither skate nor shoot and, in fact, could barely move under shirts that hung to their knees and pants that dragged at their ankles, he said, "Okay, Lisa, what's the harm?" Then he brought his excited daughter to Sears for a tiny pair of hockey skates and doll-size equipment. Lisa's mother, Jean, shared the driving to early morning practices and games, and shocked a few parents in the stands with her loud and enthusiastic cheer, "Go Lisa!"

For four years, during both the winter and spring seasons, petite Lisa Brown played in boys' hockey leagues in Michigan, where inspired coaches like Gary Root always encouraged her and silenced her detractors. Root could tell that this child's enthusiasm wasn't a statement about gender. Lisa just loved to play—with the guys in the neighborhood, the kids at the Lakeland Arena, and the boys on opposing teams. Committed and self-motivated, she would give 110 percent and leave the rink smiling. Little Lisa Brown was a coach's dream.

When Lisa reached the midget level in high school and chose not to play boys' hockey, she switched to girls' teams and tried to attract the attention of college coaches who were starting women's ice hockey programs. Many schools were adding women's teams to move into compliance with Title IX. Lisa picked Providence College, which had a women's team with corresponding scholarships. She excelled at Providence from 1984 to 1988 and then moved to the varsity women's coaching position at Princeton University.

Lisa loved coaching Princeton's women's hockey team and stayed for seven years. Between seasons, she played on every U.S. National Women's Ice Hockey Team. She left her job in the Ivy League to try out for the first Olympic team. For twenty-six years, in her quiet but tenacious way, Lisa Brown from West Bloomfield, Michigan, had redefined girlhood and offered living proof that Title IX was justified. Although she loved her job at Princeton, there was no way she would miss the opportunity to compete to be an Olympian.

Ben Smith learned about Lisa's tenacity on the day before he started his audition for the Olympic coaching position. USA Hockey officials hired him in August 1995 to select twenty women, organize practices for four or five days, and then coach their team in Finland during a four-game series with the Finnish national team. While preparing to leave for this assignment, Smith received a call from Art Berglund, the senior director of international administration at USA Hockey. Berglund said, "Ben, one of the candidates for the trip to Finland, a woman by the name of Lisa Brown, has a problem with the training camp. She's getting married on Saturday and the camp starts on Sunday. She can't be there until Monday. She needs one day for a honeymoon."

The neophyte women's hockey coach, who at that point had neither coached nor mentored a single woman player, wasn't sure what Berglund was proposing that he do about Lisa's timing conflict. Smith responded, "Hell, who cares, Art? I certainly don't. If she wants to come late, fine. It's no skin off my nose. If she wants to play hockey that bad, let her come. I'm not going to tell her she can't. But, if you don't think she should be allowed to come late, well . . ."

Realizing that Smith was unclear about what he was suggesting, Berglund interrupted, "No, no, Ben, you misunderstand what I'm saying. She's a terrific player! She's the women's hockey coach at Princeton! What I'm saying is let's give her the weekend for the wedding. Let's tell her it's okay."

Smith agreed, never having met Lisa. He wondered if she would be as dedicated as Berglund had suggested. Two days later, much to Smith's amazement, the blushing bride was doing skating drills with him in Lake Placid. He couldn't have been more impressed. Like Gary Root in Michigan, he realized he was dealing with a special type of athlete, a coach's player.

Now, while Lisa Brown-Miller sat in the penalty box, newscasters Digit Murphy and Mike Emrick showed clips of Lisa and John Miller's wedding for the television audience. Murphy pointed out that Lisa and John had not been able to celebrate their first anniversary together because Lisa again had to be at hockey camp in Lake Placid. John stayed in Michigan, where he worked for General Motors.

John Miller knew the road to Nagano would be unforgiving, but he respected his wife's abilities and dedication and did not want her to have any regrets. Lisa wanted John to be proud of her, to know she had done the best she could to fulfill her dream. And they both wanted to be positive role models for the little Millers who would hopefully come along one day. As Murphy and Emrick reminded the television audience, Lisa Brown-Miller and all the amateur athletes on the women's national team were constantly sacrificing their personal lives to qualify for the Olympics.

Team Canada would not make the sacrifice any easier. With Lisa still in the penalty box, and the American team short-handed by one player, Jayna Hefford scored a power-play goal to Erin Whitten's left, making the score 0–1. Hayley Wickenheiser and Danielle Goyette assisted. These three—Hefford, Wickenheiser, and Goyette—were the most potent offensive line in women's hockey. Team USA feared and respected them. Smith preferred to put out regular lines rather than special units of penalty killers to stop them when they had a power play.

As the action continued, Tara Mounsey took a hard shot on her foot and skated to the bench to shake off the pain. Trainer Jeanna Schepman tried to assist her. Jeanna could tell the injury hurt. The coaches watched Tara closely. They could not afford to lose her. Tara was as tough as they get, but she had already suffered a number of serious injuries. In high school Tara had torn her anterior cruciate ligament (ACL), a major supporting ligament of the knee, which had required reconstruction. The ACL tear had kept her on the Concord High bench instead of on the ice for over a year.

Karen Nystrom of Canada hooked Sandra Whyte and was sent to the box. Team USA set up the power play with Karyn Bye at the point rather than wing. The rest of the team looked tentative, but not K.L. She skated deftly behind the Canadian net and passed to Chris Bailey at the right point. Chris fired a perfect pass to Gretchen Ulion in the slot. Gretchen beat Manon with a backhand to tie the game 1–1.

The eruption in the stands was deafening. Girls in black-and-yellow Rutland Area Hockey Association jerseys screamed, "We will, we will rock you!" while boys standing near them waved a huge sign that read NOT BAD FOR A GIRL! Security guards in University of Vermont uniforms slapped each other on the back and a little boy in a red-and-white sweater with a Christmas tree embroidered on the front kissed his father. Beside him, a brother and sister dressed in purple joined a wave that moved quickly around the arena. The cry "U-S-A!" reverberated through the building.

Team USA's power-play unit hugged Gretchen in the corner and skated to the bench for high-fives with teammates. There would be no shutout for Manon, who wore number 33 like her idol, the legendary goalie Patrick Roy. Tara thought, This game is winnable.

The pace picked up immediately. Team USA was gaining confidence. The offense and defense attacked in waves of five. Everyone was digging. Everyone was skating hard. An all-out American forecheck annoyed the Canadians, who preferred a neat and tidy game where they controlled the action. The Americans, who knew that a controlled game would be a losing one, picked up the pace with a helter-skelter style that confused Canada's defense.

The strategy worked. With about five minutes left in the period, American forward Laurie Baker broke away at center ice and passed to wing Katie King on her left. Katie, who had scored two goals the night before against Finland, came barreling down on the left. Katie was a premier American forward and the all-time leading scorer at Brown. Laurie was also a sniper and a sophomore standout at Providence. Katie returned the pass to Laurie, who outskated her defender and tipped the puck past Manon, who was waiting instead for Katie to shoot. Pandemonium ensued as Team USA went ahead 2–1.

When the period ended shortly thereafter, the atmosphere was jubilant. Two UVM Zambonis, each with a pouncing catamount painted on its chassis, glided across the ice quickly and efficiently. Mike Eruzione, Lifetime Television's celebrity color commentator, quickly interviewed Ben Smith before he escaped into the locker room. Smith told Eruzione that he thought the women's teams had come out flying. Commenting on the fabulous crowd involvement, Smith added that he and his team were happy to be in Gutterson Fieldhouse in the wonderful environment that outstanding Vermont teams, coached by Jimmy Cross and Mike Gilligan, had helped to build. Eruzione agreed. The Vermont crowd was extremely enthusiastic.

Earlier in the television broadcast, the audience had been shown clips of Mike Eruzione's historic game-winning goal against the Russian Olympic team in Lake Placid in 1980. The Burlington audience recognized Eruzione immediately and mobbed him when he stepped into the stands, making it difficult for him to interview an excited group of girls from Middlebury who wore red-white-and-blue face paint. The girls' face paint radiated light under the hot television cameras. Their spokesperson, a young woman with a starry face that mimicked Chris Bailey's bandanna, told Eruzione that the Middlebury girls went all out with their makeup because the U.S. women's team had inspired them. The girls then mugged for the cameramen and television audience.

During the break, feature commentator Maura Driscoll interviewed Shannon Miller about the two teams' intensifying rivalry. Dressed in her signature black sweater, black jacket and pants, Miller explained to Driscoll that Team Canada had defeated the Americans in four final games in the annual world championships, and to date led them, once again, in contests being played in a pre-Olympic tour. She also told Driscoll that because she was the only woman coach in any venue of the 1998 Olympic Games, she was receiving enormous support. People wanted her and Team Canada to prevail. She was paving the way for women coaches everywhere. She intimated that she was the sentimental favorite.

In the Team USA locker room at the end of the first period, Tara consulted the trainer about her bruised foot while her teammates rested and rehydrated. Tara could hear the crowd outside singing the Village People's ever-popular song "YMCA," and envisioned children awkwardly spelling out the letters of the title with their bodies and extremities.

Smith walked into the locker room and told his players to pick up the pace and stay out of the box. He said they needed a strong second period to hold the lead. He then escorted Team USA back onto the ice amid cheers of adulation.

Much to Smith's delight, his players responded immediately. Two minutes into the second period, the referee sent Canadian Therese Brisson to the penalty box for hooking. Katie King, skating on the power play, converted a pass from Shelley Looney and Laurie Baker into a goal. The score was now 3–1! Fathers in colorful Christmas ties, who had rushed to the game with their kids after work, gave high fives in celebration. Katie, Shelley, and Laurie hugged each other. They sensed they were getting stronger.

Laurie and Katie had been on the same line since March, when they played in the 1997 world championships in Kitchener, Ontario. The American team had lost a heartbreaker in overtime to the Canadians, but these two young players, who complemented each other so well, believed that the Americans had put the Canadians on notice.

Laurie Baker, the younger linemate, was only twenty-one years old. She had stepped out of her junior year at Providence to try to make the historic Olympic team. Laurie had grown up in Concord, Massachusetts, and started as a figure skater. After six months in figure skates she switched to hockey and learned to play on boys' teams. Her brother David included Laurie in street hockey games, in which she liked to play goalie. Laurie enjoyed stopping tennis balls fired at her by David and his friends. The challenge made her competitive. While David helped improve her hockey skills off the ice, her dad, David senior, helped instruct her on the ice, sometimes acting as Laurie's assistant coach. Meanwhile her mother, Sharyn, supported and encouraged her as the only little girl on several Concord Youth Hockey teams. Eventually Laurie switched to the Assabet Valley girls' teams. She also switched from Concord schools to Lawrence Academy, where she excelled in soccer and softball as well as hockey. By the time Laurie reached Providence, she was a national star. She was voted the Eastern Collegiate Athletic Conference's 1995–96 Rookie of the Year and, following an outstanding performance on her first national team, the 1997 USA Hockey Woman of the Year.

Katie loved having Laurie on her line; the two forwards always played well together. Adding Shelley Looney as the third forward, with her speed and playmaking ability, made the line extremely dangerous for every opposing goalie.

Seconds after the face-off following Katie's goal, Cammi Granato gave the Americans further cause to celebrate. Canada failed to clear their zone as Angela Ruggiero and Karyn swarmed at the blue line. Karyn stole the puck, paused for one second, and then passed it to Cammi, who redirected it. The puck richocheted off Manon's skate and into the net.

While the American players congratulated their captain, Shannon Miller wiped her brow and exhorted Team Canada to get more aggressive. Before the arena announcer could enumerate the points on Katie's goal, Therese Brisson grabbed the puck at her own blue line, skated around the entire American team, and pumped the puck between Erin's skates. The end-to-end dash and score through the five-hole instantly quieted the Gutterson Fieldhouse spectators. The Canadians had turned a formidable 4–1 lead into a manageable 4–2 score in less than thirty seconds.

Shannon Miller patted her returning players on the back and Ben Smith grimaced. But the crowd would not be silenced. Teenagers with T-shirts that read PLAY WITH PRIDE, PLAY WITH PASSION jumped up and yelled, "*U-S-A! U-S-A!*" Younger kids sang and danced the macarena during a stoppage in play and then joined the teenagers' chant.

The American fans' enthusiasm did not diminish the Canadian athletes' aggressive attack. Nancy Drolet squirted out of a two-on-one scrum to the right of Erin Whitten and fed a pass to Stacy Wilson, who was circling the net. Wilson beat the unprotected Whitten to make the score USA 4, Canada 3.

There was no time to regroup. It was all-out energy on both sides.

With 8:50 left in the period, Geraldine Heaney grabbed Karyn and pulled her down onto the ice. The official called hooking and gave Team USA a power play. The partisan crown screamed, "*USA, all the way!*" while the American power-play unit fought to control the action. Their efforts were neutralized when Team USA was called for too many women on the ice during a line shift. Smith asked his dependable forward, Allison "A.J." Mleczko to serve the penalty.

Initially Team Canada could not capitalize on its advantage, but it was given a second chance when America's youngest player, Angela Ruggiero, affectionately referred to as "Rugger," hooked an opponent and was given the gate. Angela skated to the penalty box unhappily and joined her teammate A.J.

With five minutes left in the period, the momentum shifted in Canada's favor. Both teams became more physical. Danielle Goyette cross-checked Tara in the back and Tara retaliated with a push. The ref called roughing and told Tara to join Angela, who was still in the box. Tara shook her head in frustration and skated to the box to serve her penalty. Canada had a five-on-three advantage. Tara and Angela watched Erin barely hold off a flurry of opportunities by the advantaged Canadians.

As the final minutes of the second period disappeared, it became clear that the all-out fore-check and cranked-up tempo that had taken the Canadians out of their game earlier were now less effective. The officials didn't like the chaos or physical contact that the Americans' strategy created. The referee was intentionally calling penalties and slowing the tempo. The subsequent power plays—when the team skated up by a player—and penalty kills—when the team skated down by a player—were becoming a problem. The Americans were fatigued. They played better five-on-five with their regular lines than with one player down on special units.

The Canadians had a well-oiled power play. The Americans needed one. Team USA had barely survived two impressive power-play attacks in the last minute of the period. The reversal in the action left the audience thinking Canada was in full control of the game as the teams left the ice for the second intermission. But the Americans were hanging on; they still had a 4–3 lead.

In the Team USA locker room, the personal stress, which had been less apparent during the first break, returned. Things weren't going well. There were errors and lapses. The coach witnessed all of them. Tara wondered, Which mistakes is Coach most upset about? She took a silent inventory of her own performance and that of her teammates.

Stephanie O'Sullivan stepped out of the room for a prearranged interview with Lifetime. The producers were moved by her tragic family history and asked her to share it with the television audience. While photos of John and Ann O'Sullivan and their eleven offspring appeared on the screen, Maura Driscoll asked Stephanie about her father's death from cancer and her mother's terminal brain tumor. In a strong Bostonian accent, the O'Sullivans' oldest daughter explained that she wore two shamrocks on her helmet in honor of her parents and, in their memory, rubbed both shamrocks before each game. After their parents' deaths in the early 1990s, the members of the O'Sullivan clan became a team in and of themselves. They supported each other religiously, providing comfort and counsel. The older siblings coached the younger kids to adopt their parents' values. Stephanie told the interviewer that her dad had told his kids to "work hard and good things will come." Stephanie was living proof. The skinny little girl John O'Sullivan had lovingly called Stephen was now a college graduate who, by the end of the week, was expecting to be an Olympian.

At the end of the interview Stephanie promptly returned to the locker room, where she heard the coach give his third-period instructions. "Okay, folks," Ben Smith said. "This is it. Do us all a favor and stay out of the box so we can roll our lines and tire the Canadians out. The D needs to play tough and give Erin some help. Remember, go fast, but don't hurry. Let's hear 'The Star-Spangled Banner' when this thing is over. And, by all means, let's have fun."

Tara listened and decided to skate with the pain in her foot rather than sit on the bench. After all, she was needed on defense and still felt that she was on the bubble. Everyone was anxious, Tara included. All I need is to be injured and become a factor in a losing game, she thought. Mistakes at this point could have double consequences.

The jarring clatter of cowbells interrupted Van Morrison's "Moondance" as the players reentered the arena. Suddenly the stadium was divided. Canadian fans, who had been somewhat quiet during the early periods, were now ready to be heard. As the athletes stepped onto the ice surface, a war of words and a battle of banners began. A St. Albans girls' team waved Old Glory and chanted *"U-S-A! U-S-A!"* Beside them, a Canadian family fanned the maple leaf and countered with *"Can-a-da! Can-a-da!"* Meanwhile, somewhere in the audience, a would-be peacemaker jingled Christmas bells.

But things were anything but peaceful. Erin skated to her net and looked at the scoreboard. Twenty more minutes to a conclusion. Her team wrapped themselves around the net to listen to Cammi's pep talk. Erin slapped her stick on both goalposts as her teammates broke out of their huddle and wished her good luck. She need to bear down and preserve her one-goal lead.

The Canadians placed their good-luck charm, a plastic doll named "Princess," at the end of their bench. The Americans scoffed at the

Canadian's symbol. The little pampered princess was the antithesis of everything the American women stood for. Cammi hoped her team would soon find a mascot that would represent strong, independent females.

Cammi and Nancy Drolet took the face-off. The wet ice glistened. Every player hustled. Hayley Wickenheiser, the Canadian ace who had thus far been contained, came up with the puck, sped toward Erin, and fired. Erin made a clean save. Team USA broke back up the ice. Sue Merz saw daylight and sent a blistering shot at Manon. The Canadian goalie blocked it spectacularly. Her teammate Jennifer Botterill, Canada's youngest player, found open ice and put a hard shot on the American net. Erin saved it.

Suddenly Katie had a breakaway. She crashed the net at very high speed from the right side. Manon positioned herself; she could see that the "big train" was coming. With no other option, Fiona Smith grabbed Katie from behind and pulled her down. Manon stopped Katie's shot as Katie simultaneously slammed into the boards and Fiona landed on top of her. The referee and several hundred partisan fans immediately signaled for a penalty. Team USA had a power play at 14:06.

Canadian Danielle Goyette, an emotional and outspoken player, lost her head and made remarks that irritated the ref. Trash talk was tolerated, but not insults and arguments. Danielle earned an un-sportsmanlike-conduct penalty and joined Fiona in the box. Team USA now had a five-on-three power play. Smith put out his five best shooters. Miller put out her three best penalty killers.

Erin saw five blue uniforms facing off against three red ones and anticipated an American goal. But she was wrong. Hayley Wickenheiser stole the puck, escaped the zone, and skated in alone. Erin swallowed hard. The nineteen-year-old Canadian was a sniper. Hayley fired. Erin made the save!

Manon braced herself. Five American shooters headed her way and set up in her zone. The forwards passed to their points. Karyn fired a slap shot. Save! Tara rifled another one. Save! The rebound came back to Tara. Save! Sue worked the puck to Shelley. The speedster targeted the right side. Wham! Manon sizzled. Save!

The crowd was buzzing. They could feel the momentum shifting back and forth. Smith tightened his lips and wondered if his defensemen and goalie could hold on. Could his team possibly blow a five-on-three power play?

Jayna Hefford grabbed the puck and came back toward Erin with a vengeance. Jayna wound around the net, knowing she'd be tough for Erin to see. She fired a wrist shot from the right. Erin grabbed the puck efficiently and covered up. The penalties ended. Both sides were now even, but the Americans had squandered a five-on-three advantage.

The face-off took place in Erin's end. Lisa hustled. Stephanie hustled. Chris hustled. But Team USA couldn't get the puck out of the zone. Nancy Drolet launched a missile at Erin, who made a fantastic save. The frenzied pace lit up the crowd. Back-and-forth play was everything they had hoped for. The natives quickly agreed that the game was a "barn-burner."

Again the Americans had trouble clearing the zone after the face-off. Hefford took advantage, but Erin stuffed her. Angela came to Erin's aid in front of the goal mouth by shoving two Canadians face-first into the ice. Kathy McCormack took exception and retaliated. The referee gave Rugger and Kathy a penalty.

There were less than ten minutes to go. The next goal would be critical. Lisa, Shelley, and Katie created a three-on-one rush after the face-off but lost the puck in center ice and watched Danielle Goyette take off in the other direction. Danielle skated hard with Hayley Wickenheiser on her right. Defenseman Sue Merz was the only American playing back. Sue committed and Danielle went around her. Erin now faced two sharpshooters, both with perfect angles. With Erin guessing, Danielle fired the puck through her legs, tying the game and stopping the clock. Danielle did a knee-bending pump for the delighted Canadian fans and embraced her fired-up teammates. Canada was back from a three-goal deficit!

Ben Smith took a deep breath and considered whether or not to pull Erin Whitten. The tournament rules dictated no overtime. Erin had eight minutes to go. She'd be embarrassed if he yanked her on national television when she still had a chance to win the game and be a hero. He decided to give her the opportunity. She deserved it.

Gretchen Ulion and Fiona Smith tangled shortly after the face-off and the official called simultaneous penalties: Fiona for a cross-check, Gretchen for roughing. With seven minutes left, the game would be played four-on-four.

Both teams stepped up the fore-check. Two face-offs took place on Erin's right, first outside the blue line, then inside and close. Both teams battled. Finally A.J. and Sue got the puck over the Canadian blue line. A.J. fired on Manon, forcing a save. At last the Americans had a face-off in the Canadian end.

Team Canada wasn't impressed. They broke the puck out, controlled the neutral zone, and barreled over the blue line toward Erin Whitten. Erin stopped a blast from Brisson and then took a direct shot from Wickenheiser. Smith's mind raced: Can Erin hold on? She's got to. This is what it's all about. We've got to stop the Canadians in situations like this to win a gold medal.

Shannon Miller sensed her team's confidence. Nystrom, Brisson, and Dupuis were flying. Whitten was being shelled. Miller thought the American team looked tired. They were consistently failing to clear their zone.

A.J. won the face-off on Erin's right, but Jayna Hefford grabbed it. She wheeled behind the American net until Angela confronted her. Jayna stickhandled around the American rookie, who then dove to try to stop her. With Angela on her belly, Jayna took aim and sent the puck sailing over Erin's right shoulder. Score!

Jayna's heroics gave Canada the go-ahead goal with only 2:08 remaining. The Canadian bench went crazy. Four unanswered goals!

Ben Smith's heart sank. His facial expression conveyed complete composure, but his gastric juices were churning. You've got to be kidding me! he thought. We were up 4–1. How can this happen? What are we doing wrong? What am I missing? Shit, this is aggravating.

With everything on the line, Smith consulted his assistant Tom Mutch and put out Karyn, Chris, and Lisa. The partisan crowd wanted a win for the Americans. While the appointed players took their positions, the American fans stood and formed a chorus. "U-S-A! U-S-A!" they chanted. "U-S-A! U-S-A!"

Karyn made a crisp pass to Chris, who sent a quick feed to Lisa. Even though Lisa's redirect was perfect, Manon somehow stopped it. The audience took a deep breath. Time was melting away.

Sandra Whyte picked up the puck and zeroed in on the Canadian target. Manon deflected a zinger and the crowd gasped. There were forty seconds left. Smith pulled Erin and sent in another shooter.

The puck stayed in Canada's end, but no one could get off a shot.

Two players tied up the puck and the referee called time with four seconds on the clock.

The cheers became louder while the coaches sketched their strategies. Tommy Mutch helped to mastermind the face-off. This one was critical. The situation called for power. He suggested A.J. at center with Sandra, Katie, Karyn, Tara, and Angela to support her.

The chosen players positioned themselves carefully. The face-off was on Manon's left. The rafters were shaking. Flags were waving madly. The American chant became deafening: *"U-S-A! U-S-A!"* Undeterred, Canadian fans gathered behind Manon's net and screamed over the glass, *"Can-a-da! Can-a-da!"* Mleczko and Wickenheiser, two of the strongest forwards on each team, squared for the face-off. A.J. and Hayley had battled each other many times and in February expected to be facing off again in Nagano.

The referee dropped the puck. This time Wickenheiser prevailed. She muscled the puck to the corner as the final buzzer sounded. Manon leapt into the air as her teammates engulfed her. The joyous Canadians tapped their shiny red helmets while embracing. Shannon Miller hugged her players and shook hands with her associates. What a great win! What a perfect comeback!

The Gutterson Fieldhouse crowd went silent, except for the cheers of the Canadian minority. The atmosphere felt like a balloon losing air or, more accurately, popping. Kids gathered their handmade signs and folded their banners. They knew there would be no autograph session or picture-taking. They watched dejectedly as the two teams shook hands at center ice, then separated to each blue line. With a sense of profound sadness, the Americans in the audience listened while "O Canada," the melodious Canadian anthem, was played for the winners.

The American skaters, avoiding eye contact with each other as well as the spectators, listened remorsefully. Not again, Tara thought, and not on national television. She felt terrible and she knew her teammates did, too. They all knew they had screwed up and disappointed an enormous audience. They knew their coaches would be furious. For certain people, the repercussions would be almost unthinkable.

As the Canadian anthem faded, the two teams hurried to their dressing rooms and the hoarse Gutterson Fieldhouse fans and cheerleaders headed to the exits. In the broadcast booth, Mike Emrick named Canada's Jayna Hefford Player of the Game for scoring two goals, including the winner. With the cheerful, neutral expression that broadcasters assume, he noted that "sixty hard minutes had been fought in Burlington" and the Canadians had prevailed 5–4. He then said good night to his audience as the program's credits and the game's action highlights flashed on the screen. The Lifetime Television technicians synchronized the highlights with the lyrics of Chumbawamba's pop favorite "Tubthumping." Instead of closing with what Ben Smith had hoped would be joyous images of a Team USA celebration, the historic broadcast to American viewers ended with spectacular footage of Team Canada's impressive comeback victory.

After shaking Shannon Miller's hand, Ben Smith marched off the ice thinking, I want the whole thing back. This isn't what was expected and everybody's accountable, including me. Especially me! How could we lose? How could we blow a three-goal lead? For cryin' out loud, this game was our dress rehearsal for Nagano—with the cameras, the press corps, the fanfare, the screaming audience. I can't believe we lost it. I can't believe we let them come back. What a pain in the ass! The whole meltdown happened on national television! What an embarrassment! Smith knew these angry thoughts had to be stifled. Ten paces away cameramen and reporters were waiting. He had to think straight.

Smith's experience now served him well. He grabbed Tom Mutch, pulled him aside, and said, "Tommy, while I'm with the press, lock our dressing room and make the players wait outside the Canadians' locker room. Don't let our players change. Make them stand in their sweaty uniforms. This was a major screw-up. I want the team to decide if they like the outcome. Let them listen to their opponents' celebration and think about the winners' locker room for a while. If one of the players asks, tell them I said to do this." Tom followed orders and locked the door.

Humiliated and disappointed, and with no idea why they could not enter their locker room, Team USA stood awkwardly in the Gutterson Fieldhouse hallway. No one spoke. What was there to say? The staff stood at the back of the line waiting for a cue. Nothing happened. Players leaned against the walls to take pressure off their legs. Perspiration dripped off their chins onto their already soaking hockey jerseys. Their equipment chafed.

Collectively the American women were becoming irritated. Tara's foot was aching and she was anxious to remove her skates. She thought, What's going on here? Is there some kind of problem? This never happens. Our locker room is never locked. Coach won't like this.

Tara could hear the Canadian team celebrating through the open door of their locker room a few feet away. Skaters were screaming patriotic remarks about the significance of their victory. Individuals complimented each other, pointing out the highlights of their comeback. Kudos were exchanged for outstanding plays. Tara recognized certain voices and shook her head. Listening to Team Canada's yelling and screaming on the runway at the start of the game is one thing, she thought, but this is too much. Where is the key? Open the damn door!

Tara shifted her weight. She could tell that her teammates were just as annoyed as she was. The jubilant words pouring into the hallway were grating on their already frazzled nerves.

Team USA's sports psychology consultant, Peter Haberl, watched thoughtfully at the end of the hallway. The American players' facial expressions were revealing. Haberl knew there was a lot to be learned from Benjamin Smith, and it wasn't all about hockey.

Finally the locker-room door opened. Coach Smith stood on the threshold intentionally preventing anyone from entering. He said nothing.

Meanwhile the Canadians continued to scream as though they had just been presented with the Three Nations Cup or the Olympic gold medal. Although thoroughly irritated, Tara was starting to be impressed by the Canadians' pride in themselves and their country. The Canadian women were delighted that they had come back from a three-goal deficit, psyched that they had beaten a great team. They were happy they had done their best and won in front of a huge American audience. Tara rested her injured foot on top of her healthy one and thought, Listening to the Canadians celebrate is painful. It's not that we hate them. It's that we resent them. They're tough and they're competitive, and for that we respect them. But why do they always win the big ones? Why do they always get the prize? After a while, losing to them gets old.

Suddenly Tara realized why she was standing in the hallway. Obviously it wasn't about a key. She stared at her coach. He was making his postgame point without opening his mouth. She didn't like the look on his face. She'd seen it in New Brunswick when he'd kicked a can in the locker room.

When Smith sensed that most of the players had gotten his message, he stepped off the threshold. Team USA immediately spilled into the two-room dressing room. The forwards turned to the right and the defensemen and goalies to the left. Each player went directly to her stall.

When all of his players were settled, Smith started pacing between the two sections of the locker room asking rhetorical questions. Speaking slowly and clearly, he paused after each question. His face was flushed but his voice was calm. "Did you hear the Canadians' postgame celebration?" he asked. "Did you like it? Did you enjoy what they had to say? Do you want to hear it again? Would you like to listen to it seven more times? Would you like to hear the gold-medal version?"

After the final question Smith stopped and looked intently at his players. Very few looked back. No one said a word. In a tone that dripped with disdain he said, "Let's not have to do that again." Then Smith turned, glanced at Peter Haberl, who was standing in the doorway, and left.

Several women unbuckled their chin straps and threw their helmets into their hockey bags. Bob Webster noticed their behavior but decided not to comment. The majority stripped their jerseys and equipment quickly, grabbed their street clothes and towels, and went to the showers in silence. Jeanna attended to the injured players. Bob collected the equipment and bags. Peter observed the scene and made mental notes for later.

Once Tara's injury had been treated, she started feeling terrible, not for herself, but for Erin. Forwards and defensemen never blamed their goalie for a loss. The responsibility was shared by everybody. But goalies were different. They felt they were responsible for the "game-within-the-game," defending the goal, and, therefore, they blamed themselves when the team suffered a defeat. Tara regretted every goal scored when she was out on defense. But at the end of the game the goalies weren't thinking about the five players trying to protect them. They thought only about their own decisions and whether or not they were the right ones.

Even though this game felt extremely important to Tara, she wondered if Erin placed more importance on it. As long as her foot and knee held out, Tara felt she would have one more chance. But this was it for Erin, her last start. Tara leaned over to Erin's stall and said, "Erin, it's all right. You played well. We lost as a team."

The goaltender didn't look up. She was weeping softly while she methodically removed her equipment. Erin didn't appear ungrateful for the soothing words. Rather, she was processing the loss and preferred to do it privately. Tara understood. Erin's tears were blending with her perspiration and burning her eyes and cheeks. Tara turned away sadly and continued her own postgame ritual.

Tara imagined what Erin was thinking. Since she had had a difficult night against Finland the previous Tuesday, Erin had needed to post up a big game tonight. This meant that she had come into Burlington under incredible stress. Two or three of tonight's goals had been tic-tac-toe perfect and virtually unstoppable. Maybe Erin thought the other goals were weaker. But the defensemen and forwards had made mistakes. Tara was pretty sure that Erin wasn't thinking about those errors and wished she could comfort her. Now was not the time.

When Tara had showered and dressed, she grabbed her duffel bag and hustled out of Gutterson to the waiting bus. She didn't see any cheerful children waiting at the exit. Unlike the scene after the big win in Concord, this was a downer. She noticed a few players' parents huddled with their daughters near the bus, exchanging hugs and packages. The bitterly cold wind off Lake Champlain bit their hands and faces.

Tara pulled her weary body up the three stairs of the coach and shuffled to a seat near the front of the bus. She threw her duffel bag onto the overhead shelf and lowered herself slowly into an empty place. As she settled in for the long ride to Lake Placid, she could see Karyn chatting with Cammi and the bus driver checking with Bob about the equipment.

Tara looked across the aisle and noticed that Lisa was seated to her right. Lisa pulled her legs close to her body to conserve heat. Her face was turned toward the frosty window and she was staring at Christmas lights glistening in the windows of homes that abutted the parking lot. Lisa wiped the condensation off the window with her hand so that she could see the houses more clearly. From the picture windows of the houses, beautifully decorated Christmas trees threw colored light onto the snow. Tara thought Lisa looked sad. The fluorescent light on the ceiling of the bus made her appear pale. Lisa pulled the collar of her jacket around her ears and closed her eyes.

Freezing, Tara adjusted her seat to a reclining position and placed her injured body in the most comfortable position possible. Fighting to stay warm, she pulled her jacket close to her body and then rubbed her hands together. She wondered if this was the end of her road to Nagano and, if so, whether the whole thing had been worth it. She had deferred her sophomore year at Brown even though she was a premed student hoping to become an orthopedic surgeon. She had trained as an amateur without financial support. She'd suffered repeated injuries. Tara immediately regretted these thoughts and dismissed them. Other people had given up more than she had. She needed to refocus.

Okay, I'm injured and exhausted, she told herself, but there's no point in getting depressed. I'm still on the roster and I have one more chance to prove myself. This is a brutal process but I know I can handle it if I can just get through tonight. If I can survive this stress and loneliness and make the team on Saturday, it will all be worth it. I need to put tonight behind me.

As Tara ruminated about the future, she watched Coach Smith approach the bus. He stepped inside the door and asked Amie Hilles if everyone was on board. Amie, who had completed the roll call, said that everyone was present. Smith thanked her, sat down in the front seat of the bus, and directed the driver to depart. The bus driver closed the door, turned off the overhead lights, and drove his lumbering coach out of the Gutterson Fieldhouse parking lot. Tara shivered, put her hands in her pockets, and hoped she'd fall asleep long before the bus reached Lake Placid.

3

THE OLYMPIC HOPEFULS

"On the Bubble"

LAKE PLACID, NEW YORK ~ DECEMBER 20, 1997

In her room on the first floor of the Olympic Training Center, Lisa listened to her favorite CD while she packed her bags. At five-thirty the next morning, a chartered bus would be taking everyone to Boston's Logan Airport, and then it was home for the holidays. Marc Cohn's ballad "True Companions" reminded her of John. She thought of all of the separations they had endured while she tried to earn a place on the Olympic team and hoped they would all be worth it. But she was unbearably anxious. That night at nine o'clock, Coach Smith was to announce the roster for the Olympic Team. Three players' names would not be on the list. Would hers be among them? She certainly didn't want to leave the packing for later. Once the roster was announced, she would be concentrating on the list and nothing else.

Between the layers of clothing in her duffel bag, Lisa packed the Christmas presents she had bought in Lake Placid for her husband and the presents she'd received from her "Secret Santa," Sara De-Costa. The players' Secret Santas' names were revealed during the team's holiday party, organized by Amie Hilles as an antidote to a stressful week.

It had been held the night before, on the eve of the Winter Solstice, at Goldberries Restaurant on Main Street. The day had been bitter cold and short-lived, punctuated by an icy Adirondack wind. Team and staff members gathered beside Goldberries' magnificent Christmas tree to shake off the chill and celebrate the season. The tree's sparkling lights and beautiful decorations warmed their spirits. After placing their gifts at the base of the tree, people congregated around tables of hors d'oeuvres. Beverages flowed freely. For the first time in days, Team USA and its attendants relaxed.

Amie had suggested a Secret Santa gift-giving ceremony for the women on the team. When everyone arrived, women's Olympic team chairman Bob Allen, dressed as Santa Claus, called each player's team number at random. The player stepped forward, read a statement written on a small rectangle of paper about her secret friend, and let the others guess who the person was. As each sheet was read, it was added to a paper chain that symbolized the players' connectedness.

Sara DeCosta, Lisa's Secret Santa, gave her perfume and candles as well as a prepaid phone card; no one made longer or more frequent phone calls. Lisa had picked one of her favorite teammates, Shelley Looney, in the draw. Her special message to Shelley said, "You have extraordinary talent. Believe in yourself. You have no limits!"

Lisa's relationship with Shelley went back to their younger years growing up in Michigan. Shelley had been captain of three sports at Trenton's Carlson High School, but struggled in school because of a severe learning disability. Lisa's strength as a disciplined student as well as a gifted athlete inspired Shelley, who attended tutoring sessions to become a more successful learner and eventually earn admission to Northeastern University.

The admiration was mutual. Lisa respected Shelley as a sensitive and caring person who always used her self-deprecating humor and happy-go-lucky personality to support her teammates. Lisa also admired the fact that Shelley was tough. In the overtime period of the 1997 world championship game against Team Canada, Shelley threw herself in front of an opponent's shot. The puck shattered her helmet and broke her cheekbone in three places. Sitting on the bench after being attended to by the team's physician, Shelley actually asked the doctor if she could go back in the game. When Shelley stepped forward to receive her Secret Santa gift, Lisa presented her with a book of motivational sayings by elite athletes.

Halfway through the Secret Santa ceremony, Bob Allen decided to lighten up the proceedings. As players came forward to make a presentation, he invited them to sit on his knee. He interrupted their readings with daffy one-liners and peeked into their packages, playing a silly St. Nicholas, much to the women's delight.

Bob Allen was the heart of the women's program and its officially designated godfather. Bob loved having the women athletes train in Lake Placid, his hometown and the place where he was known as "Mr. Hockey." He had chaired the board of directors of the United States Amateur Hockey Association for the 1980 Winter Olympic Games. He had also overseen planning and management of the town's Olympic skating facilities. Bob had always felt that it was only a matter of time before women were Olympic skaters, and for ten years he had worked toward that goal. When women's ice hockey became an Olympic sport in 1992, all the players recognized Bob Allen as the patron saint of women's hockey.

The team chipped in to buy everyone on the staff something nice. Tom received a gift certificate to Abercrombie and Fitch. Ben received a limited-edition print of his idol, Bobby Orr, flying through the air as he scored the overtime goal to win the 1970 Stanley Cup. Amie, Jeanna, and Kris received gift certificates for massages. Peter Haberl, who was completing his doctoral dissertation, received a bookstore gift certificate. And then there was equipment manager, Bob Webster. As "Webby" was much loved and appreciated, the team decided to give him something special.

From a Colorado "Beer-of-the-Month Club," Cammi had arranged for a twelve-pack of microbrewed beer to be sent directly to Bob's home every thirty days. Bob opened his card, read his gift certificate, and immediately looked confused. Where the hell is my beer? he wondered. Are they going to roll it in here?

Cammi saw Bob's confusion and said, "Webby, reread the card and you'll figure it out."

Bob made another attempt. Once he understood that his favorite beers were going to be delivered to his home in the Rockies, he broke into a big smile and shouted, "You've got to be shittin' me! That's awesome!" and while the entire group convulsed in laughter, added, "Thanks a lot! This gift is perfect!"

When all of the staff had opened their presents, Amie said she had a special gift for everyone from USA Hockey, Inc. She handed small, beautifully wrapped packages to the coaches, staff, and players. Inside were gold wristwatches with white faces bearing the "USA" logo that appeared on the team's official uniforms. The recipients gasped when they opened the boxes and immediately strapped their new watches on their wrists.

If Bob Allen was the designated godfather of the team, then Amie was its designated godmother. Her official title was team leader of the U.S. women's national and Olympic teams. In this role she organized and performed all of the tasks that kept Team USA moving. Amie was Coach Smith's right arm, and he would not have taken on his responsibilities without her. Amie had remarkable experience and was known to be outstandingly competent. She was director of USA Hockey's team and event marketing. She had operated regional and national tournaments and assisted with world championships, pre-Olympic Tours, and world cups. Smart and articulate, Amie could persuade, cajole, and convince. No one could cut red tape faster. Coach Smith insisted that Amie lead the women to the Olympics. The presentation of the watches at the Christmas party was one of Amie's consistently smart and thoughtful suggestions.

Before the Christmas party ended, Cammi, Karyn, Sandra, and Alana announced that they had prepared a surprise Christmas skit for their friends' entertainment. They quickly disappeared into the ladies' room and changed into costumes that consisted of sunglasses, construction paper grass skirts, spandex shorts, flip-flops, and plastic flowers. They tied their USA T-shirts in a knot under their breasts and dropped a tape into a boom box. When the music started, a lovely Hawaiian melody filled the room. Then, with bare midriffs and skirted hips swaying, the four entertainers lip-synched "Mele Kaliki-maka," Bing Crosby's tribute to a Hawaiian Christmas.

The skit caught the audience off guard. People had seen Cammi and Karyn act crazy; they were jokesters and pranksters. And dark-haired, exotic Alana was well known for her wonderful sense of humor. But Sandra Whyte, the Harvard anthropology major, was another story. No one had ever seen her let down her hair and get wacky. Quiet and reserved, she rarely did anything unladylike. She was more likely to be found reading than playing cards or watching movies. Sandra was definitely not your average "rink rat."

So when Sandra started to shake a hula with her three teammates, the crowd shrieked and whistled. The song was nutty, the lip-syncing was terrible, and the outfits were falling apart, but the dancers were hilarious—especially Sandra. She was a natural comedienne and held nothing back. Wiping tears of merriment from their cheeks, the on-lookers gave the hula girls a boisterous cheer and loud applause as the final strains of "Mele Kalikimaka" signaled the end of the party.

That was last night. Now it was time to depart for today's game, the final match of the Three Nations Cup tournament. Lisa checked her new watch, not wanting to be late, and thought about the next time she would be looking at it. At nine o'clock that evening she would find out whether the watch was merely a memento of a team she was once part of or the watch that would accompany her to Nagano.

Grabbing her gear, Lisa rushed down the hallway, met her team-mates in the lobby, and boarded the players' shuttle. The trip to the 1980 Rink at the Olympic Center took only a few minutes. Once there, the players braced themselves against stinging blasts of wind and swirling squalls of snow as they hurried through the players' en-trance to the rink. It was early. The game did not begin until four P.M. A few friends and relatives were hanging around inside the entrance, but no one was standing outside the building. It was the coldest, short-est day of the year. But, for many players, it felt like the longest and the most stressful day of their lives.

Coach Smith announced in the locker room that Cammi, Tara, and Erin would not be dressing. Cammi deferred to Karyn, whom Smith had selected to be the team's assistant captain prior to the start of this game, to handle the captain's responsibilities. Tara's foot injury made her effectiveness questionable. Erin had moved out of the rotation. Twenty-year-old Sara DeCosta would start in the net. With so many key players out of the lineup, everyone would have to "play up" to beat the Canadians.

The anxiety that had characterized the locker room in Burlington returned. Tying her skate laces, Lisa wondered, Why is he sitting down Cammi? It's the final game in the Three Nations Cup. We need her out there. Is it possible that our captain could be on the bubble, too? After thinking over her question, Lisa decided, No way. Of course he's going to take Cammi. She's in.

Lisa secured the laces and pulled her other skate on. While she did so, she continued to mull over the lineup: What about Tara? She's one of our most consistent defensemen. Does Coach think she's too fragile? Will he take someone else who can play both offense and defense? She rejected that possibility. No way. Of course he's going to take Tara. She's in, too.

Lisa banged the end of her blade onto the floor to slide her foot to the back of her boot and continued to speculate: And what about Erin? She can stand on her previous performances. But will her experience outweigh Tueting and DeCosta's better records in this tournament? Lisa shook her head and dismissed the notion of Erin being cut. Of course Erin's experience will matter. He just needs to see the other young goaltender again. Erin's in, too.

Lisa tied the laces of her second skate slowly. The ankle she had injured in July was sore. She decided not to make an issue of it with Jeanna. There was no point in giving Coach another reason to cut her. She would play through the pain. She could tie the skate tighter and give the injured area greater support. While continuing to consider why certain players might or might not be in the lineup, Lisa pulled her skate laces until they were taut. Yeah, she thought. Granato, Mounsey, and Whitten have already made it. They don't need one last game to prove their worth. Tonight's lineup is for Coach's unfinished decisions.

A sudden wave of nausea poured over Lisa. I'll bet everyone in this room is on the bubble. I'll bet the unlucky three are tying their skates right now, just like me, not knowing it's for the last time. She sat up straight to let the nausea pass.

When she started to feel better, Lisa thought, This anxiety is ridiculous. She rolled her shoulders, twisted her neck, and tried to work some of the tension out of her muscles.

Lisa saw Kelly, Karyn, and Stephanie tidying their stalls. Sara DeCosta was consulting with Sarah Tueting, and Bob was sharpening skates. Colleen was wrapping her stick. The other players were going about their business, preoccupied with the importance of the game and its outcome. Lisa started thinking about her career: This may be my last game in a USA jersey. I'm extremely thankful for the long period of time I've had the honor to wear it. I'll give the game everything I've got today. If this is it, then I have a lot of great memories. If not, then I'll have more memories, Olympic memories. Lisa started getting teary. She turned toward her stall and pretended to rearrange her clothing while she composed herself.

Coach Smith entered the room and asked for full attention. Lisa knew exactly what he was going to say before he started. Her seven years as Princeton's coach, eight seasons on the national team, and two and a half years with Smith offered sufficient experience. She turned around, sat down, and looked him in the eye, unafraid to engage him.

For, whereas Smith now controlled Lisa's destiny, she knew that at one time, she had had a very strong influence over his. When she first met Ben Smith in 1995, two days after she and John were married, she sized him up as the team prepared to depart for Finland. She missed the first day of practice because Smith and Art Berglund had given her the day off. When she arrived on Monday, her teammates said, "Brownie, wait till you meet our new coach. You won't believe this guy. When we got on the bus at Logan Airport, he didn't even introduce himself. We had no idea who he was. He looked down the aisle from the front step of the bus and asked, 'Do you guys like hockey?' We all yelled back, 'Yes.' He immediately responded, 'Well, this must be the right bus,' and stepped off. While he stood outside the bus talking to people getting on, somebody already on the bus whispered, 'Hey, guys, that's our new coach, Ben Smith.' We all started chuckling. Karyn said, 'What a bozo!' and everyone laughed.

"Then we went to practice. He watched our entire practice without saying a word. At the end of the day he called a team meeting. He sauntered in and with his hokey Boston accent said, 'I'm pretty impressed with how you skate. I'm pretty impressed with how you shoot the puck. And I'm also pretty impressed with how you pass the puck.' Then, he left!

"We all thought, 'What a jerk! Impressed with us? He should know what we can do. He's coached at Dartmouth and Northeastern. He's seen excellent women's hockey. He should have a clue. What's wrong with this guy?'"

Lisa had laughed at her friends' description of the new coach but withheld comment. Privately she wondered, Could USA Hockey have really blown it? This guy has no experience with women. If this is Smith's tryout for the Olympic job, he's really given a bad first impression.

She decided to judge him for herself. It wasn't going to be easy for a new person to step in and coach the team. Players had a lot of loyalty for some of their former coaches as well as the aging veterans in the program. A new guy could mean a shake-up. He would undoubtedly hit some resistance.

Four days later the team was sitting in a Finnish locker room waiting for Smith's inaugural pregame pep talk. It was their first big game with their brand-new coach and everyone was eagerly anticipating what he was going to say. He walked in the room, looked around quickly, and said, "The hay's in the barn! Let's go, girls!" Then he walked out.

When the door closed, Karyn looked at her equally perplexed teammates, including Lisa, Cammi, and Kelly O'Leary, and with a grimace asked, "What? Girls? The hay's in the barn? That's all he has to say, the hay's in the barn?"

A vociferous debate ensued and all types of theories were floated about the meaning of his words. The players finally agreed that Coach Smith's metaphor meant that they knew what to do and simply needed to go do it. Lisa decided she was starting to like the new coach.

By the end of the Finland adventure, the entire team was enamored with Ben Smith's quirky, low-key coaching style. He was knowledgeable, organized, and confident. Karyn had started recording his crazy, often incomprehensible one-liners and Lisa was quietly analyzing his effectiveness. He was different, but he certainly wasn't a clown. In fact, he was quite the opposite. The team decided on the flight back to the United States to write their thoughts about the trip on one sheet of paper as a memento of their outing with Coach Smith. The consensus seemed to be that while they had no idea who this Ben Smith was, they would really like to have him back as their coach.

Shortly after Lisa returned home from that 1995 trip she received an unexpected phone call from Art Berglund at USA Hockey headquarters in Colorado Springs. Sitting in her office in the Hobey Baker Rink at Princeton, she thanked Berglund for the day off after her wedding and then laughed when he asked very seriously, "So what did you think, Lisa? How do you think Ben Smith did?"

Lisa responded enthusiastically, "Oh, he did great, Art."

Berglund wanted details. "Well, what did the women on the team think of him? Did they like him?"

Lisa chuckled. "Everybody loved him, Art. If you could hire this guy to take the team, I know everyone would be excited about it." Lisa had no misgivings. She thought Smith was the person for the job.

Art was pleased. "Well, he coaches a Division One men's team at Northeastern, Lisa, but we'll see what we can do."

Lisa had no idea how USA Hockey actually persuaded Smith to throw down what he was doing, place his career in jeopardy, and take a three-year contract to coach the women's national and Olympic teams. All she knew was that she was a factor in his being in Lake Placid making the final selections. Now he controlled her fate. She was a mature adult. She looked him in the eye. She could deal with his decisions.

Smith's remarks were, as usual, abbreviated. He said, "We worked hard to get to this final game and you all know we can win the cup. We need good concentration, tight defense, and a few goals. Let's not fast-forward into the second and third period, but play in the present, shift by shift. We all know that we have a good team, so let's stick to doing what we do well. Play your very best. Let's go and have some fun." Then he swept back his bangs, nodded his head at Tom, and left.

Lisa noticed that Cammi, Tara, and Erin—the inactive players—had been asked not to come into the locker room. She thought it was strange, but not as strange or annoying as the Canadian television delay that made both teams wait for their game to begin. She was glad the players could leave the locker room and sit on the bench. The pause gave her an opportunity to think about the place she would soon be leaving.

The Lake Placid Olympic Center was an exciting complex in which to skate. The buildings oozed the history of the 1932 and 1980 Winter Olympics. To enter the complex, spectators had to pass the speed-skating oval where Eric Heiden, in a golden racing suit, had set 1980 Olympic records in four races and then broken the world's record—by six seconds—in the fifth. If you stood in the 1932 Rink you could close your eyes and envision the charismatic Norwegian teenager Sonja Henie mesmerizing judges and winning her second Olympic gold medal. If you walked into the 1980 Rink, just yards away, you could easily recall twenty euphoric American hockey players piling on top of their goalie while commentator Al Michaels screamed into his microphone, "Do you believe in miracles?" Somehow Michaels's question, the cheering, and the applause continued to echo, as if the building could preserve historic moments. Lisa sat on the bench where Mike Eruzione and his teammates had counted down the last thirty seconds of their game against the Russians, and wondered how they had felt. She wanted to experience that emotion. She too wanted to do something remarkable.

Sitting in the stands high above the bench, Cammi and Tara waited for the television delay to end. While USA Hockey staff members handed pucks to waiting children in the audience, the two players, dressed in street clothes, bided their time by analyzing the team's recent performance and discussing the dreaded announcement that was pending. Tara said to Cammi, "Burlington was a painful reality check. We've got to get better. We've got to move forward."

Cammi agreed. "When you're winning four-to-one and lose five-to-four, people start asking questions. They say, 'You're doing something wrong, but what is it?'"

The question was a tough one. It made Tara nervous. She responded, "You can bet Coach thinks part of the problem is defense, and that really concerns me. He's carrying seven defensemen. Six are healthy. I'm the one who's injured. Why not get rid of the one who's injured? He knows my knee's a problem. He may be concerned about my durability. He has to think of what's best for the team."

Cammi immediately protested. "You're not the one he'd cut, Tara. You're one of the best defenders. Not just on our team, but in the world. Stop worrying. There are other things he can do."

Unpersuaded, Tara asked, "Like what? He's got so many solid players. Injuries are a special problem. They slow you down, wear you out, and make you less effective."

Cammi could understand Tara's worry. She had suffered with back pain for a long time and knew it sometimes hurt her performance. But she couldn't see Coach cutting Tara. To cheer her up Cammi said, "Hey, Tara, try to relax. Look, Coach probably won't cut you because your face is on our tournament posters!" They both laughed, knowing her logic made no sense. Ben Smith would cut anyone he thought couldn't do the job, including poster girls and captains.

Cammi and Tara were relieved when the hockey game finally started. Erin joined her teammates in the stands, choosing to sit a few seats in front of them.

Tara thought Erin looked drawn and remembered all the stories Erin had told about toughing it out through the hard times. In high school, taunting fans had thrown tampons at her on the ice. During three years in the minor leagues with the Toledo Storm and Dallas Freeze, people had repeatedly heckled and harassed her. To unnerve her, some would make wolf calls. To insult her, others would scream, "Go back to the kitchen!" But Erin persevered through the insults and the taunts. She was thick-skinned and serious and, to her benefit, well educated. A degree in psychology helped her understand this sort of deviant behavior toward women.

But the face Erin wore tonight did not include the stiff upper lip she employed to face down hecklers. It was expressionless. She barely spoke. Tara said to Cammi, "I've never seen Erin like this before. She seems so down."

Cammi responded knowingly, "She's scared, Tara, just like the rest of us."

The audience for the final game of the Three Nations Cup tournament was disappointing in size. Lake Placid was too far for most Americans to drive on a blustery winter night, and Canadian fans could see the game on TSN television. The fans who had ventured out, however, were noisy and enthusiastic. The Canadians evenly matched the Americans with horns, hats, bells, whistles, and banners. Like Gutterson Fieldhouse in Burlington, the atmosphere in the 1980 Rink was festive.

The game started almost forty-five minutes late. While Teams USA and Canada were quickly introduced on television, Tara and her teammates noticed how attractively dressed many of the Canadian spectators were. Large numbers of the women wore long leather coats with matching leather boots. Men wore "hero jackets" with leather sleeves and university names like MCGILL and TORONTO sewn in block letters on the back. Just as in other cities on the tour, the children rooting for both sides wore hockey jerseys and face paint. Many of the girls in Lake Placid wore baseball caps with small American flags stuck through their ponytails. The flags looked like plumes. The girls' brothers and boyfriends wore Santa caps and jester's hats with colorful bells hanging from every point on the brim.

The players were impressed by the number of children who traveled as a team to see them play. Groups of girls from the Plattsburg Road Runners; the Lake Placid Rockets, Sparklers, and Firecrackers; the Rutland Raiders; the Louisville Lions; the Potsdam Silver Blades; the Dixhill Rebels; the Ogdenberg Silver Leafs; the Syracuse Stars; and even the Washington, D.C., Little Capitals approached Cammi, Tara, and Erin in the stands for autographs. When the groups of girls left, the players watched them conduct cheering matches in the stands with equally enthusiastic groups of girls' teams from Canada.

The confidence and energy of the young girls asking for autographs inspired the American skaters. Whereas Cammi, Tara, and Erin, as children, had admired men like Dennis Savard of the Chicago Blackhawks, Cam Neely of the Boston Bruins, and John Vanbiesbrouck of the Philadelphia Flyers, these adolescent girls had the women on their national team to emulate. They could take home posters with images of the women and buy T-shirts emblazoned with the national team roster. They could even read girl-positive mottos and slogans in the stands. An enormous Canadian banner read SHE SHOOTS! SHE SCORES! A JOFA advertisement read JOIN THE WOMEN'S HOCKEY REVOLUTION. T-shirts featured sayings like REAL GIRLS PLAY REAL SPORTS! One of the favorite shirts was Louisville Hockey Products' DON'T TELL ME WHAT I CAN'T DO! Another was VISA's GIRLS WILL BE GIRLS! Not only did the three pioneers notice how much times had changed, they liked being part of the progress. Cammi signed a fan's program with the words *Follow your dream! Cammi Granato #21.*

Everyone was delighted when the game finally started. Paul Romanuk and Margot Page called the game for TSN. Marina Zenk refereed while Deb Parece and Isabelle Giguerre served as linesmen. Sara DeCosta defended the goal for the United States and Manon Rhéaume, who now had nine wins, one loss, and no ties in pre-Olympic play, took the goal for Canada. Team Canada's other goalie, Lesley Reddon, who had also played well during the tour and tournament, was ready to substitute if necessary.

Romanuk and Page speculated for the Canadian audience about

what Ben Smith might do in choosing goaltenders. Romanuk said, "This is last call for a few of the U.S. players, including perhaps the goaltenders. The veteran is Erin Whitten. She is not dressed for this game."

Page responded, "It's going to be tough because all of the goaltenders have looked good. The young kids, DeCosta and Tueting, have great stats."

Her partner added, "Whitten is the veteran, but she has had a lack of success against Canada."

The Canadian broadcasters chatted about the question both Canadian and American fans were asking: Would Ben Smith take youth over experience, or would he select purely on the basis of wins and losses, save percentage, and goals-against average?

Ben Smith was factoring everything into his decision about the goaltenders. He had told his goalies that their body language during a game was as critical as their stats. "An important but subjective part of your performance is your body language. If you give up a goal, can you continue to dig in and show maturity and focus, or do you let it bother you? Do you let something that's behind you hurt what happens next?"

Smith wanted to see confidence. He felt that the mental game is the most essential element in a goalie's performance. He was watching for how a goalie behaved if the opponent got one by her. Did it shake her up or did she move on? He knew that the best teams in the world were going to score goals. Could a goalie show confidence in every conceivable situation?

Sara DeCosta and Sarah Tueting had no idea how Coach Smith was leaning when they dressed for the final game of the Three Nations Cup tournament. "Sara D." was due to play in the rotation and looked forward to impressing Ben Smith. "Sarah T.," also known as "Teeter," had been solid in preseason play and was ready to stand in if necessary. Both young goaltenders felt confident.

The same could not be said for all of their parents. Nancy and Frank DeCosta were so excited they could hardly speak. They were used to seeing their daughter excel, but to start in the final game of a major international tournament was absolutely thrilling. They were also excited for Stephanie O'Sullivan and the other players they had gotten to know well personally.

Sara's brothers, Frank Jr. and Matthew, were rooting also. Frank, in his early twenties, and Mat, a senior in high school, had become fixtures at the national team's games. Like many of the other players' brothers and sisters, they wore replicas of their sister's official jersey with the family name embroidered on the back. Frank and Mat, both hockey players, were what cultural observers were starting to describe as "Title IX brothers," male siblings who had grown up watching their sisters do things that were unthinkable for girls a generation earlier. The DeCosta brothers were their sister's biggest fans.

The DeCosta family had learned to expect lots of excitement watching Sara play hockey. She was a natural athlete blessed with agility and speed. Sara had grown up in Warwick, Rhode Island, playing on boys' teams. As she ascended through the various levels of youth hockey and her coach, Joe Cavanaugh, let her play against strong boys' teams, her reputation spread across New England. Sara became the "girl goalie" from Rhode Island every boys' team wished to face, often to their chagrin.

By her junior year at Toll Gate High School in Warwick, Sara was a legend. She was the starting goalie and the first girl to play in Rhode Island's demanding Interscholastic League's Championship Division. As a senior she backstopped Toll Gate to the title game in the state championship against the never defeated, always champion Mount St. Charles Academy. "The Mount" had won eighteen consecutive Rhode Island state high school hockey championships and produced many outstanding players including the New York Rangers' Matt Schneider, the Phoenix Coyotes' Keith Carney, and the New York Islanders' Calder Cup winner as the 1997 NHL Rookie of the Year, Bryan Berard. Sara helped the Toll Gate Titans become the first public-school team in fourteen years to reach the title round against the perennial champions. Mount St. Charles won the three-game series 2–1, but Sara also became the first goalie in eighteen years to shut out Mount St. Charles, with a 3–0 defeat. In the final game of that series Sara lost in spite of a forty-save performance.

When Sara's spectacular high school career was over, she moved to Providence College, where she changed her sense of timing for women's play and posted a 2.66 goals-against average on her way to an 18–7–2 record her freshman year. She failed to earn a spot on the U.S. women's world championship team that competed in Kitchener,

Ontario, in March of that year when Sarah Tueting and Erin Whitten beat her out. So she decided to train with Boston University's strength coach Mike Boyle, who was preparing other women hopefuls for the national and Olympic team tryouts.

By the August 1997 trials Sara was physically and mentally ready. She recorded a 6–1 win, a 4–3 loss, and the only shutout in the trials. She also made spectacular saves in the final game, which finished with a ten-round sudden-death shootout. While performing a sensational sudden-death save on her friend Stephanie O'Sullivan, Sara pulled her hamstring muscle off her pelvic bone, which also sustained a small fracture. The injury was serious, but Ben Smith appointed her to the national team anyway. She had the best statistics of anyone at the try-out and showed outstanding confidence in the clutch. Sara was ready to take on the world's best women.

Sara's injury, however, created a special challenge for making the Olympic team. While Erin Whitten and Sarah Tueting rotated on the national tour, Sara was forced to miss the team's opening trip to Sweden and Finland and several early games back in North America, thirteen games in all, while completing the rehabilitation of her fractured pelvis. When Sara was given medical clearance to play in early November, however, she made a dramatic comeback. She defeated the Canadians 3–2 in her second game back and first start against Canada. She stopped twenty-six shots. Erin and Sarah T. had both lost in two previous games against Team Canada. The questions tonight were, could she do it again, and, if so, would she impress her coach enough to guarantee a place on the Olympic team?

Sarah Kristen Tueting was asking herself the same questions. Would Coach Smith take the young superstar DeCosta and the veteran Erin Whitten? Sarah T. felt she was competitive with both of them. She had made the national team in 1996, traveled with the team to China, and made the 1997 women's world championship tournament team. Before competing nationally and internationally, she was a standout at Dartmouth College, earning Ivy League Rookie of the Year honors in 1994–95. Six outstanding Sarahs had played hockey for Dartmouth that year: Sarah Tueting, Sarah Devens, Sarah Lenczner, Sarah Hood, Sarah Howald, and Sara Vogler. All of them were excellent. But Tueting made an unusual decision. At the end of her sophomore year, she decided to withdraw from Dartmouth and dedicate herself to making the Olympic team. She set aside the study of neurobiology and a difficult sequence of premedical courses and focused her energy on earning a trip to Nagano. She joined the U.S. Women's Training Program, moved to Boston, and started training with a passion.

Doing things with passion was Sarah Tueting's way. As a child she had obsessed about becoming a goaltender. When her parents, Pat and Bill, brought their pigtailed six-year-old to her older brother Jonathan's youth hockey games in Winnetka, Illinois, she spent the entire time behind the net staring at Jonathan's goaltender. Her parents thought she had a crush on the boy, but, as she explained later, "I liked the position, not the guy."

Her mother and father bought her a pair of used goalie pads, which she slept with initially and then wore as her Halloween costume. She quickly became serious about using them properly and joined the boys' youth hockey team. Jonathan, her mentor, encouraged and inspired her in the tradition of other Title IX brothers. He would pull Sarah in a sled containing their skates and sticks to an outdoor rink where they would play with local kids. She competed with the boys all the way to a state championship at New Trier High School ten years later. Along the way her parents taught their precious pigtailed tomboy to believe in herself and give 110 percent. They told her she could do and be anything. Along with her coaches and teammates, they tried to protect her from anyone who might dampen her love for the game. Once, when a skeptical opponent asked why a girl was on the ice, a teammate responded matter-of-factly, "That's not a girl, that's Sarah, our goalie."

With Sarah's passion for the game came an intensity that she often channeled inward. When she was younger she would sometimes stay up all night after a bad game or react impulsively during a contest. Once, in a tournament in Detroit, the opposing team scored on her sixteen seconds into the game and the coach pulled her. Sarah marched off the ice and into the locker room, where she threw down her jersey, undressed, and stomped off to the lobby to call her parents to come and get her. A teammate's parent witnessed her frustration, intervened, and saved the day. Like many young athletes, Sarah often found it hard to separate her self-worth from her performance. She had to learn first that no one is "in the zone" all the time and that who you are as a person is far more important than how you play as an athlete.

Sarah truly learned to enjoy the intensity of the game in the summer of 1996, when she joined the national team. She had never felt more challenged and, at the same time, more secure. Under Coach Smith and his staff, hockey became both more intense and more relaxing, like her beloved music. Sarah, an accomplished cellist, played in the Dartmouth Symphony Orchestra. As she told her teammates, "Cello rejuvenates my soul. It's just like being in the zone in hockey where nothing else matters and you can't think or worry about anything else. You walk away with a lighter step."

As a double bonus, Sarah's music kept her hockey in perspective. She loved hockey, but the music reminded her that she also loved and excelled at cello, science, writing, and other important activities, some of which, unlike hockey, would be the foundation of her life's work.

While Sara DeCosta rehabilitated her injury during much of the pre-Olympic tour, Sarah Tueting concentrated on staying relaxed and focused. On October 25, 1997, in Salt Lake City, in front of 7,306 fans—the largest crowd ever to watch a women's hockey game in the United States—Tueting led Team USA to a 5–4 win in shootouts against Canada. It was Team USA's first of thirteen contests against Canada on the pre-Olympic tour. Sarah made twenty-five saves and denied five sharpshooters in sudden death. At the end of the game Coach Smith said Sarah had "raised her stock."

By the start of tonight's game, the last game of the fall tour, Sarah Tueting had proven she could play with the best. Her athleticism, passion for the position, and hard-driving commitment to excellence placed her in a highly competitive stance in comparison to DeCosta and Whitten. And she was truly having fun. Selected or not, she would have no regrets.

The Canadian broadcasters' banter about who might become the Americans' Olympic goaltenders, forwards, and defensemen continued throughout the first period. Meanwhile Lisa and her teammates tried hard to shake the jitters and play good hockey. The Americans employed a tight fore-check to try to force Canadian errors. The large international ice surface made every play more demanding, but Lisa and her teammates were used to it by now. Lisa decided that if this was potentially her final game in a national team uniform, she would truly skate her heart out. I'm going to enjoy this game, she said to herself. I'm going to play hard and contribute. Seconds later she made a great move to stop Canada's Nancy Dupuis from breaking to the net.

The period was marked by senseless penalties and unsuccessful power plays on both sides. Canadian penalties for boarding and interference yielded no power-play points for the United States. Manon Rhéaume, as usual, was solid. Three American penalties, two against Angela Ruggiero and one against Vicki Movsessian, put pressure on Sara DeCosta. The Canadians were constantly crashing the net and drawing penalties. But they could not capitalize on their man-up advantage. Sara made thirteen excellent saves for a first period shutout.

Lisa slapped Sara's pads as she left the ice at the close of the first period and headed into the locker room. "Nice job, Sara," Lisa said. "You look great tonight. You made some nice stops and you look confident."

Sara smiled. "Thanks, Brownie," she gushed breathessly. "They had a couple of opportunities toward the end, but the defense made it easy for me."

The former Princeton coach knew better, but liked Sara's modesty. She said, "If you keep this up, you'll win the cup, Sara, and Coach will be extremely impressed."

Sara appreciated Lisa's feedback and said, "Yeah, I hope so. My family is rootin' for me upstairs and they're more nervous than I am." They both chuckled, knowing that goalies' families endure a unique kind of agony when their child is in the net.

After the break, the team poured out of the locker room in numerical order with number 1, Sara DeCosta, first. When Sara paused to let her teammates line up behind her, Lisa patted her helmet and said, "You're hot. Just keep it up." Sara smiled under her face mask and slapped Lisa's outstretched glove.

Lisa could see Bob Allen kissing A.J. Mleczko's newly taped stick, which she had handed to him as she waited for the entire team to get in line. Every player had superstitions, many of which involved their equipment. Bob touched A.J.'s stick one night before she scored three dramatic goals and, from that night forward, he became her good-luck charm.

It was important for A.J. to feel lucky. More and more often her prowess as a face-off specialist and goal scorer were becoming factors in the team's success. At Harvard College, where she would have been a senior if she had not stepped out to try to make the Olympic team, A.J. had been named an Eastern Collegiate Athletic Conference and Ivy League Rookie of the Year as well as a perennial All-Star. By the end of her junior year, she was the school's all-time leading goal scorer, having in three years broken records previously held by her teammate Sandra Whyte. A stunning five-foot-eleven-inch beauty, A.J. was easily able to dominate other women in the Ivy League physically. Ben Smith felt that her size, strength, and skill could be tremendous assets against the world's finest players. When A.J. decided to leave school, he recommended that she train in Boston with strength coach Mike Boyle. In the fall of 1996, A.J. left her home in Nantucket, moved to Boston, and committed herself to becoming an Olympian.

Living in Boston was a mixed blessing for A.J. She enjoyed being near Cambridge and her college friends, but she had to face the prospect of not making the national team in August or being cut in December and returning to school midyear. Sliding back into Harvard's strenuous academic program wouldn't be easy.

Plus, Allison Mleczko loved competing internationally. She had skated on three national teams and was becoming a world-class player. Hockey was her passion. She had played field hockey and lacrosse as well, but ice hockey was the sport that thrilled her.

Like other teammates, the thrill started when she was a child. As a little girl growing up in New Canaan, Connecticut, A.J. had watched her talented older sister Wink figure skate. When A.J. decided that figure skating wasn't the right match, she turned to hockey—the sport her father coached. Tom and Bambi Mleczko supported their little girl's preference in spite of the fact that some parents were appalled. One rudely remarked that A.J. was "Tom's favorite son." Tom and Bambi didn't care. They affirmed and encouraged A.J. because they realized that their child loved the game. It didn't matter that A.J. was one of the first little girls to play hockey in New Canaan. Allison was happy, excited, and *good*! Of course she should play!

With her mother and father's support, A.J. never looked back. She played hockey for twelve years on boys' teams, including her father's bantam and school teams, before making the transition to the Taft School's girls' team and the Connecticut Polar Bears, an outstanding girls' youth hockey team. The Harvard College varsity and U.S. national teams followed. The little girl who loved the game became the young woman who excelled at it.

When A.J. made her second national team, she made two hard decisions: to set aside her senior year at Harvard, even though she was captain-elect of the hockey team, and to become stronger. She knew she wasn't the fastest skater, but felt she could offer exceptional strength and scoring ability. Like so many other Olympic hopefuls, she was an amateur. That meant sacrifices. During the summer she worked with her father, who ran a charter fishing boat off Nantucket. During the rest of the year she trained with Mike Boyle in Boston. Each day, as A.J. grew stronger, she hoped her decisions had been the right ones.

They were. In August 1997, A.J. made her third national team. She now had one more hurdle, the most important and difficult one, making the Olympic team. The final competition was fourteen world-class forwards. A.J. made one more very hard, very critical decision. She would use her strength to become one of the most proficient players at some of the least glamorous plays in the game: winning face-offs, digging the puck out of the corners, and muscling people in front of the net. These were not the high-profile skills that had made her a record setter at Harvard. They were difficult, bone-crunching skills. But A.J. knew that they were also critical to the success of the team. And she knew she had the size, strength, and courage to execute them.

A.J. entered tonight's game with thirteen goals and twelve assists in twenty-nine games on the tour. But, more important, Ben Smith had started relying on her as his face-off specialist and go-to-girl when strength was imperative. She knew she was no longer the center of attention on a good team. But had her decision made her invaluable on a great team?

A.J. would find out the answer in a few hours. In the meantime, she saw tonight's game as a great opportunity to avenge the Burlington fiasco. As luck would have it, Bob Allen was in the building and ready to kiss her stick. A.J. felt hopeful that something good would happen.

When all of Team USA was in line, Sara led them to the bench. Tara, on the sidelines, watched her teammates file down the runway and wished she was marching with them. She wanted to hear the conversations on the bench and follow the coach's strategy. But Coach Smith had directed the three players who were not dressing to stay out of the locker room between periods and away from the bench during the game. He said he wanted them on the ice for the awards ceremony, but until that time they were to make themselves scarce.

On the bench the tension was tangible. The Canadian coach shuffled a few players to give her lines more life. Ben Smith made a few adjustments to account for those changes and the absence of Cammi and Tara.

Within minutes of the opening face-off, Canadian Danielle Goyette was called for a penalty. The Americans had been crashing the net and threatening. Shelley challenged Manon, forcing her to split and butterfly to protect the cage. While the Team USA fans screamed for a power-play goal, Ben Smith put Sandra, Gretchen, and Jenny out as forwards, with Kelly and Karyn on defense. When play started, Karyn got the puck on the left side of the Canadian blue line and fired a blistering slap shot at Manon. Sandra picked up the ricocheting puck and passed it to Gretchen on the right side of the crease. Gretchen immediately roofed the puck past Manon for a dramatic go-ahead goal! Gretchen leapt into the air and celebrated while the partisan fans rocked the building with their cheers.

A few moments later the Canadians were penalized for tripping and Smith sent out a similar power-play unit, substituting only Sue on defense. That group, as well as the second power-play unit, failed to score a goal and the action moved quickly in the opposite direction. Sara braced herself but no shots materialized. Team Canada skated around the periphery and looked disorganized. With almost ten minutes gone in the period, the Canadians finally managed a shot on goal.

The Americans were dominating play. Tricia Dunn was setting the pace with outstanding fore-checking. Everyone was playing aggressively and trying to make things happen. Lisa was one of the aggressors. After a physical play on hard-driving Hayley Wickenheiser, which left Hayley shaken up on the ice, Lisa was called for a penalty. She skated to the penalty box while Hayley limped to her bench. Hayley had thirty pounds and eight inches on Lisa and was twelve years her junior! So, while she regretted the penalty, Lisa felt good that she had temporarily slowed down the young superstar.

Smith launched four veterans—Tricia, Shelley, Sue, and Sandra— to kill off the Canadian power play. The Americans buzzed around the Canadians, who had trouble setting up and shooting. The penalty killers' speed and aggression frustrated the Canadians, whose fans were shaking cowbells, waving flags, and chanting for the tying goal. With only seconds left in her punishment, Lisa stood up and prepared to rejoin the action. She saw Vicki, Karyn, and Gretchen headed up the ice. When the penalty-box attendant released her, Lisa jumped out of the box and joined them, evening up the sides and adding pressure to the rush. She covered a wing while Vicki fed Gretchen, who pulled the puck around Manon's outstretched stick and poked it past her. The Americans went wild! Vicki, Lisa, and Karyn hugged Gretchen, who was euphoric. They had killed off the Canadian power play and pulled ahead by two!

Gretchen's teammates embraced and congratulated her as she approached the bench. Some encouraged her to go for a "natural hat trick," three goals in one period. She laughed and jumped over the boards, happy and breathless.

The thought of producing a hat trick was not farfetched. Gretchen Ulion, whom her teammates liked to call "Greta," was a natural shooter, a sniper. As an undergraduate at Dartmouth she had been the 1991 Ivy League Rookie of the Year and the 1993 and 1994 Ivy League Player of the Year. She set four Ivy League and eleven school records on her way to being named an Eastern Collegiate Athletic Conference All-Star. At five feet, two inches and 130 pounds, Gretchen was pure energy. During her senior year in college she scored forty-nine goals and assisted in thirty-six others. She loved to go to the net, over, under, around, or through people who were usually a lot bigger than she was. She prided herself on being a pain in the rear to defenders around the net. She would squirm, wiggle, twist, and shove to gain position, and then "deek", deflect, or redirect for the point.

Gretchen was the kind of skater with whom other scorers like to play. She was unselfish and creative around the net. If a teammate had a better position, she'd make the textbook pass for the assist. Gretchen was elated about her two goals in the final tournament game and desperately wanted to win. She had decided that, as a twenty-five-year-old with a master's degree and teaching certificate, this was her only shot at being an Olympian. On Halloween her boyfriend, Steve Silverman, had surprised her with an engagement ring. If she could make the team and compete in Nagano, she could then build a life with Steve.

Gretchen had quit her teaching job in Massachusetts to train for the national team in 1996. She had learned that she could not work full-time and train properly when she was cut from the 1996 national team after playing on the 1994 and 1995 squads. Devastated, she decided to sacrifice her career and income for an Olympic opportunity. She had played the game for twenty years, eight of them as the only girl in the Glastonbury and Central Connecticut boys' youth hockey programs. She spent one year with the Connecticut Polar Bears girls' team and the Columbia Youth Hockey Program before entering Loomis Chaffee for high school and Dartmouth for college. During three years on the national teams she realized that her lifelong dream of being an Olympian was in sight. Why not give up one more year to fulfill it?

Like A.J. Mleczko, Gretchen did not give up her precious year without devising a plan. She decided that she would be a greater threat against world-class athletes if she could stay composed and make intelligent decisions every time she touched the puck. And, like A.J. and so many other stars on the team, she resolved to become an unselfish role-player. She had scored only six times in the fall after missing the Scandinavian tour, but she had become a smarter opponent. And she had grown particularly effective against Team USA's top rival, Canada. For months she had been hoping that Coach Smith had noticed her evolution. Tonight she would find out.

Gretchen's excitement inspired the entire team. They picked up the tempo, which made the Canadian defense look listless. On her very next shift, Gretchen broke in on Manon Rhéaume, who was forced to make a spectacular pad save to deny Gretchen's natural hat trick. Team Canada was zero for four on power plays and looking tired. It was the perfect time to pounce.

The opportunity to do so presented itself moments later. Shelley had a breakaway. Stickhandling beautifully, she came straight in on Manon. The Canadian goalie made another remarkable save to keep her team in the game. But her prowess was immediately retested. Shelley, Tricia, and A.J. hustled to keep the puck in Canada's end. Tricia grabbed it high on the right side of the Canadian zone and crashed in on Manon's left. With A.J. busting in at center, Tricia made a pretty pass in front of Manon's crease. A.J. stretched her five-foot-eleven-inch frame to its full extension, with her stick extending her reach by almost six feet. The timing was absolutely perfect and A.J.'s stab sent the puck sailing over Manon's shoulder! A.J.'s teammates mobbed her and Tricia and celebrated their three-goal lead. A.J. kissed her stick and told her linemates Bob Allen was a verifiable secret weapon.

A.J. and Tricia's play was lowlight material for TSN's not-so-happy Canadian audience. Three unanswered American goals did not leave TV watchers or the Canadian fans in Lake Placid with very much to cheer about. With approximately one minute to go in the period, Kelly and Stephanie peppered Manon, whose defense was collapsing in front of her. When the buzzer sounded, Rhéaume had fifteen shots on net to DeCosta's four.

The members of Team USA were sky-high emotionally as they poured into their dressing room to rest before the final period. Karyn yelled, "We can do this! We can beat them tonight!" Lisa added, "Great defense, we've all got to continue to play great defense. That's all we need to do. They're wiped out. They're struggling out there."

Everyone was psyched. In the absence of Cammi and Tara, Coach Smith was trying new combinations and they were working. The Canadians were back on their heels with only twenty minutes left in the contest.

The brief lapse in the tension surrounding the cuts was helpful. If the teammates could only be together for another half hour, at least they were having fun. They were about to conquer Team Canada for the first time and in the perfect place. Lake Placid's 1980 Rink, with its dark blue walls, bright red seats, and wide white stairs, reeked of American victory. Team USA had tried out, trained, and often competed in this beloved space. The thought that this was where they were about to defeat their nemesis and plant seeds of doubt about the Olympic champion created an ebullient mood that was contagious.

The only person not celebrating exuberantly was Katie King, Tara and Tricia's roommate. Katie had contracted a virus earlier in the week and was struggling to keep herself healthy enough to remain in the lineup. With Cammi in the stands, Coach Smith could not afford to sit down another forward. Katie, a critical playmaker and intimidator, was much needed by her team, but she was feeling physically and emotionally stressed. Earlier she had asked her roommates and her close friend A.J. if they sincerely believed Coach Smith would put her on the Olympic team. At twenty-two she was making her first appearance on the national team. Katie did not have the international experience of most of her teammates. She wondered if Coach Smith would possibly think her worthy.

But Katie's lack of extensive international experience was offset by her remarkable athleticism. At five feet eight inches and 165 pounds, Katie was both powerful and gifted. She had excelled in three sports—field hockey, softball, and basketball, all of which she captained—at Salem (New Hampshire) High School. She then acquired an out-standing reputation at Brown University, where she was the women's ice hockey Ivy League Player of the Year three consecutive times and the ECAC Player of the Year as a senior. Few Ivy Leaguers competed as varsity athletes in two sports, but Katie also lettered in softball. She was Brown's much-heralded pitcher and the Ivy League Softball Player of the Year.

Salem, New Hampshire, and Providence, Rhode Island, had rarely seen anything like Katie. She followed her older brother David into Salem's Youth Hockey Program as a five-year-old and then played on various coed and single-sex ice hockey teams outside school while playing three other sports at school. Katie knew Coach Smith was watching her carefully and studying what she could do when her entire focus was on one sport, her favorite.

Katie was watching him back. Hoping one day to be a coach, she observed her many coaches closely. There was a lot to observe with Coach Smith. He was quirky and reserved but knew how to teach the game. He used silly, memorable expressions to convey important principles. He'd say, "Go fast, but don't hurry"; "Get your thumb out of your bum and your mind out of neutral"; or even, "Think fast; you weren't sure whether to shit or go blind, so you farted and blinked." One way or another he made sure players were listening.

Once Smith—an accomplished sailor from Gloucester, Massachusetts—interrupted a dismal practice on the road in Walpole, Massachusetts, to explain his thinking on a series of losses. He gathered his players at center ice and said, "I know why we played poorly in St. John's, New Brunswick. The weather was stormy, the tide was low, and there was the full moon. Do you know what roughly fifty percent of your body is made of?"

Wondering where he was going with the question, Katie and her teammates answered, "Water."

"That's right," Smith said. "A storm from the northeast bit you in the ass in New Brunswick. How can anyone expect to play well in a full moon? The whole world is upside down." He then skated away happily.

Katie knew it didn't matter that what he had just said didn't make any immediate sense. His comment was a Smithism. If you thought about a Smithism long enough, it would yield wisdom worth remembering.

Along with his odd sayings, strange analogies, and complicated metaphors, Katie found Smith's off-ice expectations interesting. He had some unusual requests. For example, he insisted that the entire national team memorize a verse that Peter Haberl had introduced during a sports-psychology session. It was from Rudyard Kipling's *Second Jungle Book*. The players were told to be prepared to recite it during their common meal at the Olympic Training Center. Smith would select one player randomly and ask her to recite the poem. She would have to stand and repeat Kipling's words:

> *Now this is the Law of the Jungle—*
> *As old and as true as the sky;*
> *And the Wolf that shall keep it may prosper,*
> *But the Wolf that shall break it must die.*
> *As the creeper that girdles the tree trunk,*
> *The Law runneth forward and back—*
> *For the strength of the Pack is the Wolf,*
> *And the strength of the Wolf is the Pack.*

Smith would then give his approval and she could sit down. It was Psychology 101, but Katie liked it. Smith was a master at conveying simple philosophies about individual and collective excellence without hitting people over the head with them.

Katie also admired Smith's appreciation of other coaches. He knew he wasn't perfect and there was a lot to be learned from his peers. He would sometimes say to his charges, "You're sick of hearing my voice. I don't see and understand everything, so I think it's nice for me to bring some of my colleagues out here who will see things differently and give us good feedback."

When the team practiced in Walpole, Katie met Jack Parker, Boston University's men's coach; Brad Park, a former Boston Bruin; and 1980 U.S. men's Olympic team members Mike Eruzione and Jim Craig. Keith Allain, a Yale goalie Smith had coached during his days with Timmy Taylor's Bulldogs and as an assistant coach with the 1992 U.S. men's Olympic team, also met the women in Walpole. Tim Taylor, the 1994 U.S. Men's Olympic Ice Hockey Team coach, was a constant resource. Old friends and hockey players John Gummere and Tom Babson helped out in Lake Placid. New York Ranger Mike Richter and his wife, Ronnie, skated with the team at Chelsea Piers in New York. All of these visits were a chance for the team and its coaches to hear other comments. Smith was secure. He would listen carefully to others' thoughts about his team and then use some of their observations to make improvements.

One trait Katie particularly liked was Smith's sense of humor. Naturally reserved and somewhat mysterious, he did not let down his guard often or yuk it up with his players. He also did not have favorites or establish personal relationships. But he knew when something was humorous and could poke fun at himself and others.

Once in Nokia, Finland, during the team's Scandinavian tour, the hotel's laundry service mistakenly left one of the players' clean laundry—including her bras and panties—on Coach Smith's bed. The next morning at breakfast he decided to approach A.J., Stephanie, and Katie. He said, "Are you missing any laundry? I think I may have your things in my room."

The three players grimaced and ran to his room. A.J. and Stephanie were relieved. Katie was mortified. She turned crimson, swiped up her clothes, and ran down the hall saying, "Oh, my God, Coach saw *everything*!"

The word passed quickly that Katie and Coach were sharing laundry. Smith decided to give the team a reason to laugh with rather than at him. Katie was the perfect foil. She would laugh, as he said, "at the drop of a puck." She made him feel like Leno or Letterman.

When the players were resting in their hotel rooms later that afternoon, Smith yelled down the hallway, "Hey, Katie, can I call your mother tomorrow to see what you're wearing? Maybe we can be twins."

Katie started laughing. Her teammates jumped in and called out from their rooms, "Are you and Coach the same size, Katie? We hear you're swapping jeans."

Smith soon heard hysterical laughter in every room and thought, "There's no way I could crack up a bunch of guys that fast with a lousy load of laundry."

Coach Smith's comic behavior almost always made Katie smile, but not tonight. Her coach's optimism and her teammates' cheerfulness about entering the final period with a three-goal lead couldn't lift her spirits. Katie's illness was debilitating. Exhausted and weak, she feared that tonight's performance might destroy her chance to make the Olympic team. She drank as much fluid as she possibly could, wiped the sweat from her brow, and challenged herself to persevere. In fact, Katie was struggling not to lose her dream.

The other Team USA players were poised and ready for the third period. Coach Smith delivered a brief final-period monologue. "Okay, listen up. I want to remind you that three nights ago in Burlington, Vermont, we had a similar three-goal lead. We do not need any more goals in this game to win it. We need to shut them down with solid defense. It would be very nice to enter the two-week break with a win under our belt. Let's have no Burlington meltdown. But let's have fun." When Smith finished, Karyn, as Cammi's stand-in, led a cheer in the center of the locker room. Then Sara DeCosta, like a mother hen, guided her chicks down the hallway and onto the ice.

A battle of banners accompanied by cowbells, air horns, and applause greeted the two teams as they slid onto their benches. In the highest seats, a group of teenage boys waved an enormous American flag, twelve feet high and twenty-four feet long. Meanwhile young girls flapped smaller flags and homemade signs and chanted patriotic slogans.

The referee called the two teams into position and dropped the puck. As she did, young girls sang, "I'm bored to death, I want to be a ref."

Contrary to this irreverent message, the referee's job was anything but boring. The American women had learned a great deal from their loss in Burlington and did not want to witness another Team Canada celebration. Each one set aside her personal problems and fears and played uncompromising defense. Shifts were shortened so that everyone could play harder. Players sprinted to the bench and made precision line changes. No opponent's stick went undisturbed. The metal shafts clicked and clattered as the American players banged every Canadian player's stick in an attempt to disrupt passes or steal the puck. The officials scrutinized the intense fore-checking and back-checking but let the women play.

Sara DeCosta was inspired. Danielle Goyette broke through the American defense and fired a rocket to Sara's left. Nancy DeCosta's heart skipped a beat as Sara made a huge save. Running on empty, Katie charged back up ice and made a beautiful pass to Laurie, who discharged the puck at Manon. The legendary goalie made a spectacular save. But Angela kept up the pressure by sending a hard shot at Manon from the blue line. Sandra caught the puck waist-high with her stick and tipped it slightly wide to Manon's right. The audience gasped.

In frustration a Canadian player hit Tricia and was sent to the box. Once again the players on the points quarterbacked the American power play while the forwards crashed the net. Shelley, Stephanie, and A.J. charged and threatened while Chris, Sue, and Kelly looked for shots. When the power play ended, the Americans intentionally slowed down the pace to kill time.

Tom Mutch screamed directions to the defensemen as the Canadians picked up speed to try to score. Shelley, Katie, and Laurie executed a nice drive on Manon but came up empty-handed. Nancy Drolet escaped the American defense and shot on Sara. Again Sara made the save!

Moments later Manon coughed up a puck to Shelley, who was in alone. Fearlessly, Manon stood up straight and came right out to meet her. Shelley aimed and fired, but Manon made a fabulous stop. The crowd was delighted. Cheers of *"U-S-A!"* and *"Can-a-da!"* filled the building.

Team Canada was losing time and patience. A hard-charging forward boarded Lisa behind Manon's net. Lisa was prone face-first on the ice but received no call. While American fans berated the ref, Canada's stars Jayna Hefford and Hayley Wickenheiser pounded their blades into the ice and sped toward Sara. The DeCosta family held its breath. The fearless forwards attacked. With split-second tim-

ing, Sara extended to a full spread-eagle to protect against both forwards. The puck bounced off her pad and fell into the crease. As Lisa
pushed Jayna out of the goal mouth, Jayna kicked the puck into Sara's
net with her skate. The Canadian players went beserk until Marina
Zenk ruled, "No goal!" Canadian coach Shannon Miller was furious,
but Zenk would hear none of her objections.

Play continued with Karyn and Jenny rushing on Manon but failing to connect. Colleen, Alana, and Vicki pressed and were denied.
Eventually a scrum occurred in front of Sara's net. She covered up
nicely to give everyone a breather.

Smith told his Americans on the bench that they were playing great
and just needed to remain composed. Seconds later, with three and a
half minutes left in the game, Therese Brisson and Vicki collided in
center ice. Vicki crashed backward, slamming her head on the ice.
Therese ricocheted off Vicki into the air and then landed on top of
her. Stunned and struggling for air, Vicki skated to the bench. A
penalty was called, but no plays or points materialized. The Canadian
skaters were demoralized. As the clock ticked down, Team Canada
made silly passes and struggled to break out of the zone. The Americans controlled the play. They had no trouble skating in on Manon,
who seemed to be the only red jersey playing defense.

When Lisa jumped on the ice for her final shift in the game, she was
trembling. She thought, This may be my last shift. My career as a
player may be ending. The team was about to win a huge victory. Her
excitement blended with her anxiety and the suspense.

When the buzzer sounded, Team USA exploded onto the ice and
embraced its goaltender. The twenty-year-old American had just
handed Team Canada its first defeat in a major international tournament! While the American fans screamed "U-S-A!" at the top of their
lungs, Cammi, Tara, and Erin raced to the bench to join the celebration. They slid onto the ice in street shoes, grabbed Sara around the
neck, and congratulated her. She had stopped twenty-three shots and
registered a shutout! Her teammates had assisted her by firing forty-
one blasts on Manon Rhéaume. Even the Americans agreed that
Manon had played remarkably and kept the contest from becoming
an embarrassment. When the two teams shook hands at center ice,
Sara and Manon exchanged knowing smiles.

A red mat was thrown on the ice. Upon it was placed a table covered with a black cloth. A Lake Placid attendant set the large silver cup out along with forty-three tournament medals with red, white, and blue ribbons.

For the first time in seven years of international competition, Team USA, standing at attention along the blue line, heard "The Star-Spangled Banner" emerge from the sound system. None of the players broke into a smile. A few sang the words quietly as they stared at the American flag hanging from the ceiling. Above it, in the rafters, Lisa could see a lighted Christmas tree.

Bob Allen hosted the ceremony. He awarded the coveted Three Nations Cup to Cammi and Karyn, who together held the large trophy above their heads. Bob then handed a gold medal to each American player and shook her hand. When A.J. took Bob's hand he gave her a wink. He then handed silver medals to the women of Team Canada.

When Bob had finished, USA Hockey official Ron DeGregorio announced the all-tournament team, which included Tara and Katie. Gretchen was named the tournament's most valuable player. As American fans roared, TSN broadcasters wondered if twenty-year-old Sara DeCosta had just played her way onto the U.S. Olympic Team.

Cammi asked her teammates to remember to thank the fans. As the Canadian players skated to their locker room, the American skaters formed a circle at center ice, turned to face the audience, and raised their sticks in a hearty salute. Team USA's fans cheered, ecstatic to have seen an important American victory. When Team USA lowered its sticks, Amie Hilles called them together with the staff for a team photo. When everyone was in position, Coach Smith said, "Okay, winners, let's get everybody in the picture. I want big smiles and, as my buddies on the Bombers—Gloucester's team of mostly aging amateur hockey players with rapidly deteriorating skills—refer to the champions' pose, the 'Bomber lean.' On the count of three. One, two, three!"

The players and staff leaned in on one another and smiled as newspaper photographers and a couple of eager parents snapped photos. Lisa could barely smile. In the back of her mind was the realization that this was the last official representation of the 1997 national team. By nine o'clock the national squad and three of its players would be history.

Sara DeCosta, Gretchen Ulion, and Ben Smith were surrounded by reporters when the team started to scatter. Smith told reporters, "We had a setback the other night in Burlington that I think was instrumental in getting us ready for tonight." Gretchen added, "Beating Canada anytime is great, but beating them in a game like this, a tournament final, is extra special. We learned from the other night and came out with something to prove."

Television commentators and cameramen accosted Sara. In the seven years of women's international competition, no one had recorded a shutout against the reigning world champions. Her parents watched proudly from the stands while their daughter completed her interview. She said, "It definitely was tough to be injured and miss part of the tour. At first I was nervous and I just wanted to get better and get back on the ice. But I respect Coach Smith and had confidence that he was going to give me a fair shot."

Within a few minutes, the audience and reporters had vacated the Olympic Center. It was dinnertime on a stormy winter night and no one was waiting to gather autographs. Parents, relatives, and friends walked to the vestibule outside the players' locker room and waited for the two teams to emerge. The smell of sweaty people and equipment mixed with the fresh scent of soap and shampoo.

The Canadian players' families were subdued. Losing was a phenomenon with which they had very little experience, and clearly they didn't enjoy it. Tomorrow their team would face serious public scrutiny for losing to the upstart Americans. It would be a long ride home to Calgary for Shannon Miller and her players.

The American families' mood was cautiously optimistic. The team had won and everyone had played well. Relatives buzzed about the victory and the stress of waiting for the selections. They noted that Ben Smith hadn't said much to their daughters or sisters, so they weren't really sure what to expect.

Ben Smith had made it a point to distance himself from his players' relatives. He had met some of them over the years, but some bitter experiences had taught him to avoid personal relationships. The bottom line was that families love their children and have a biased opinion about their abilities and performance. No measure of a coach's time or attention in the interest of a child can ever be sufficient. No rationale for a coach's decision to release a child is ever acceptable. Smith had decided long ago that it was his job to coach athletes and not their families. If a player introduced a sibling, parent, fiancé, or spouse, he was respectful, but that was where it ended. Especially tonight, when heartbreaking announcements were imminent.

Lisa showered, dressed, and rushed out of the locker room. Many of the players were celebrating the win, but Lisa was more excited about seeing John, who was waiting in the vestibule with the other players' families. He had driven from Detroit to be with his wife on the night of the selections. Lisa ignored all of the other people in the waiting room, wrapped her arms around John's neck, and gave him a kiss. Holding him close, she whispered, "I'm so glad to see you. I'm so happy you're here. This has been the most difficult week of my life." Then she started sobbing.

John held Lisa tightly around the waist and let her cry. He wasn't sure what to say. After a few seconds he spoke to her softly, "I know it's been rough, Lisa. Everything is coming down to these few days. I'm worried about you. Are you okay physically? I saw you flatten Hayley Wickenheiser and then get checked by someone else. Are you okay? Are you sore?"

Pulling back and looking into his eyes, Lisa said, "Believe me, John, it's a lot easier to deal with the physical stuff than with the mental. I'm really stressed. I'm really sad. It's starting to get to me. I need to talk to Webby for a minute before we leave."

Bob Webster had already started his postgame chores: washing uniforms and underclothing, repairing equipment, and cleaning the locker room. He had hours of labor ahead of him. Tomorrow was a departure day and everything had to be ready. Bob looked up casually as Lisa approached, studying her face. With a sorrowful voice that cracked when she spoke Lisa asked, "Webby, if by chance I don't make this team, could I have my jersey?"

Bob stared in her eyes, nodded, and said, "I'm sure something can be arranged, Lisa."

Lisa felt some relief. At least she would retain her pre-Olympic tour jersey, a meaningful memento of a remarkable year. "Thanks, Webby," she said. "I know you understand what it would mean to me." Then, fearing she would once again lose her composure, she hurried to find John.

Team USA spilled out of the locker room and then out of the

Olympic Center to have dinner with relatives and friends. All the players knew they had to be back for the nine o'clock announcement.

For virtually every player, the wait was unbearable. They wondered why the coach didn't make the selections in the locker room immediately after the game. At dinner tables all across Lake Placid players asked each other, "What more does he need to do? Do you think he has to call the USA Hockey office and consult with the selection committee? Why can't he just get the cuts over with and let us go home?"

The waiting heightened tension and destroyed many appetites. Most of the players who had joined their friends and relatives for dinner finished early, scribbled their relatives' hotel telephone numbers on a napkin, and returned to the Training Center.

Karyn was dropped off by her buddies at around eight-thirty. She wandered down to the training room for about ten minutes to kill time making small talk with Amie and Jeanna. When she ran into Lisa being dropped off by John, there wasn't much to say. She muttered, "Hang in there, Brownie," and Lisa nodded.

At 8:45 P.M., all of the players started shuffling into the Skylight Room on the second floor. On a regular day this was a totally benign conference room filled with nondescript tables and chairs where coaches, trainers, and sports psychologists gave instructions.

Tonight Lisa thought the room felt eerie. The veterans sat in silence listening to the young players' nervous chatter. Lisa envied the rookies at that moment. If their names weren't called there would be a second or perhaps third try. None of them would be as devastated as the veterans if they didn't make it. She took the first seat in the front row. Kelly came in and sat down beside her.

Some of the USA Hockey staffers were conversing in the hallway before entering the room. Remembering the team's terrible experience in New Jersey, when Barb and Jeanine were cut, Sarah Tueting took Cammi aside and said, "I don't think all of the staff should be in the room when Coach announces the cuts. It would be more compassionate if the staff weren't here. We're all really vulnerable and it shouldn't be a spectacle. If you agree, as our captain, could you talk to Coach?" Cammi listened carefully and agreed. She found Ben Smith in the hallway and shared Sarah's suggestion. Smith immediately agreed and said he would take care of it.

Lisa tried to wait patiently. Now was the moment of truth. She folded her hands together on the table and thought of all the times she had sat in a similar position in the past and survived both the stress and the selections. Rarely had she received bad news. She wondered if this, her last selection announcement, would be the one that would break her heart. She tried to calm herself down: I'm thirty-one years old. I've been through this process many times. If I am cut, I will congratulate my teammates and go back to my room and call John. No overreaction. I can do this. I'm prepared not to hear my name.

Lisa's maiden name was near the start of the alphabet, so she'd know her fate right away, unless Smith used her married name, as he sometimes unexpectedly did.

Amie entered the room at nine and gave simple instructions for the next morning. She said, "The bus will depart from the front door of this building at five forty-five A.M. sharp. Everyone is expected to be on it. Bags and equipment must be in the lobby by five A.M. Your rooms must be left immaculate. Strip the linen from your bed and put it in the laundry. The bus is going to Logan Airport where you will each be given tickets to fly or bus home. Family members and friends can pick you up there if you live near Boston. If you are selected for the Olympic Team, plane tickets for the Olympic Training Center in Colorado Springs will be sent to your homes." Amie then gave a few details about the itinerary for early January, when the team would begin its pre-Olympic tour using Colorado Springs as its new home base.

Coach Smith poked his head in the room, interrupted Amie, and asked her to join him in the hallway. While they conversed for several minutes behind a closed door, the women started to become anguished. Some rubbed their foreheads. Others bit their fingernails. A few looked out the window at the winter darkness and prayed for the night to be over. Tara muttered what everyone was thinking, "What's going on? Let's go."

Coaches Smith and Mutch entered the room before Tara's question could be answered. Smith stood at the front of the room alone. The staffers remained outside, as Cammi had requested. Ben Smith looked up and down the rows of athletes seated before him and rubbed his chin. All eyes were riveted on his face. He took a deep breath, put his hand in his pocket, and pulled out a sheet of paper. Then he said, "You are all outstanding athletes and I have tremendous respect for all of you. The tour was great. I could probably take any of you to the

Olympics and you'd play well. But I can't do that. I can only take twenty. And obviously I want to take the twenty people who I think will give us the best chance to win the gold medal."

Many of the players felt their heartbeats start to race. Lisa thought, Make it fast. *Please* keep your comments short.

The coach continued, "So here is the list of the twenty names of the women who have been selected for the 1998 United States Olympic Ice Hockey Team. After I read the list, those twenty people are excused, and I want you back here in thirty minutes to meet with Amie to discuss logistics."

Sara DeCosta said a prayer. Karyn Bye sat up straight in her chair. Several players crossed their fingers. Others closed their eyes. Some put their faces in their hands. Tara said to herself, Focus, listen carefully. Lisa told herself, Be prepared not to hear your name.

Smith looked at the paper in his hand. The names appeared alphabetically by position: goalies, defensemen, and forwards. He cleared his throat and started reading.

"So here is the list:

"Sara DeCosta and Sarah Tueting.

"Chris Bailey, Colleen Coyne, Sue Merz, Vicki Movsessian, Tara Mounsey, and Angela Ruggiero.

"Laurie Baker, Alana Blahoski, Lisa Brown-Miller, Karyn Bye, Tricia Dunn, Cammi Granato, Katie King, Shelley Looney, A.J. Mleczko, Jenny Schmidgall, Gretchen Ulion, and Sandra Whyte.

"You twenty people are excused."

He folded the sheet of paper, placed it back in his pocket, and stood in silence.

Lisa heard her name and thought, Is it true? Am I sure? Did he say it? I think he did. Oh, my God, he said my name! What a relief! What a relief! She was so excited that she could not focus on the other names he was reading. It was a moment of complete self-absorption. When Smith excused the twenty Olympians, Lisa arose weak-kneed from her seat and quickly stepped out of the room, anxious to see who would follow.

The women who walked out behind her were silent. She smiled as she saw Cammi and Karyn, old friends, move through the doorway along with some of the young rookies she was so fond of—Sara, Angela, and Jenny. Lisa was thrilled when she saw Shelley and Tara and so many others who were worried enter the hallway. All of the players looked spent. When the hallway appeared to be filled, Lisa turned to Cammi and Karyn, both of whom looked sick, and said, "So who's left?"

Sandra Whyte, whose name was at the end of the list, was among the last to leave the room. She was stunned when she saw who did not stand up to leave. She placed her hand gently on the player who had been sitting beside her and said, "I'm so sorry, Steph." Sandra wanted to cry. She walked out feeling helpless.

What Lisa, Cammi, and Karyn saw when they looked back into the room shocked them. Three veterans like themselves—Kelly O'Leary, Stephanie O'Sullivan, and Erin Whitten—remained seated, and each looked absolutely stunned. Lisa, Cammi, and Karyn looked at Sandra's face as she walked through the door and realized what had happened. They could not believe it. Ben Smith had cut three of the most experienced players, women who had persevered for many, many years just as they had! Kelly, Steph, and Erin! Kelly, Steph, and Erin!

Sandra looked at Cammi, Lisa, and Karyn and was speechless. They knew what she was feeling. Friendships that had been built over many years, friendships that had been sincerely celebrated at the Christmas party twenty-four hours earlier, were now going to change irrevocably. A tremendous sense of grief overwhelmed the four of them.

Cammi ran to her room and sat on her bed trembling. When her roommates, A.J., Tricia, and Chris, came in, she was shaking. Cammi felt like she had just witnessed an accident, something terribly frightening. The coach had cut Kelly, Steph, and Erin! Their dreams were destroyed! She almost felt as though it had happened to her.

In reality, neither she nor the other players selected for the Olympic Team could understand what the others had lost. At first each of the three unselected veterans wondered if she hadn't paid enough attention or if the coach had made an embarrassing mistake. But as the truth sank in, their faces first grew pale and then rapidly began to color as disbelief, bitter disappointment, and a fearful sense of panic engulfed them. It was as if the enormous pressure that had lifted almost magically off the twenty who had been excused descended with a vengeance on the three left behind, shattering their dreams and breaking their hearts.

When the last of the excused players had left the room, Ben Smith addressed the three silent, shaken women who sat before him. "On behalf of USA Hockey, I want to thank you three for your contributions. I know that you have put in a lot of hard work over the years and I thank you for that effort. Obviously this isn't the news you wanted. I don't expect you to be thrilled about the decision. If you would like to discuss my decision now, just stay here. If you'd like to discuss it in a half hour or two hours or two days, I'll be available. I've got to do a press conference downstairs, but then I'll be in room 102." When he had finished his remarks, he waited.

Erin Whitten arose, walked up to Smith, and thanked him for the opportunity to play on the national team. Privately, his heart went out to her. A lump formed in his throat as he took her outstretched hand and thanked her for all that she had done. He saw tears well up in Erin's eyes. She quickly composed herself, said good-bye, and left the room.

Simultaneously, Kelly got up and walked out without a gesture or a word.

Stephanie waited. When Kelly was gone, Smith said, "Would you like to talk now, Steph?" and she said, "Yeah." He walked over and sat down beside her.

Stephanie asked for an explanation. Smith described his reasons for not selecting her. He said, "Hey, Steph, I can imagine how difficult this is for you. I know you have all been working your asses off to make this team. Obviously it didn't turn out the way you wanted it to, but you've got to know that I tried to select a team that will give us the best chance to be successful. If you want to talk about this in a couple of days, give me a call when you get back to Boston."

In shock, Stephanie simply said, "Okay."

Stephanie had started processing the decision while Smith was speaking to her. She looked like she wanted to interrupt him and tell him he had made a huge mistake. She seemed to be contemplating what his decision would mean—that she would not be going to Nagano or marching in the Opening Ceremonies or fulfilling her lifelong dream. How could he select twelve forwards and not her? Why? Stephanie listened, trying to understand. But what her coach was saying didn't seem to make sense to her. How could this be his decision? How could this be happening?

When Smith finished speaking, Stephanie looked at him from what appeared to be a whole new perspective. She said she would call him and walked out.

As she left the room and passed her teammates in the hallway, Stephanie's frustration and disappointment showed on her face. She looked stunned and disillusioned, as though she were asking herself, How could so much happiness and anticipation have come to this?

When Stephanie got to her room, Sandra was waiting. Sandra asked if she was okay, knowing full well that she was not. Stephanie appeared to be in shock both physically and emotionally, too stunned to cry and too hurt to become hysterical. She exhibited the calm of a person who is traumatized. Sandra wanted to lessen her friend's disappointment but had no words or solutions.

Sandra too was surprised at the selections and didn't want to make matters worse by suggesting the coach's reasons. Instead of saying anything, she sat quietly with Stephanie in friendship and support.

Kelly appeared not to be interested in either a handshake or an explanation. When Smith finished speaking with Stephanie and walked down the hallway to attend the press conference, Kelly confronted him. She challenged him to defend his decision. She pointed her finger in Smith's face to emphasize her comments. Smith responded calmly, "You don't belong on the team, Kelly. We can talk about it later." His brief retort infuriated her.

Kelly wanted answers. She was a veteran of six national teams. Along with Cammi and Lisa, she was one of the only players who had been with the women's program since its inception. She was around long before Ben Smith was hired. She had been named to three all-tournament teams in the world championships. In Auburn, Massachusetts, she had been a high school standout. At Providence College she had received numerous athletic honors. She had experience and credentials. As Smith walked away from Kelly, her ire seemed to increase. She grabbed a phone to call her family.

Ben Smith knew the reporters could hear the euphoria that was starting to break out in the hallways. He followed Kris Pleimann's instructions and hurried downstairs to release the names of the Olympic team members to the press. Passing Tom Mutch in the hall, he said, "Tom, I'd appreciate you staying around and dealing with the fallout." Tom agreed to do so.

What Tom saw in the hallways was not what he thought Smith anticipated. As the scope of the coach's decisions became clear, many of the chosen twenty became uncontrollably emotional. A flood of pent-up fear and misgivings poured out in a stream of tears. Joy mixed inextricably with sadness to create a whole new array of emotions.

Among the players whose emotional reaction was most dramatic was Colleen. Her legs collapsed beneath her when she stepped out of the Skylight Room. Tara grabbed her to prevent her from falling. Leaning on her friend for support, Colleen whimpered, "Oh my God, Tara, I can't believe I made it. I had myself cut before I entered the room."

Struggling to bear her friend's weight, Tara said, "Colleen, I can't carry you. You've got to try to walk." Shoving open the door to the first-floor stairwell, Tara asked, "How could you cut yourself, Colleen? What made you think that?"

Choking on tears as she descended the stairs, Colleen sobbed, "You've got to understand. I'm twenty-six years old. This was my only chance to make the Olympic team. If I didn't make the team this time I knew that I could not come back to try again in four years. I was frightened."

Passing teammates who were lining up to use the hallway telephones, Tara said, "But you did make it, Colleen! Congratulations!" Tara deposited Colleen near one of the phones and hurried to find her parents' number. Sue and Mike Mounsey could not be in Lake Placid; they were in Connecticut with Tara's younger brother. Tara couldn't wait to call them and her grandparents, who would then spread the news in Concord.

Tara wasn't teary. Rather than feeling joyful, she was relieved. The pressure to make the team had become distressing, as people who admired her assumed that she would make it. She worried about disappointing them, letting them down. She was young enough that she would get a second chance at the Olympics, but that was not the issue. People had come to expect a lot from Tara. Her family and friends would love her and understand if she didn't make the team, but what about the people around the state and region who had been so kind and encouraging?

The enthusiasm of Tara's fans was not misdirected. She was one of the most highly skilled defensive players in the world. She was unusually strong and athletic, and she was gifted handling the puck. Every coach who worked with her knew she was a big-game player, offensively and defensively. She was the come-through kid, the player you wanted on the ice in a must-score or must-stop situation. She could win a game for you at either end of the ice. Every goalie who faced her feared her slap shot. She had a tendency to throw herself in front of other people's hardest shots to protect her own goalie. She and Karyn Bye gave Team USA two world-class players on the power play. The only question was Tara's health. Would her injured legs survive the grueling schedule that lay ahead? Naming her to the team meant that Ben Smith was willing to monitor her health rather than not select her.

Smith had scared Tara by reading "Movsessian" before "Mounsey," but she could forgive him her two seconds of panic. She was going to Nagano and she was elated. She'd tell him about his problems with the alphabet later.

Lisa had decided not to wait for a telephone. She dialed John's number on her cell phone in the stairwell while she walked toward her bedroom. Like Cammi, she was trembling. When John picked up the phone and said hello, Lisa started bawling. John held his breath. His wife was usually stoic. With bated breath, he asked, "Lisa, are you okay? Did you make it?"

He heard more intense crying on the other end. Lisa was so upset she could barely talk. After a few worrisome seconds John heard her tearful voice whisper, "Yes, I made it."

Interrupting her sobbing, John asked, "Lisa, why are you so upset? What's going on?"

In a voice drenched with sadness, Lisa said, "Oh, John, Kelly, Stephie O., and Erin were cut."

John understood his wife's reaction. The personal news was wonderful but the news about her longtime friends was devastating.

Just then Kelly rushed into the room, gathered her bags hastily, and rushed out without interrupting. Lisa could see that Kelly was terribly upset. She could hear her friends who were with John cheering in the background but knew she had to go after Kelly. She put down the phone and hurried to find her friend. But Lisa was too late. Kelly had already departed.

Tom Mutch had never seen a group of athletes so profoundly affected by a coach's decision. He started to think about how this moment was different from others he had witnessed in competitive athletics. One difference was that the selections were for the Olympics, but the major difference was the individual relationships. The athletes were like sisters suddenly forced to separate. The paper chain they had constructed at the Christmas party the night before to symbolize their sisterhood was now smashed and scattered.

Tom noticed Colleen on the reception-desk phone. She was speaking with her father, who was waiting in a hotel room in Lake Placid. "I made the team, Dad! I made it!" she gurgled. Still unsteady, she was leaning against the wall. "I'm so happy I can't stop crying!" And then, "Yes, I know you're proud, Dad. I love you, too." Colleen hung up the phone, looked at Tom, and attempted to smile. "My dad's so excited," she said. "I have to call my mother at home to calm him down." She dialed her mother and started crying hysterically all over again.

Tom realized that he hadn't genuinely understood what it meant to these women to make the team. For many of them it was a validation of many years of self-sacrifice. For some, like Colleen, it felt like a reversal of fortune.

Six months earlier, on June 22, Colleen Coyne's family home in Falmouth, Massachusetts, had burned to the ground. The four Coyne children and their parents, Dennis and Donna, had to pick up and start over. Two sons and two daughters started rebuilding the house with their parents board by board. Petite Colleen, who was a five-foot-three brunette weighing only 131 pounds, did her share while gathering new equipment and preparing to try out for the national team in August.

Colleen was determined to make the national team in spite of this setback. She had faced adversity in the past and prevailed. As a young child, Colleen had dreamed of being a great athlete. Her parents built up her confidence and encouraged her. She was a tomboy who loved hockey, baseball, and lacrosse. After starring at Tabor Academy, Colleen became an All-American in lacrosse at the University of New Hampshire while also helping the Wildcats' women's hockey team win two ECAC titles. In 1994, Colleen fractured her jaw in a hockey game when a puck hit her in the face. Three weeks later she tried out for the Colorado Silver Bullets women's baseball team—as a pitcher with an eighty-mile-per-hour fastball! She was cut, but the following year pitched for a men's team in the Cape Cod Baseball League, the

Wareham Gatesmen. Along the way Colleen skated on four national teams as a solid, stay-at-home defenseman. At the 1996 Pacific World Hockey Championship in China she broke her arm, but she bounced back and made the next national team.

Ben Smith selected Colleen for a fifth national team in August but then did not give her much encouragement. Often during the thirty-two-game tour she found herself in warm-ups in the stands rather than in her uniform on the bench. Colleen didn't complain. When she did dress, she followed her coach's simple directions and played text-book defense, nothing fancy. Other defensemen were bigger and more versatile. They wandered from the blue line rushing the puck and try-ing to score. But Smith didn't want Colleen to do that. So she per-fected her defensive skills the way her sister Cape Codder, A.J. Mleczko, perfected her face-off skills. What Colleen didn't quite re-alize during the tour, but understood clearly tonight, was that she had worked her way onto the Olympic team by becoming the unselfish and dependable role-player her coach felt he needed.

While Tom Mutch continued his walk through the corridors, Erin approached him crying. Tom felt awkward and tongue-tied. He wasn't responsible for her sadness, but he was a part of it. He thought, What can I possibly say? I don't want to hurt her by saying something stupid.

Erin said nothing. She put her arms around her assistant coach and gave him a hug. Tom fumbled for words. All he could find were, "Hang in there, Erin. We're all going to miss you." There was so much more to say, but he felt hopelessly inarticulate.

Erin neither spoke nor smiled. She let go, wiped her eyes, and joined her fiancé, Tim Hamlen, who was waiting. Then she was gone. Tom sighed deeply and thought, This is such a roller-coaster ride. So many highs and lows. Coach needs to see this. But Ben Smith was still with the news reporters clarifying his decisions.

Nancy and Frank DeCosta burst through the front doors of the Training Center and rushed into the lobby. Sara ran to meet them and melted into the warmth of a tandem embrace. Mom, Dad, and daugh-ter cried unabashedly. The fractured pelvis and weeks of physical ther-apy were behind them. The DeCosta clan was euphoric until they heard about Stephanie, whom they adored. Stephanie.

The King, Baker, and Mleczko families rushed in behind the De-

Costas. Their daughters ran into the lobby to hug them. The Granatos arrived a few moments later, followed by an ecstatic Dennis Coyne. Dennis hugged Colleen and Vicki, whom he was very fond of, and said, "I've won the lottery!" As more and more family members arrived in the lobby, the players started to relax, accept the news, and rejoice.

Ben Smith barely had enough time to finish his press conference and hurry back to the Skylight Room by the appointed time. The Olympic team was slowly gathering in the seats. Though many of the players looked drawn, Smith could tell from their expressions that they were in a better mood than the last time he had seen them. He knew the disappointment about their friends had not been easy and wanted to say, "Hey, it wasn't very pleasant for me either, but it's my job." He also knew that they understood and were grateful to be present.

While Smith was waiting for everyone to arrive, Tom came up to him and took him aside. Tom said, "Coach, you wouldn't believe the emotion of the kids who made it. They've been bawlin' on the phones to their mothers and fathers. They've been calling home and sobbing their eyes out."

When everyone was seated, Smith cracked a smile and said softly, "Congratulations." The players smiled back and gave him their full attention. "Tomorrow you are going home," he said. "I want you to spend the time with your families. It's very important.

"I also want you to enjoy the experience of being an Olympian. People are going to know who you are and you will start to hear how excited they are about the Olympics. I want you to appreciate how special that is. After I was part of the 1988 Olympics, I woke up one morning and the birds were chirping and I asked myself, Where did it go? I do not want that to happen to you.

"Now, remember, you are no longer civilians. We can't live like them. We don't eat like them, and we can't consume the beverages that they consume. Have fun with your families and friends, but remember you have something very important to do when the two weeks are over.

"So get yourselves all packed up and I'll see you at five-thirty in the morning. Good night." Smith rubbed his neck and felt weary. He had scores of details to take care of before departure time. He asked Tom and Amie to handle any last-minute questions.

Lisa and Karyn congratulated their Olympic teammates as they left the Skylight Room. Returning to their bedroom, they both wondered what to do about Kelly, who had left everything that she hadn't yet packed when she rushed out of the building.

Lisa started making a pile of Kelly's belongings. "This is the worst part about being an athlete," she said. "You give everything you've got and then you listen to someone read a list. If you are not on it, everything is over. If you're a woman athlete, it may be really over."

"I'm so glad we made it, K.L.," she added as she gathered the last of Kelly's possessions.

Karyn thought, How could he not take you, Brownie? Nobody wanted to be on this team more than you and nobody worked harder to make it. Karyn considered how during every shift, practice, and game Lisa demonstrated to her coaches, teammates, and opponents her pride in wearing the USA uniform. Ben Smith had put pressure on Lisa during the tour, but nobody, including Smith, had pushed Lisa harder than she had pushed herself.

Feeling a need to do something helpful, the roommates decided to pack Kelly's personal effects and send them home to her. They listened to people laughing in the hallway and realized that the players were coming together as a team.

While Karyn addressed the box to Kelly's home, Lisa picked up the cell phone and called John in his hotel room. Coach Smith had given Lisa permission to spend the night with her husband. John, who said he had put champagne on ice, was coming right over to get her.

As Karyn walked Lisa to the front door of the Training Center, she dropped Kelly's package with the clerk at the reception desk. Sending their friend's package home made both women melancholy. So much was ending and so much was beginning.

Entering the lobby they saw teammates reveling in happiness. The two young goalies, flushed with excitement, were talking together on a couch. As Lisa and Karyn walked toward the door, they overheard the goaltenders saying, "We can do it! We can backstop this team to a gold medal!" The two veterans started laughing. What an amazing thing to be twenty years old and headed for the Winter Olympics!

The two young revelers gave the veterans renewed hope. They smiled at each other, realizing that the years of sacrifice had finally paid off. "We're going to Japan, Brownie," Karyn said joyfully. "As members of the first women's Olympic hockey team!"

Lisa hugged her close friend and said, "Be sure to pack your flag, K.L. I have a good feeling we'll be needing it in Nagano."

4

THE INNER CIRCLE

"For a Higher Purpose"

San Jose, California ~ January 20, 1998

Cammi unfastened her seat belt and leaned over to pull her carry-on bag from beneath the seat in front of her. She heard her teammates and the other passengers in the plane chattering as they wearily arose from their cramped, uncomfortable seats, opened overhead compartments, and removed their stowed gear. In the sardine-can intimacy of the cabin, curious passengers stared at the players' travel clothes and politely asked questions. Cammi eavesdropped on these friendly conversations, which inevitably ended with hearty congratulations and wishes of good luck. She chuckled each time she heard a well-dressed business traveler opine that the women on the plane "sure don't look like hockey players." Some of the players were genuinely glamorous women whose striking good looks suggested that they might be models and not athletes. A casual observer might be fooled by the baby blue nail polish, glossy pink lipstick, or red-white-and-blue grosgrain ribbons. But a closer look made it clear that, to paraphrase the Women's College Coalition slogan, their "role models weren't models." The twenty women in navy blue Nike travel suits were clearly very serious athletes. Cammi loved the way her teammates' healthy appearance and no-nonsense demeanor shattered stereotypes.

The pilot and copilot joined the cabin crew in wishing the players good luck as they disembarked at the front of the plane. Cammi's pace quickened as she walked down the tarmac toward the section of the airport terminal where her older brother Tony, his wife, Linda, and their four young children—her darling niece and nephews—were waiting. For Cammi, seeing Tony and his family was going to be the highlight of the Olympic team's trip to California.

Tony, a professional hockey player with the San Jose Sharks, was delighted to see his sister. Team USA was scheduled to play an important game against Team Canada in Tony's home rink, San Jose Arena, better known as the Shark Tank, on Tuesday, and then remain in the city for several days of pre-Olympic events and activities. The Sharks had two big home games during the women's stay, and the Sharks' organization had provided complimentary tickets to Cammi's team. After not seeing Tony and other members of her family for several weeks, Cammi had five precious days to be near them.

As Cammi hurried up the passageway toward the terminal, she scanned the waiting crowd. Suddenly, four small heads peeked around a corner. The children caught a glimpse of their aunt moving toward them and immediately started waving American flags to welcome her. Cammi stopped squinting, broke into an enormous smile, and started jogging. The welcoming party was cuter than any of her pictures or memories. The children were dressed patriotically for the occasion. Eight-year-old Michael and six-year-old Nicholas had thrown on blue jeans and jerseys. Four-year-old Dominic was red, white, and blue from head to foot. Two-year-old Gabrielle, or Gabby, as her parents called her, wore red. Linda had Gabby in red clothing, shoes, and, of course, nail polish. Cammi threw her arms around her four favorite fans, kissing each one and thanking them for being there.

Tony extended his hand to Ben Smith, his old friend and hockey coach. Tony held fond memories of the 1988 Calgary Olympics, when Dave Peterson and Smith coached a group of young hopefuls to a seventh-place finish. Tony Granato had been a much-heralded All-American out of the University of Wisconsin when he was selected for the 1988 men's Olympic hockey team. Some of his buddies on that Olympic squad were now experienced NHL players like himself. Many favored the idea of "Smitty," as they called him, coaching the first women's Olympic team.

Acknowledging his former player, Smith took Granato's hand and said, "Hey, Tony, it's great to see you. How are you doing? I can't tell you how much fun it is to finally coach the *good* Granato."

Tony laughed. "Everything is going well. Linda and I are enjoying Northern California. The kids are growing fast. I'm feeling fine."

Tony Granato had suffered a serious injury in a hockey game while playing for the Los Angeles Kings two years earlier. He was checked into the boards and hit his head as he fell. Initially he shook off the hit as a routine part of the game. But when he started having severe headaches a few days later and could not recognize the people on Christmas cards posted on his refrigerator, his wife became seriously worried. Doctors eventually diagnosed a blood clot in his brain. He was given medication to try to shrink the clot, but after a subsequent X ray showed that the clot was continuing to grow, he was scheduled for immediate brain surgery. Within hours of the decision his family was by his side. His sisters were devastated. The nature and immediacy of the surgery were frightening.

Tony's operation was successful, but his recovery was painful and difficult. Sitting at his bedside one day Cammi tried to inspire him to be tough by reminding him of the day he hit her with a fastball. He was about twelve years old and she was five. He wanted to practice pitching but didn't have a catcher. So he made Cammi put on a glove and provide a target. The first time Tony threw a fastball he hit Cammi in the stomach. She crumbled into a ball and fell to the ground gasping for breath. To his amazement, she didn't cry or run to tell her mother. Tony crouched over his sister to assess the damage. Cammi was struggling for air but wasn't bawling, so he said, "Okay, Cammi, get up and get ready. I'm throwing ya another one." The brave little sister staggered to a standing position and took the next fastball. Cammi reminded her bedridden brother that, even though she was scared to death and suffering, she stood up and took another pitch.

Tony laughed and tried to deny his behavior but knew the story was true. Eventually, with the love and support of his wife and family, he persevered and made a full recovery.

Bob Webster said, "You're lookin' great, buddy. We were worried about ya for a while." Tony and Bob were also old friends. Bob had served as the equipment manager for several USA Hockey teams on which Tony had played.

Tony slapped his old friend on the back. "It's great to have you guys here. Your team will enjoy playing in the tank."

"Will we see you in Nagano?" Ben Smith asked.

"I wouldn't miss it," Tony responded. "I'm excited to see the women make Olympic history."

Smith and Webster described the great job Cammi was doing both as captain of the team and spokesperson for women's ice hockey. They promised to meet in Nagano, where Tony and Linda would be joined by many members of the Granato family.

Cammi and Tony's parents, Natalie and Don, raised four sons and two daughters in a home filled with unqualified love. Cammi remembers a household constantly filled with siblings and cousins. Don worked two jobs to meet expenses and Natalie kept the family's support systems running. To keep the children healthy and occupied, Natalie and Don emphasized athletics and provided both structured and unstructured opportunities to play. In every season there were sports commitments—football, softball, soccer—but year-round and at all hours of the day and night, there was hockey.

Across the street from the Granatos' home, when Cammi was little, there was a baseball field where her father and uncle would play softball. The brothers and their wives would gather their children and bring them to the games to serve as batboys and -girls, provide water, or, every kid's favorite, change the numbers on the scoreboard. When summer faded into fall and autumn rains flooded the field, it became a perfect little pond. When the pond froze, all the children in the neighborhood pulled on skates, grabbed a stick, and spent the best hours of each day making up teams and playing games. Natalie couldn't drag her brood off the ice until darkness fell and the skaters could no longer see the puck. Cold was no factor. The colder the day, the rosier the cheeks. On the best days, the Granato kids, like racers entering a pit stop, would gobble dinner without removing their skates and hurry back to their contests. Those wintry afternoons on the pond, when the hot chocolate was steaming, the snow was crunchy, the air was still, and the ice was painted with a purple sunset, were the backdrop for many happy family memories.

Other happy hours were spent playing hockey in the basement or attending Chicago Blackhawks games as a family. The indoor contests were played with ferocious intensity in an empty cellar converted to an arena. Tape marked the lines. Nets stood at each end of the room. The goalies wore masks hand-painted by brother Don. Full-body checks were allowed under the house rules. On a typical day, first the 1980 U.S. Olympic team battled Russia and then the Chicago Blackhawks challenged the Minnesota North Stars. Vicious fights broke out at the start of each game over who would be Mike Eruzione, number 21 for the Olympians. Cammi and her three older brothers played two on two until three Granato cousins, all boys, showed up and created a three-on-three contest with a "bench." Players on the bench sat on a mattress propped against the wall until their turn to rotate into the game.

The unwritten rule for the Granato arena was "If you want to play, you don't tell Mom when something goes wrong." Natalie Granato was a disciplinarian. Telling her what was going on downstairs was like inviting a referee to hand out penalties. And Mother Granato's punishments could be harsh. So, as the Olympians attempted to crush the Russians, the rule was that a call to Mom earned a long wait on the bench or elimination from the game. Cammi learned fast to absorb body checks, play hard, and keep Mom out of it.

The basement gladiators' fantasies were fed by frequent trips to see professional games in Chicago. If a child took a good nap on specified days, he or she might merit a ticket to the Blackhawks game that night. The two Granato families had six season tickets between them. Their nine kids begged to be invited if their health and hockey schedules permitted. Christina, who didn't join in the basement shenanigans, did join the chorus begging for Blackhawks tickets. She and Cammi loved the action of the games and had crushes on favorite players. In short, the Granato kids enjoyed an active, family-centered childhood.

After a wonderful dinner in the city, Tony and Cammi hurried to a live interview at a San Francisco television station. Tony was a sports hero in California, so having the duo in the San Francisco Bay area was newsworthy. Tony's children watched with total fascination as their father and aunt were prepped and presented on camera. The children understood that their dad was famous and were only beginning to realize that Aunt Cammi was a celebrity, too.

The players' hotel was a three-block walk from the San Jose Arena. The hotel's proximity to the arena, a gym, and local restaurants made its location highly desirable, so it was no surprise to Cammi when she discovered that Team Canada was staying there also. She chuckled. Ben Smith and Shannon Miller would have to be polite to each other in very close quarters, an objective that was becoming increasingly difficult as the Olympics approached.

When Cammi reached her hotel room she shared her day's adventures with her roommates, consulted with Kris and Amie about the next day's jam-packed schedule, and called her mother and sister, who had flown into San Jose from Chicago.

Cammi's mother's presence was felt by all of her teammates. Natalie Granato was "Mrs. G." to the veterans as well as the rookies. During the eight years Cammi had played on the national team, Natalie had traveled to as many games as possible, sometimes alone, sometimes with her husband and other children. Over time, she had become one of the women's team's most enthusiastic supporters. As the mother of four players, she had a unique perspective on the evolution of the sport for both men and women.

As her older boys moved from the basement to prep school, college, semi-professional, and in Tony's case, Olympic and professional hockey, Natalie watched and learned. While her boys ascended to higher levels, her hockey-playing daughter tried to achieve as well. Cammi and her older brother Robby were close in age and the best of friends. When they entered adolescence they had similar aspirations, including some day becoming Chicago Blackhawks. Their idol was Keith Magnuson. Cammi had a set of autographed knee pads from Magnuson, a treasured gift purchased at a charity benefit.

One day when Cammi was about thirteen years old, she had a conversation with her mother about playing in the National Hockey League. Nonchalantly, Cammi said, "I want to be a Blackhawk when I grow up, Mom. I'm going to be a Chicago Blackhawk."

Natalie was startled and replied matter-of-factly, "Cammi, you can't be a Blackhawk. You can't play in the NHL. You're a girl."

Cammi became upset and said, "What do you mean I can't play because I'm a girl?" She was shocked. It had never occurred to her that she couldn't play the game at a higher level because she was a woman. She competed with her older brothers and they were considered skilled players. Why couldn't she play with older guys?

Natalie felt terrible when Cammi started crying. Until that moment,

Natalie had never told her daughter she couldn't do something specifically because she was a female.

But unlike a lot of adolescent girls who receive negative messages about being a woman, Cammi never gave up. She continued to play hockey and look for opportunities that included women. Her parents became her anchor, providing emotional and financial support; her older sister Christina became her confidante, listening when she was down and giving advice when she was discouraged; and her brothers became her allies, determined to help their sister reach the top of a sport where women were considered outsiders.

In early adolescence the Granato boys didn't yet realize that their younger sister and her love for the game of hockey were special. She was just their little sister and she liked to play a game. Tony recalled that it wasn't until he was about seventeen that he first noticed that his buddies' little sisters weren't playing hockey. Their little sisters were playing with dolls and their teenage sisters were cheerleading or playing a "girl's sport." At that point Tony and his brothers became aware that Cammi was different.

Tony's buddies also noticed Cammi's impressive talent. The Granato boys started to worry. What was Cammi going to do when the biggest guys started to hit her? It was inevitable that if she played with the boys, guys would take runs at her. And what was she going to do if she could no longer play? Their local high school didn't offer girls' hockey and their parents would never send her away from home to attend a high school that did. Cammi's brothers decided that the one thing they could do was to continue to include her as an equal in their games. In that way, as they got better she would also.

When Cammi reached adolescence the three older Granato brothers had a second revelation; not only was their little sister an impressive hockey player, she was a beautiful woman. When Cammi attended her first dance and came downstairs in a dress, her "allies," like typical brothers, started teasing. Leaving their whistles and comments behind, Cammi hurried off to the dance with her boyfriend.

Although Cammi's physical appearance was irrelevant to opposing teams by the time she reached fifteen, the facts that she was a girl and a star athlete were not. As she told her brothers, "Everyone is taking aim at me." Fools tried to injure her because she was a girl. Serious competitors tried to stop her because she could put the puck in the net. The most discouraging part was that some of the coaches condoned the fools' behavior.

When Cammi received in one game a concussion from what was alleged to be an intentional injury, Cammi's parents became concerned. Her brothers' prediction had come true; guys were taking runs at her. Although Cammi's parents knew she was as tough as the other kids her size and could handle the common injuries that are natural to the game, they worried about uncommon and potentially devastating "get-the-girl" injuries. Cammi could have eighteen or twenty allies, including Robby, on her own team, but they could not possibly protect her everywhere on the ice from a troublemaker on the other team.

With sadness but good judgment, Natalie and Don encouraged Cammi to switch to basketball for her final years of high school. Cammi, already a star in soccer, tennis, and volleyball, was disappointed and angry that her parents felt she should give up the game she loved. She wondered if anyone understood what it meant to her. But she acquiesced and switched to basketball.

Cammi was the Downers Grove North High School basketball team's most valuable player, but she never gave up hockey. When she finished a basketball game, she grabbed her skates and stick and headed for the rink. And between her junior and senior years in high school, she applied to colleges that offered not only the curriculum she desired but also competitive intercollegiate women's ice hockey. She wanted to be with other women who loved the game, played it well, and wanted to promote it. She felt that more girls would play if given the opportunity, and if more girls played there'd be less tolerance of discriminatory behavior.

By the time Cammi was eighteen years old, Natalie was well aware that her daughter's commitment to following her dream was as impressive as her talent. Natalie's boys were supported by existing systems: state and regional public and private high school programs, AHAUS/USA Hockey programs, NCAA Division I and III men's hockey programs, the U.S. men's Olympic program, and even the National Hockey League and its feeder teams. When Cammi went off to Providence College there was a brand-new national team for women and a young intercollegiate women's program, but no NCAA national championship, and no women's Olympic program.

Cammi's first step toward reaching her goal was earning a place on the 1990 national team. Four years after her memorable conversation with her mother, the International Ice Hockey Federation (IIHF) announced that it would sanction the first women's world championships in Ottawa, Ontario, in 1990. Cammi tried out for the American team and made it. Natalie was thrilled. On the day Cammi turned eighteen, she played for the very first international gold medal in women's ice hockey. At a team dinner on the night before the game, the captain of the national team, Cindy Curley, surprised Cammi with a birthday cake. All of a sudden, being young and female didn't seem like a limitation.

The first world championships in women's ice hockey illustrated how gender stereotypes and limited resources affected the evolving women's game. Finland, Sweden, Norway, Switzerland, West Germany, Japan, Canada, and the United States qualified. The Canadian hosts decided to create a bright Pepto-Bismol–pink environment for their women guests. The Ottawa Civic Centre's ushers and usherettes wore pink tuxedoes with pink bow ties and handed out pink-and-white souvenirs. Canadian fans waved pink and white pom-poms for their national team, which was dressed in pink satin hockey pants with white shirts and socks featuring a pink maple leaf. The American team had its own uniform problems. The tournament was the first time USA Hockey had to outfit a women's team for a prominent international competition. Instead of formal travel uniforms, the women received inexpensive sweat suits and lightweight jackets. The sweatpants drooped in the rear and at the knees. The jacket was too flimsy to provide warmth. Cammi and the rest of the American team froze while their Canadian hosts looked ridiculously precious in pink. Yet the women athletes recognized that it was important to celebrate what had been accomplished: The International Ice Hockey Federation had established a world championship. There was no point in dwelling on the mistakes. The more serious objective at hand was gaining approval for a women's competition in ice hockey from the International Olympic Committee (IOC).

The first American request to make women's ice hockey a medal sport occurred in 1971, the year Cammi was born. The American Girls Hockey Association made the petition directly to the IOC. In 1975 the Amateur Hockey Association of the United States (AHAUS),

USA Hockey's predecessor, formalized the American request to the IOC. Before it would approve the sport, the IOC insisted that there be at least five petitioners with nine organized teams in each country. Regrettably, political and economic problems in the late 1970s derailed many petitions for five more years. In 1980, however, new petitions were launched as the sport grew. During the next decade the Canadians were frequent hosts and enthusiastic organizers of international competitions, with the Ontario Women's Hockey Association leading the way.

By 1990 a sufficient number of nations had the prerequisite number of skilled players and teams to qualify for Olympic competition. The pink-and-white Ontario tournament was the prelude to the next IOC petition. In 1992, Cammi turned twenty-one and the IOC approved an Olympic medal competition for the 1998 Winter Olympics in Nagano. Cammi could not try out to be a Blackhawk, but she could sure enough try out to be an Olympian.

By 1992, Cammi was prepared to push hard to gain gender equity in her sport. She had always been extremely competitive, with complete confidence in her ability. Title IX became law shortly after she was born. Twenty years later, the moment was right to earn the respect of the wider sports community. Within that community were men whose mothers, wives, and sisters had taught them that in the new culture of womanhood, females are active rather than passive and outspoken rather than silent. Many of these same men had daughters who expected to be treated equally, and sons for whom that expectation was a given. The culture of manhood had also changed in twenty years. Many older men were self-consciously antisexist. Young men instinctively supported civil rights. They all wanted their female loved ones treated fairly and, if they were not, would help them figure out how to make it happen.

The national team was the conduit to the future Olympic team. From 1992 to 1997, Cammi worked extremely hard to qualify for each one. To qualify she had to excel on her college team. She did so, leading Providence to back-to-back ECAC championships. When she graduated from Providence in 1993 she enrolled in a master's program at Concordia University in Montreal and played for Concordia's women's team. The postgraduate play was, to a certain degree, similar to the opportunities many men had in junior hockey leagues.

By 1996, Cammi was recognized as a standout. USA Hockey named her their Woman Player of the Year. In 1997, Cammi was elected captain of the national team. She was also selected, along with her brother Tony, now a nine-year NHL veteran, as the spokesperson for the sixtieth anniversary of USA Hockey. Less than ten years after hanging up her skates for fear of being injured, Cammi was America's most-honored woman hockey player. Natalie was proud once again, not only because her child had done something remarkable, but because she had never given up her dream.

When Cammi and her teammates awoke the day after their arrival in San Jose, they found that Coach Smith, Amie, and Kris had placed them on a busy and exciting schedule. They had a morning practice and afternoon clinic in the San Jose Arena, a nap before dinner, and then the West Coast showdown with Team Canada at seven-thirty P.M. Kris had arranged for lots of media coverage in the sports-crazy California market. Cammi and Tony were the stars, although the reporters also loved team shots with the little girls who turned out for the players' afternoon clinics.

Team USA discovered that the West Coast girls were as enthusiastic about hockey as their East Coast, Midwest, and Canadian peers. Through their braces and retainers the girls told reporters that they loved the game because "playing it proves we aren't wimps." They came to listen to the players because "we really wanted women role models." And, they were "psyched for the Olympics because the Americans were ready to kick butt." The clinic interviews of the players and their young disciples were a huge hit on the evening news.

The Olympic team's San Jose game was one of five showcase games with Team Canada that Ben Smith had scheduled in important American and Canadian cities throughout January to prepare his players for the Olympics. In addition to the event in San Jose, the teams were playing in Cleveland, Vancouver, Calgary, and Colorado Springs. Smith wanted the women primed for the intensity of representing their nation in front of enormous audiences with high expectations. He wanted them to practice dealing with difficult public situations. He wanted to see how well they'd handle pressure, to borrow a phrase from Billy Joel.

The coach didn't drop his players in front of the media and fans in January without initial introductions. He had three opportunities to do so in Boston and New York during the pre-Olympic tour. The first introduction followed an invitation from Harry Sinden and the Fleet Center to be guests of the Boston Bruins. Sinden suggested that the team perform in a brief exhibition between periods of a Bruins game.

When Smith told the women, they were insulted: "Between periods? That's like Little League, Coach. That's mini-one-on-one. We don't want to do that. It's demeaning."

Smith disagreed and said, "I think it might be fun. It would be neat. We could expose the women's game to a lot of people who love hockey."

The women weren't convinced, so Smith said, "Okay, we'll all go in and watch the Bruins and Ducks game and we'll have some food. We'll wear our blue-and-white team uniforms and we'll be introduced. That will be it." His players agreed.

Halfway through the first period on the night of the game, the Bruins' public-address announcer told the huge Boston audience that the 1997 U.S. women's national team was in attendance and asked the players to stand. The applause was enormous, and minutes later children started showing up for autographs. The kids' faces were sweet and shining. Behind the youngsters, mothers and fathers lined up in the aisles seeking signatures for children who weren't at the game. The players were amazed at how much attention they were receiving from what was essentially a men's audience.

When the Bruins game ended and Team USA moved toward the exits, people on the escalators recognized the players and called out, "USA! USA! Go get 'em! Good luck in Japan! We love you, USA! Good luck, girls! All the way USA! Miracle on ice! Go for the gold!" The excitement grew as they passed through the crowd.

Riding back on the bus to Lake Placid, Coach Smith heard his players saying "Gee, these people really care about us. They don't even know who the hell we are and they're rooting for us."

The next day the coach asked his players how it felt to be "America's team" and whether they'd like to return to Boston for an exhibition. Cammi said she had canvassed the team and they felt great about it.

Three weeks later Team USA played between the periods of a Bruins game and then signed autographs in groups of four at six tables placed around the concourse. Deep lines formed at every table as young boys, college guys, businessmen, fathers, grandfathers, and, of course, girls and women in the building came to meet them. The Fleet Center had to shut off the line when it wrapped around the entire building, causing egress problems. The local press loved the exhibition and open access to the players. One reporter wrote the next day something to the effect that there had been "great two-way action for ten minutes at the Fleet Center" the night before "and then the Sabres and Bruins came back on the ice." When Smith read the article he decided his team was ready for the next venue, the Big Apple.

When the team had arrived in the New York City area in early December, Ben Smith shook everyone up by cutting Jeanine and Barbara shortly after their arrival. The players had to put their disappointment aside and move on. The New York City schedule and media attention offered the perfect dress rehearsal for Nagano. For three days the team went from seven A.M. until midnight without a break. Among other activities, they played an exhibition game before fourteen hundred people at Chelsea Piers, had lunch at the NHL offices, visited St. Luke's Hospital, and were hosted at a New York Rangers game in Madison Square Garden and a New Jersey Devils game in the Brendan Byrne Arena, where they were once again introduced and celebrated. Team USA did ABC, CBS, NBC, CNN, ESPN, and FOX news programs, as well as various other media appearances.

In New York and New Jersey, Ben Smith's players spoke with journalists, politicians, and celebrities. From each they received the same questions over and over again and learned how to fine-tune their answers. Before the trip, the players had interacted mostly with small-town media in small doses. New York, New Jersey, and Boston gave the players an introduction to high-power media in high doses. It was very important practice. Boston was two nights. The New York/New Jersey trip was three and a half days. The Winter Olympics would bring constant interaction with the international press corps for sixteen days and nights.

Ben Smith knew American women's Olympic teams had traditionally not received a lot of media attention, but he had an inkling that the women's hockey team would be different. For starters, the gold medal U.S. women's basketball, gymnastics, soccer, and softball teams had emerged, after the fact, as the story of the 1996 Summer Olympics. Furthermore, the hockey team was participating in a new Olympic sport and one that was not commonly played by women.

Smith knew there was a dichotomy between the average sports fan's perception of the men who play hockey and the women who would play on the Olympic team. Every reporter assigned to cover them was fascinated to learn that the women who were playing this very rough game were not big, strapping females but indistinguishable from the other attractive young women in the stands. And, unlike the NHL all-stars who would compete for the other gold medal in ice hockey, the women athletes were amateurs. The male professionals would bene-fit from NHL player association contracts, high salaries, and special perks. But in the end, the women and men would play the same game for the same prize. The contrast between the NHL all-stars and the all-American girls grabbed every reporter's attention, especially when they realized that the women's games were going to be no less im-portant than the men's.

Ben Smith had come to the conclusion that his colleague at USA Hockey, Art Berglund, was correct when he said, "Ben, this is going to be big, big, big!" Smith recalled that Art had added, "Gold medals change lives."

By January, Ben Smith and Art Berglund's conviction that this was a big story was proven right. The media covering the NHL All-Star Game in Vancouver during the January 17 to 19 weekend also had a chance to see a USA-Canada women's game. Reporters started mak-ing male-female comparisons and speculating about his-and-her medals. Many asked Smith to comment on what made coaching women different. He wisely stuck to his standard response: "The blue fingernail polish under the gloves, the Beanie Babies in the hockey bags, and the perfume in the locker room." Once in a while he'd throw in "the sports bras under the T-shirts." The writers got his point: Hockey is a woman's game as well as a man's; drop your sex-ist biases and report on how well these athletes play this extremely fast and physical sport. Smith knew that if the media concentrated on the players as athletes, they would be impressed.

And they were. The women's teams played before fourteen thou-sand fans in Vancouver and, even though the American team wasn't the favorite, Cammi and her teammates loved the intensity of the au-dience's reaction. The Canadians won the game, raising Canadian hopes for a gold medal, but the Americans played well also. It was a great preview for the world press.

The Vancouver game was an excellent opportunity for Smith to watch how his team handled being in the presence of sport celebrities. The women players met NHL luminaries whom they had admired. Tricia Dunn, who idolized Eric Lindros, endured merciless teasing at the All-Star Game. Smith knew that in the Olympic Village the famous blend with the anonymous, and he wanted his players to get used to being around superstars. He also wanted to help his players understand that their own medal competition was as significant as the celebrities'.

Ben Smith knew that his players would need more than these limited experiences dealing with fans, media, and sports notables in order to handle the pressure of being an Olympian. He had seen players, coaches, and even teams lose their focus under the pure strain of Olympic competition. He asked sports psychology consultant Peter Haberl to help him prepare Team USA for the psychological stress of performing under pressure. The 1998 U.S. Women's Olympic Ice Hockey Team had existed for less than one month. Ben Smith, however, had hand-picked Peter Haberl two years earlier to act as the national team's sports psychology consultant. Haberl had worked hard to build trust among the players during that time.

Prior to San Jose, Peter had taught the national team specific principles of sports psychology. Goal-setting, staying focused under pressure, and team-building exercises in December and early January were precursors to important concepts and exercises Haberl planned to introduce in San Jose. As far as Peter was concerned the countdown to Nagano was ticking off quickly. He was not scheduled to go to Japan and needed time in San Jose to finish the team's preparation. He hoped the San Jose game with Canada would provide instructive moments the players could carry into the Olympics.

When Cammi finished a series of pregame interviews, she hurried to join her teammates in the locker room. As always, Bob Webster had every piece of her equipment in perfect condition. The San Jose locker room looked as well-equipped and orderly as when the professional men's teams used it. Cammi was comforted to find that her stall, like every other, bore the sign of Bob's special attention to detail. Every item, including each skate, was not only in the correct place but also pointing in the same direction. On the training table in the center of the room Bob had placed the team's new Olympic mascot, a replica of the Statue of Liberty.

Lady Liberty, as the team had christened her, was a gift from Providence College alumnus Vincent Martello. After reading about Team USA and what they were trying to accomplish, he sent the statue to them in Colorado Springs with a letter enumerating the reasons why it should serve as their symbol. He argued that, most important, the statue represented freedom, but in addition, it had come to symbolize the nation as a land of diverse and independent people. Appropriately, he continued, it also represented the power of a woman—a strong, fearless female who could stand up to adversity and prevail.

When Martello's package arrived, Team USA still had no official mascot. They groused about Team Canada's highly visible symbol, the Princess, a Barbie look-alike dressed in a long blue gown and crown. The Americans felt that the Princess was a mismatch for the Canadian team specifically and the sport in general. "Hockey," they said, "is a game for everyone, a sport free of class distinctions and rank."

The Americans quickly agreed that the Statue of Liberty represented them well; they not only gave her a name but also a uniform. Gretchen cut the fabric from a USA jersey and Cammi drew the USA Hockey emblem and the name and number—LIBERTY 98—on it. When Laurie finished making a stick and helmet, the Americans welcomed Liberty as their new teammate.

After Liberty's formal designation as mascot, Bob saw to it that she was placed in the center of the locker room at the start of every game. The team surrounded her during their pep talks and some players touched her before every period. Gretchen held on to Liberty during the captain's comments for good luck and inspiration. At the end of each game Bob packed Liberty safely with the rest of the women's equipment so that she would be ready to take her place on the next locker room's training table.

While Cammi changed into her underclothing and a Prodigy tape blared on a boom box, Karyn yelled, "Hey, guys, five minutes to team stretch." Then she looked around for Lisa and said, "Okay, aerobic queen, get ready to lead."

Lisa pulled several CDs off the top shelf of her stall and walked over to the disc player. She shut off the Prodigy CD, much to Angela's dismay, and replaced it with a *Dance '97* CD. Adjusting the volume, she walked to the center of the room, and within a matter of moments, her nineteen teammates, dressed in the spandex and cotton they wore under their uniforms, formed a circle around her. Lisa asked, "Is everybody ready?"

Her teammates screamed above the music, "Yes, Brownie, we're ready!"

"Okay," Lisa said, "I've got two fast songs, one slow stretch, and a cool-down. You will each have nice loose muscles when these dance aerobics are over. So let's go!"

For the next fifteen minutes, as Lisa guided her team through a series of strenuous exercises, the locker room echoed with laughter. Bob stood in the hallway sharpening skates and tapped his toe to the beat of the music.

When Lisa was finished, the team gave her a cheer and then scattered to finish getting ready. Some checked in with Jeanna while others lined up to see Bob. When Cammi was dressed she looked around to see how everyone else was doing. Jeanna was taping Gretchen's wrist and Dr. Tom Carlson was reminding everyone to drink extra fluids. At the request of the USOC, Tom had volunteered to fly into San Jose from Oregon to serve as the team's physician in California. His job was to help Jeanna keep the women healthy until Dr. Sandy Glasson could take over as their doctor during the Olympics.

The USOC was responsible for appointing all medical personnel for American teams. Jeanna, Tom, and Sandy had been selected after a long qualification process that included experience working in sports festivals and world university games. Their roles were key. Cammi grabbed her numbered water bottle and waved to Tom, who saluted her for her good example.

When everyone was dressed and the pregame rituals and preparations were completed, Coach Smith came into the San Jose locker room and told his team that there were more than seven thousand fans in the building to see them, the largest American crowd ever to attend a women's hockey game. He reminded them that the game was their eleventh contest with Canada since October. "Canada hasn't got many secrets left to show us," he said. "Let's get out there, see what they've got, and have a great time."

When Smith was finished Cammi pulled the players together in the center of the room and gave them a pep talk. She said, "This is a big one. There are a lot of people here to see us. Let's show the crowd we're happy they came to support us, and let's give them a great game of hockey." Then she tapped Lady Liberty on the head and led her pumped-up teammates into the hallway.

Bob Allen and Art Berglund were standing in the hallway to greet them. While Bob kissed A.J.'s and other players' sticks, Art and Tom Carlson gave the skaters high-fives. The Canadians' locker room was so close that Cammi could see Shannon Miller pacing. She ignored her and said, "Here we go, USA!" then stepped aside to let starting goalie Sara DeCosta lead the American procession into the arena. Webby wished the players luck as they quickly paraded by him.

The San Jose Arena was jumping. The atmosphere felt truly California. Technology giants IKON, Netcom, LSI Logic, Apple, Seagate Software, and Adobe Systems had bought advertising space on the boards along with Toyota and Columbo Yogurt, a sponsor of the women's Olympic program. Vendors sold huge dishes of nachos with guacamole and salsa while techno music blasted over the skaters during warm-ups. Teenage boys with bleached-blond hair borrowed programs from buddies wearing aqua Sharks shirts and baggy jeans. The camera scanning the crowd found a group of young women in red Stanford sweatshirts dancing in the aisles. They were there to support Sami Jo Small from Winnipeg, an alternate goalie for Canada and a member of the Stanford women's club team.

San Jose's audience was as diverse as it was excited. There was an impressive mix of spectators by age, race, and ability. There were lots of older couples, young children escorted by their parents, and kids and adults in wheelchairs. An Asian couple in their twenties, one wearing a Team Canada T-shirt and the other a Team USA shirt, filed into their seats. A Caucasian couple wearing shirts that read LEAVE THOSE WHITE SKATES HOME: THE POWER OF A WOMAN slid in behind them. Ads for singer Luis Miguel's upcoming appearance in the arena flashed on the JumboTron in Spanish and English, followed by similar ads for Elton John. A group of Latino teenagers, standing in the front row next to the glass, waved a large American flag. Three well-dressed businesswomen sitting beside them joined their chanting. Cammi was pumped. This was a spectacular audience. She hoped she and her teammates could give them something exciting to cheer about.

Unfortunately, by the end of the second period neither team had done much to impress the crowd, which nevertheless remained enthusiastic. In the first period, Karyn scored a power-play goal on a slap shot from the blue line and received a penalty for body checking. The sound engineer played "One in a Million Girl" to recognize her hustle. Otherwise the period was uneventful. In the second period, Team Canada scored two goals, including the go-ahead goal on a power play. Sara DeCosta defended the net well, but the Canadians outshot the Americans 22–16. By the time the third period started, Cammi was anxious. She desperately wanted to win in her brother's home rink before this fabulous audience. Her team needed to play tough, disciplined hockey and control the play for the last twenty minutes of the game. They also needed to get lucky.

Seven minutes into the third period Katie King responded by scoring the tying goal for the Americans on beautiful assists from Laurie Baker and Shelley Looney. The crowd jumped on its feet and started singing "Everybody Dance Now" until a Canadian player checked Sue Merz, sending her reeling in pain, first onto her knees and then into a crouched position on the ice. While Jeanna Schepman attended to Sue and the American fans called for a penalty, the technician played the Rolling Stones' "Start Me Up" to applaud the trainer's efforts.

Sue was down but not out. One of the more athletic players on the team, she was extremely tough. She could play offense or defense and was usually on the ice when the team needed a power-play goal. Smith knew Sue was the perfect player to "tee it up" for the score.

Sue's real name was Suzanne, but everyone called her "Murphy." She had grown up in Greenwich, Connecticut, where for ten years she played in the Greenwich Blues boys' program. In 1988 she switched to the Connecticut Polar Bears girls' regional team and two years later won a girls' national championship. Sue excelled in softball, baseball, and field hockey in high school but decided to attend the University of New Hampshire and concentrate on ice hockey. During her four-year career at UNH she tallied fifty goals and fifty-three assists.

When she was only eight years old, Sue lost her mother, Catherine, after a sudden illness following a trip to Europe. Her mother and father, Andre, had moved to the United States from Switzerland. Andre raised Sue and her older brother, Jean-Claude, or J-C, as a single parent. He gave Sue 100 percent support when she asked to play a non-traditional sport.

Ben Smith thought Sue might be the all-around best athlete in the national competition when he took over the women's national program, but he wasn't sure how hard she would work to make the Olympic team. Like a lot of the hopefuls, she was so talented she could easily cruise. He decided to test her. He cut her from the national team before the world competition early in 1997. Sue took the gesture seriously. After working with Mike Boyle at BU, she gained strength, increased her stamina, and moved into a higher fitness category.

Smith was impressed. He needed Sue's skills as well as her commitment. When the national team was announced in the summer of 1997, he was pleased to have her on the roster. When she heard the good news, Sue put on her good-luck charms—a gold heart, a UNH pendant, and a little elephant with an elevated trunk—and asked Bob Webster for a shirt with her favorite number, 7.

As Team USA's number 7 skated to the bench with Jeanna's assistance, the San Jose crowd applauded. Moments later play resumed and Alana Blahoski was called for hooking. The music quickly changed to "Born to Be Wild." The song continued as Chris Bailey was called for roughing, forcing the Americans to play shorthanded. Good luck followed bad when a Canadian goal, scored with one and a half minutes left in the game, was nullified by the referee, holding the score at 2–2. The American fans didn't want any part of a tie. They screamed for the winning goal while their Canadian counterparts did likewise.

The Canadian fans got their wish with forty-nine seconds on the clock when Jayna Hefford scored her second goal in the game. Everyone wearing a maple leaf celebrated wildly while Coach Smith called time-out and huddled with his players. "Look, there's plenty of time left on the clock for us to score," he said. "I want a set play executed when I pull Sara out of the net. Listen carefully: I want Cammi, Karyn, Tara, Sue, and Alana out on the ice when Sara hits the boards."

When the ref dropped the puck and the clock started, Sara watched for her cue. Smith left her in, waiting for the perfect moment. As luck would have it, Canada's leading scorer, Geraldine Heaney, punched Karyn with twenty-seven seconds to play, providing another time-out and the chance to set up a two-man advantage. While the crowd sang

"Na Na Hey Hey Kiss Him Goodbye," Tom Mutch assigned A.J. to the face-off and Ben Smith directed Sue Merz and Tara Mounsey to take their places on the points. Cammi, Sandra, and Karyn were told to stay near the net just in case A.J. Mleczko lost the face-off.

Which, to no one's surprise, she did not. With the game on the line, the crowd on its feet, and twelve seconds on the clock, A.J. dug down, grabbed the puck, and fired it to Sue, who executed a precision pass along the blue line to Tara. Standing at the point, Tara planted her skates, pulled back her stick, and, when the puck arrived, blasted a stunning one-timer past Manon.

As the arena exploded, Cammi looked up. There were seven seconds on the clock and the game was tied 3–3! She sprinted toward Tara, who was flabbergasted. Tara raised her stick and arms straight in the air and simply turned to look at her cousins who had flown in from Los Angeles to see her game. Her cousins were going crazy in the stands, along with most of the other spectators in the building. Grabbing Tara to congratulate her, Cammi felt her anxiety melt away. She now felt instinctively that her team would beat Canada.

Seven seconds after the drop of the puck regulation time ended, sending the West Coast showdown into sudden-death overtime. The fans couldn't have been happier. The third period had been spectacular. Both teams passed and shot magnificently. Eight of their previous eleven games had been won or lost by a goal, and now the same would be true of this game. Patriotic zeal took over. With country music as the backdrop, the fans started waving and screaming. Chants of *"U-S-A! U-S-A!"* and *"Can-a-da!"* filled the Shark Tank.

Cammi caught a glimpse of her mother, Christina, Tony, Linda, and the children—dressed in number 21 USA Hockey jerseys with GRANATO across the shoulders—waving their homemade signs and American flags. She felt upbeat and confident. Someone on Team USA would score a goal. She just knew it. In the huddle around Sara's net she said, "This game is ours. Let's show them what we're made of!"

The overtime hockey was excellent. The play was fast, clean, and balanced. Laurie, who had assisted on Karyn's and Katie's earlier goals, was heavily defended. She took the double coverage in stride, knowing that Canada intended to leave an American player open. She watched for an opportunity. When Alana fed her the puck and the

Canadian defense collapsed on her, leaving Katie open, Laurie responded cleverly. Instead of passing immediately, she crashed in on Manon's left, taking the defensive coverage and goalie's attention with her. Meanwhile Katie barreled down the right and waited for the pass. At the perfect moment, Laurie slid the puck under the defense and across the slot, giving Katie an open net in which to score the winner. When Katie shot and the red light behind Manon came on, the American fans threw popcorn and programs in the air and hugged their neighbors while Team USA spilled over the boards and buried Katie, Laurie, and Alana under a pigpile.

Cammi was so excited she embraced and congratulated each player personally. When the crowd started clapping to the beat of the music and a film clip of Mike Myers as Austin Powers dancing down a street flashed on the JumboTron, she started laughing. Her team had come back three times under pressure and won the game in style. Cammi was euphoric.

Team USA followed their captain to the blue line and lined up randomly for the national anthem. Suddenly the song seemed terribly important. The Americans in the audience, knowing they could not join the players in Nagano, offered their equivalent of an Olympic send-off. With hats removed, hands on hearts, and vocal cords extended, they sang a rousing and emotional "Star-Spangled Banner," letting the young women know they'd be with them in spirit at the Olympics. Cammi registered the sentiment in her memory. When the anthem ended, the Americans shook hands with their opponents and saluted the audience with their sticks. The crowd roared as the players hurried to the locker room to shower.

After Coach Smith congratulated his team, he shook each player's hand and asked them to hurry upstairs to give autographs. Reporters, relatives, and fans were waiting. A line had formed around the radius of the mezzanine. Cammi hustled, knowing it was late on a school night and her niece and nephews were coming to the locker room to visit her.

When she had showered, dressed, and checked her instructions with Kris and Amie, Cammi rushed into the hallway outside the locker room. Waiting with her brother and sister-in-law were her four red-white-and-blue favorites, each dressed in a replica of her USA Hockey jersey. She kissed her brother and leaned over to hug the children, who presented her with red roses. Then, while Tony congratulated Ben Smith and discussed the highlights, including Tara's "rocket," Cammi took the kids by the hand and introduced them to players finishing up in the dressing room.

The Granato children had met the stars of the Los Angeles Kings and San Jose Sharks, including the legendary Wayne Gretzky, but they were in awe wandering among the women Olympians. Cammi could tell that meeting the Olympic team was special. The boys were as excited as she had been ten years earlier when she had met Tony's Olympic team in Calgary.

Amie escorted Cammi to the arena mezzanine, where hundreds of Team USA fans had gathered. Waiting patiently in line, the fans recognized Cammi and applauded as she hurried to join her teammates already seated at tables. Although she had had a very demanding day, Cammi signed programs, T-shirts, and ball caps until her left arm was exhausted.

The fans in San Jose were wonderful. They told stories, shared their enthusiasm, and wished the players good luck at the Olympics. One of the last groups through the line was a threesome from Northern California—one black and two white girls—who said they were hockey players on a competitive boys' team. Cammi laughed when they said one of the best players on their team was a guy from Jamaica. That's awesome, she thought. The coolest game on earth is going global.

Since the team was staying on in California for rest and a change of pace before the Olympics, they were able to attend a luncheon the next day, hosted by the San Jose Sports Authority and Visa U.S.A. The luncheon, which was attended by many San Jose dignitaries, was billed as the team's official West Coast Olympic send-off. The team listened carefully as USOC executive director Dick Schultz told the players and local guests that in official public-opinion polls rating the most admired athletes, Americans rated Olympians fifty points higher than the most respected professional, college, or high school athletes. "The most important thing you do," he said, "is make an effort to be a positive role model for young girls, young people, and Americans in general."

When Schultz had finished, executive director of USA Hockey David Ogrean gave the audience an overview of the history of the U.S.

women's ice hockey program, and Donna Lopiano of the Women's Sports Foundation expressed the foundation's best wishes for the team's success. Becky Saeger, an executive vice president of Visa U.S.A, told the audience that "girls aren't wimps in business or in sports" and that "the big story" of the Olympics would once again be the women.

The luncheon's keynote speaker was Tara VanDerveer, who had coached the 1996 U.S. Women's Olympic Basketball Team to a gold medal in Atlanta. VanDerveer told the athletes to "act, not react" and to appreciate the fact that "team is everything." She described Laurie Baker's assists in the previous night's game as being just as critical as her teammates' goals. She said the athletes should envision winning the gold medal and ask themselves, Why not us? VanDerveer described how she made her basketball players practice receiving the gold medal using an actual medal one of them had won in a previous Olympics. She told the hockey players, "There will be only sixty minutes between you and the gold medal. You must play great defense and you must play with confidence." In closing, she coached the American women, "Go for it! Kick their ass! . . . Have fun!" Cammi and her teammates cheered VanDerveer's comments and locked them in their memories.

Ben Smith followed VanDerveer. After a film clip that described him as "the man behind the women," Smith told the audience that when he took over the team in July 1996, following thirty years coaching men at different levels, he worried that he had "stepped into the abyss." Instead he found fun-loving women athletes who played with courage and modesty. And while he couldn't resist saying that "the only difference between coaching men and women is fingernail polish," he conveyed an important message. "The only thing a coach really needs is to get off the bus with the best athletes, but in this case, I am not only getting off the bus with the best players, I am also dealing with individuals who are better people than they are athletes."

The audience erupted in applause. Smith had articulated why Dick Schultz's point was so powerful: The Olympic Games expose athletes to everyone. Olympic athletes, therefore, have an important obligation to act responsibly. Smith believed that, as the coach of this particular Olympic team, he had the best-case scenario, superb athletes whom he knew to be excellent role models. Cammi understood more clearly than ever before Team USA's mission to be "athlete-ambassadors" for their country and their sport.

In addition to providing time to rest and visit with family and friends, the most important thing the team's extended stay in California afforded was an opportunity to prepare psychologically with Peter Haberl for the Olympics.

Cammi and the team liked working with Peter. He was very sensitive to the women's specific needs and was an excellent one-on-one resource for the players who needed someone to confide in. Most of the time he was a teacher and observer. He taught goal setting and the basic principles of sports psychology to the twenty women as a unit, and he observed the group's dynamic on and off the ice. Ben Smith called Peter the "mad Austrian" because of his wonderful accent, sense of humor, and history as a member of the Austrian national hockey team. Cammi, however, thought of Peter as a mild-mannered young advisor who knew the game well and had a wealth of knowledge about leadership, team building, and group cohesiveness. In her capacity as captain, she felt comfortable going to Peter to make suggestions or ask questions.

For the final pre-Olympic training sessions in Colorado Springs and San Jose, Peter consulted colleagues and then very intentionally designed an approach that was player-centered. He also worked closely with Cammi and her teammates to discern how best to prepare the players to be in a strong position to handle the stress and pressure that they were going to face at the Olympics. Peter explained to Cammi and the team that he was taking a "preventive perspective": "Together we will further develop your mental skills so that whatever happens at the Olympics, you will be able to handle the situation without disrupting your personal concentration or destroying the team's sense of cohesiveness."

Peter decided to build on the players' existing strengths: their love of the game, their experience competing under pressure, and their mutual respect. He conceptualized these strengths using three terms: "focused fun," "the circle of control," and "the inner circle."

Peter first introduced the notion of focused fun in December during the selection process. He and Ben Smith knew from experience that when there is too much pressure, athletes forget that what they are doing is supposed to be fun. They can even forget that being on a national or Olympic team is fun. Both men understood that athletes perform best when they are joyful. To have fun and be joyful they must lose themselves in the activity and become completely oblivious to everything else going on around them. At that point they stop evaluating themselves and play for the love of the game. Sometimes there are emotional barriers that prevent an athlete from achieving total concentration. Being aware of these impediments in advance and learning how to deal with them gives an athlete the ability to sustain concentration and remain "in the moment" and "totally present in time and space." "The circle of control" refers to a willingness to let go mentally of the things that can't be controlled—what the food is like, what the press writes, or whether or not an athlete gets stuck in traffic on the way to her event—and think about the one thing she can control: herself. This is the only way to maintain concentration and a sense of balance. In establishing this circle of control around her attitude, thinking, and the way in which she relates to her teammates, she contributes to her own and the team's well-being.

Peter taught the players that, in addition to controlling themselves successfully when the pressure became extreme, they could visualize a happy place filled with things that make them happy, and go to it mentally whenever the stress became unusually difficult. This was also a place they could access if they were feeling homesick or lonely.

By mid-January, Peter's preventive approach was already being utilized by many members of the team. Cammi and Peter agreed that it was now important to help people understand that the Olympics were right around the corner. As a further reality check, Haberl decided to take the athletes and staff to the Olympics psychologically before they were sent there physically. Imagery was a mental skill used to send the players to the Olympics in their mind's eye. He also planned two special activities with advice from the players and staff. The first was a viewing of film clips that addressed Cammi's concern about "being there." The second was a team bonding exercise he called "the inner circle."

Peter selected the first film clip to help the team start to visualize the Olympics and prepare for the emotional impact of being there. He chose two scenes from Bud Greenspan's famous series of documentaries on the Olympics. There was moving footage from the Opening Ceremonies at the 1984 Sarajevo Olympics. Greenspan's powerful imagery evoked the grandeur of the Olympic Games as a celebration of winter, while his narration elicited the wonder of competing among athletes who are or will become immortals—"the men and women whose exploits will live for all time." Peter knew that Mike Eruzione and other Olympic athletes whom the players had met had told them that the Opening Ceremonies were magical. He wanted the women to be moved and inspired by the spectacle but not overwhelmed by it. Peter was striving for a controlled, focused excitement.

The second film clip was Greenspan's scenes from the 1960 Squaw Valley Olympics' men's ice hockey competition. Greenspan interviewed Jack McCarten, the gold-medal goalie, many years after the Olympic Games. In 1960, McCarten's team was ranked fifth behind Canada, Czechoslovakia, the Soviet Union, and Sweden. The underdog Americans won five straight games to earn the gold medal. The press gave McCarten credit for the win, but he refused to accept it. He said, "We were a bunch of hockey players of average-to-good ability who played together as a team. I've always believed . . . since that day that teams win games, not individuals." Peter felt that it was important for the players to understand that McCarten was correct: Everyone on a team wins or loses together, a point that Cammi, as her team's captain, felt was critical to emphasize. Every member of Team USA must share Olympic disappointment as well as Olympic glory.

The third set of film clips Peter chose were from the Academy Award–winning documentary *When We Were Kings*, which relates the story behind one of former heavyweight boxing champion Muhammad Ali's remarkable fights. Peter had shown the entire film two weeks earlier in Colorado Springs. He selected the film to convey several important points he found difficult to communicate, including maintaining a sense of self and controlling the fear of failure. He believed that Ali's performance illustrated the points perfectly, but worried that the women might have a hard time relating to an African-American male athlete whose greatest athletic achievements occurred before most of them were born. He took the chance, knowing that the women shared at least one affinity with Ali: his commitment to competing for a higher purpose.

The next day on the ice at practice in Colorado Springs, Ben Smith spoke to his players about Muhammad Ali. He explained Ali's legacy as one of the greatest living athletes and gave a historical overview of the social and political environment in which he competed. Smith described the racial hatred that defined the era when Ali was pushing boundaries and questioning prejudicial practices. He explained how Ali used his sport to advance social justice.

The team was pleased that Smith had provided his perspective and enjoyed seeing the excitement in his eyes as he talked about it. The women had no context for the drama that surrounded Ali's life and knew nothing of his passion, rebellion, or moral commitment. They questioned Ali's often witty and charming but sometimes vituperative and political interaction with the media: It was the antithesis of the way they conducted themselves. But they had not experienced the hurtful reporting, exploitation, or trivialization that Ali had. They had not felt the demands of the media or the pressure to perform on the world stage. They had not yet encountered real stress. On the other hand, as athletes, the players had experienced self-doubt and fear of failure and, as women, they had struggled with unjust stereotypes. Too often they had been told they were the wrong sex, had the wrong look, or were the wrong type. They could identify with Ali's "getting in the face" of those who thought him unworthy for simply being who he was.

In San Jose, Peter used certain sections of the film to make several important points. The first point was that world-class athletes are not perfect. As Peter explained, "Elite athletes are often portrayed in the media as flawless heroes when, in fact, they are regular human beings who struggle like the rest of us to overcome physical, emotional, social, and financial problems. World-class athletes have doubts and concerns just as we have. They struggle to face their fears and overcome them."

Peter noted that early in the film Ali was shown in his prime winning a gold medal in the 1960 Summer Olympics and bragging about his talent. Peter explained that Ali, then Cassius Clay, stunned the public with his physical beauty and athletic prowess but also shattered stereotypes of black athletes by speaking out and demanding respect. On the surface Clay was a supercocky, self-assured sports hero. Underneath was a vulnerable human being putting his physical health at risk in the ring to make a public statement about social justice. The media gave him a forum. His athletic ability gave him an audience.

Peter's second point was that Cassius Clay maintained a strong sense of self despite being portrayed by the media as arrogant and—when he became a Muslim, changed his name, and refused to be inducted into the army on religious grounds—as unpatriotic. Ali consistently maintained his dignity each time the press and public criticized him.

Peter used the climax of the film, Ali's 1974 heavyweight championship fight against George Foreman in Zaire, to illustrate his third point, that it is okay for an athlete to be afraid, and fourth point, that successful athletes often compete for a higher purpose. He explained that the fight, which was billed as "The Rumble in the Jungle," was Ali's attempt to regain the heavyweight crown. Ali was no longer in his prime and he was scared. He went into the fight as the underdog. Nobody thought he had a chance to win. Nobody believed in him but himself, a situation very similar to the women's team, whom everyone considered the underdog. The only ones who believed in the team were the women themselves.

Aside from concerns about his physical condition, the fight's moral purpose—to fight in Kinshasa, Zaire, in an outdoor setting on the banks of the river Congo, before a live audience of 100,000 Africans and "uplift my brothers"—gave the contest greater importance and higher stress. The stress intensified as Ali lost control of most of the things going on around him. His accommodations were poor. His schedule was chaotic. Foreman suffered a training injury and the fight was postponed. The weather threatened. Ali even spoke to a witch doctor, who told him "a woman with trembling hands" would get to Foreman and help destroy him. But Ali remained fearful. Foreman had the capacity not only to humiliate him in the ring but to kill him. The strength required to beat Foreman had to come from within. Ali had to control his fears and insecurities and rely upon his strengths. And he had to believe in his heart that he was fighting for a noble purpose.

To illuminate for the women athletes how Ali's challenge and success related to their own, Peter then showed them film clips from several of their own games—clips that illustrated moments when pressure was enormous and emotions ran high. He showed sudden-death overtime goals, injury-producing penalties (when American players did not retaliate), and outstanding goaltending. He made the case that the women, like Ali, had a noble opponent who was also a reigning world champion. He argued further that they shared a commitment to a higher purpose than winning an Olympic medal. The athletes could prove to a world audience that women can excel at anything, including a highly physical sport that demands strength, speed, and skill. They could explode stereotypes. They could destroy prejudices. They could inspire girls. In the process, they could win greater opportunities for women.

In closing, Peter Haberl reminded the women athletes that they, like Ali, were flawed human beings who would make mistakes at the Olympics and, at some point, experience fear. He said, "Once you realize and can accept that you are not a perfect human being and will screw up, you will be in a better position to deal with your mistakes. Once you realize that it is okay to be afraid, you will be in a much better position to deal with your fear." Peter then asked the players to practice "U.S.A."—his acronym for "unconditional self-acceptance."

One day later, Peter gathered the twenty players, Ben Smith, Tom Mutch, Amie Hilles, Jeanna Schepman, and Bob Webster together in a hotel meeting room and introduced what he had decided was the final critical piece of the overall prevention strategy—team bonding exercises designed to create "the inner circle." The goal of the two exercises was to form a cohesive unit and establish team spirit.

Peter explained to the group that their strength as a unified group was imperative for their success, and that the people in the room were the only members of their "inner circle." No one else had the ability to help them reach their goal. He told them they would individually and collectively need the strength of the inner circle at the Olympics when unpredictable events threatened to undermine them. "When that happens," Peter explained, "the strength of the inner circle is what will keep you together and allow you to perform to your potential."

Peter asked everyone to join him in creating a physical representation of the circle. In an earlier team discussion in Colorado Springs, Sarah Tueting had suggested exchanging something symbolic to emphasize the notion of team. This idea was then fused with the concept of the inner circle. Peter and Amie had purchased a long, thin rope. The entire group methodically measured, cut, and then tied pieces of it onto each other's wrists. After each player, coach, and staff member, including Peter, had a bracelet, the group discussed what the bracelet meant to them.

Peter summarized their thoughts and impressions by saying, "You all now know who are the members of your inner circle, the very small group of people with the power to help you fulfill your goal of winning an Olympic medal. Your bracelets will be a constant reminder, an ever-present symbol, of who you are as a group, why you are at the Olympics, where you have come from, what you want to achieve, and how you must act individually and collectively to reach your goal. You have faith in each other. You trust each other. You can face what comes with individual and collective strength. You are mentally prepared to go to the Olympics."

After this symbolic ceremony, they followed Peter outside to the hotel parking lot. Peter directed members of the group to take the ends of a long, thick rope lying on the ground, shape it into a circle, and knot the ends.

When the knot was secure, Peter directed the entire group to pick up the knotted rope together, step back, and hold it. He explained that everyone there with their hands on the rope formed the team's inner circle. "From now until the gold-medal game is over, all that really matters is the inner circle. Everyone else—your parents, relatives, friends, the media, and the fans—are outside the circle and cannot help you to achieve your goal. In fact they can be distractions. You must rely on the inner circle for strength."

Peter then told the group to plant their feet firmly and, holding the rope tightly, lean back as far as they could without moving their feet. Everyone in the circle, including the coaches, leaned back, relying completely on the inner circle for support. They held this somewhat dangerous posture until Peter told them they could relax. When they did, they were excited. The rope had held and the entire group had been supported.

Astonished, Ben Smith said, "Let's do it again!"

Peter asked them to close their eyes and repeat the exercise. The athletes and their colleagues strained to defy gravity without injuring themselves. Knees bent, muscles twitched, and jaws tightened, but again the rope held and no one fell. When Peter said, "Open your eyes," the group started to cheer.

Peter repeated the exercise one more time from a sitting position.

The athletes bobbed in an awkward but impressive show of strength.

When everyone was standing, Cammi yelled, "We can do this! We can do this!" and gestured to the inner circle to huddle. She placed her hand in the center of the huddle and the players and staff placed their hands on top of hers. Face-to-face, leaning on each other for support, they smiled at each other and screamed, *"USA!"* Then they danced out of the huddle with their hands in the air, convinced they were ready for anything.

In a team context everything Cammi had hoped for had happened. There was an amazing sense of closeness among the team and staff members—twenty-six people who would win or lose, succeed or fail together. The inner circle was bound together metaphysically with a symbol that would strengthen and support them.

In a personal context Cammi understood why she increasingly had to sacrifice attention to her closest relationships, and why she should no longer feel guilty about doing so. What mattered at this time—until the Olympics ended—was the "family" within the inner circle. It was that special bond that provided comfort and needed to be nurtured, and Cammi felt fortunate that she had been elected to play the central role in doing that.

Ben Smith and Peter Haberl appreciated Cammi's leadership role as well. Several of the players were well-respected elders, but Cammi had the voice that each player could identify with, a voice that clearly articulated a shared vision. Cammi claimed that her experience watching her older brothers interact thoughtfully with the media had taught her to be a good spokesperson, but her coach detected other dimensions to her talent. For one thing, she cared deeply about the personal well-being of every teammate. She did not differentiate between rookies and veterans. She did not play favorites. He noticed how she consistently monitored players' interpersonal relationships and their impact on the team's general spirit. When team chemistry wasn't positive she found ways to improve it. In the dressing room she was enthusiastic. On the ice she was constructive. And, most important, she never complained—to her teammates, the staff, or her coaches.

Despite his special regard for Cammi, Ben Smith was as hard on her as he was on everyone else. He in no way granted her "most favored player" status even though she was his captain and, by Janu-

The players and staff of the 1997 USA Hockey Women's National Team in September 1997. Five of these close friends and team members were left behind when the Olympic team was selected from their ranks in December 1997. (*Photo by BBS/Scott Levy*)

Front row: Erin Whitten, Sarah Tueting, Cammi Granato, Sandra Whyte, Tom Mutch (assistant coach), Bob Allen (team chairman), Ben Smith (coach), Lisa Brown-Miller, Karyn Bye, Kelly O'Leary, Sara DeCosta. *Second row:* Amie Hilles (team leader), Bob Webster (equipment manager), Vicki Movsessian, Tara Mounsey, Tricia Dunn, Laurie Baker, A. J. Mleczko, Angela Ruggiero, Katie King, Stephanie O'Sullivan, Alana Blahoski, Jeanna Schepman (trainer), Kris Pleimann (public relations). *Back row:* Jenny Schmidgall, Gretchen Ulion, Shelley Looney, Chris Bailey, Barbara Gordon, Jeanine Sobek, Sue Merz, Colleen Coyne.

National team members line up on the blue line, eager to begin one of their games on the pre-Olympics tour. (*Photo by Concord Monitor/Andrea Bruce*)

Cammi Granato, inspirational captain and voice of the national and Olympic teams. (*Photo by Duomo/Chris Trotman*)

Ben Smith
(*Photo by
BBS/Scott Levy*)

Head Coach Ben Smith behind the bench with Assistant Coach Tom Mutch discussing strategies with their players during a pre-Olympics game in Canada. (*Photo by BBS/Scott Levy*)

Tara Mounsey signs autographs for fans. The crowds of children and adults seeking signatures from the athletes grew during the pre-Olympics tour and the Olympic Games. (*Photo by Concord Monitor/Andrea Bruce*)

A. J. Mleczko scraps for a puck with Team Canada's captain, Stacy Wilson. (*Photo by USAToday/Diane Weiss*)

Lisa Brown-Miller hustles up-ice during the 1997 Three Nations Cup tournament. (*Photo by Duomo/Chris Trotman*)

Sarah Tueting focuses on the game in a state of mind goaltenders refer to as "goalie world." (*Photo by Duomo/Steven Sutton*)

American Sandra Whyte and Canadian center France St. Louis face off in Nagano. Faceoffs proved to be a critical deciding factor between the evenly matched U.S. and Canadian teams. (*Photo by Duomo/ Paul J. Sutton*)

Sandra Whyte and her teammates were committed to winning the gold medal for a "higher purpose." (*Photo by BBS/Scott Levy*)

Team USA crashes the net against Team Canada on Valentine's Day in the two teams' fourteenth meeting and the prelude to the gold medal game. (*Photos by BBS/Bruce Bennett*)

Shelley Looney scores the winning goal in the Olympic gold medal game on February 17, 1998. (*Photo by BBS/Bruce Bennett*)

Truly "something special"—the gold medal–winning 1998 U.S. Women's Olympic Ice Hockey Team. (*Photo by Chicago Tribune/Nuccio DiNuzzo*)

Front row: Sarah Tueting, Sara DeCosta. *Second row*: Tricia Dunn, Gretchen Ulion, Jenny Schmidgall, Vicki Movsessian, A. J. Mleczko, Colleen Coyne, Cammi Granato, Angela Ruggiero. *Third row*: Shelley Looney, Chris Bailey, Karyn Bye, Alana Blahoski, Sue Merz, Dr. Sandy Glasson, Lisa Brown-Miller. *Back row*: Ben Smith, Kris Pleimann, Jeanna Schepman, Sandra Whyte, Amie Hilles, Tara Mounsey, Bob Webster, Katie King, Tom Mutch, Laurie Baker.

Three . . . two . . . one! Jettisoning sticks, gloves, and other equipment, the victorious Americans burst onto the ice. (*Photo by Duomo/Chris Trotman*)

Peter Haberl advised the American players on sport psychology principles.

Karyn Bye proudly waves the American flag she brought to Nagano from her home in Wisconsin. (*Photo by USAToday/Alan Lessig*)

Two pioneers, Lisa Brown-Miller and Karyn Bye, shed tears of joy after winning the gold medal. (*Photo by AP Wide World Photos*)

So close, but ... Manon Rhéaume, Vicky Sunohara, Laura Schuler, and Shannon Miller, the only female head coach of a women's ice hockey team in Nagano, watch the Americans celebrate. (*Photo by AP Wide World Photos*)

Great victories require noble opponents. The loss of their team's supremacy was a crushing blow to the four-time world champions, Team Canada, who, with Hayley Wickenheiser (center), set the standard for excellence that Team USA needed to surpass. (*Photo by BBS/Bruce Bennett*)

Gretchen Ulion, Sandra Whyte, Katie King, Angela Ruggiero, Vicki Movsessian, Jenny Schmidgall, A. J. Mleczko, and Sarah Tueting emotionally sing the national anthem, loud and clear and out of key. (*Photo by Duomo/Paul J. Sutton*)

The puck stops here. The 1998 U.S. Women's Olympic Ice Hockey Team was blessed with two exceptional goaltenders. Sara DeCosta and Sarah Tueting's unselfish support for each other made the duo highly effective and their victories shared triumphs. Both went undefeated in the Olympic Games. (*Photo by AP Wide World Photos/Kevork Djansezian*)

ary, the poster girl for women's hockey. Through his equal treatment of Cammi he sent a message to the team that everyone was alike and would have to work hard to earn his respect and, consequently, playing time.

Meeting her coaches', her teammates', and the media's expectations wasn't always easy for Cammi. On the morning of the Chelsea Piers game in New York, she and A.J. overslept and arrived late for the bus ride to the rink. Smith considered tardiness a cardinal sin. His response was simple: Cammi and A.J. would not play.

Cammi was upset and embarrassed. She had just spoken with Wayne Gretzky and Mike Richter, who said they would try to come to her game. Now she wouldn't even be dressed! A.J. was in a similar situation. Numerous friends and relatives had told her they were coming to watch her. Instead of asking for preferential treatment, Cammi accepted the sanction and sat down with A.J. The message was clear. Rules are rules no matter what the circumstance.

On the final day of Team USA's visit to San Jose, the coaches put the women through a series of hard skating drills in anticipation of their forthcoming game with Team Canada. It was to be held in Canada's home rink in Calgary as their official Olympic send-off. It was a win the American coaches wanted desperately. A "hell skate," a series of endurance drills, would prove to their players that they were ready.

Cammi, the little girl who wanted to be a Chicago Blackhawk, wasn't worried about a hard skate. As the coaches put the team through a battery of drills, she could see her brother Tony by the glass on the opposite side of the rink watching her. Cammi felt rested and happy. As she skated and breathed deeply she could smell her mother's hot chocolate. She could see the frozen pond in Downers Grove under a purple sunset. She could hear Tony screaming to her to skate faster and beat Donny or Robby to the puck. "Keep your feet moving!" he was yelling. "C'mon, Cammi, catch him!"

As the final drill started in San Jose, Cammi raced past a teammate on the straightaway and looked toward her beloved brother. She was radiant. Tony caught her eye, exchanged a smile, and no longer regretted asking his little sister to catch fastballs.

TEAM USA

"Games from the Heart"

NAGANO, JAPAN ~ FEBRUARY 1 TO 16, 1998

SUNDAY, FEBRUARY 1, 1998

TEAM PROCESSING

As the plane touched down on the runway of Osaka's Kansai International Airport, Sandra Whyte resolved that she would write a brief entry in her journal every day during her stay in Japan. *Even if I write only a few words, it will be enough,* she told herself. *I want to remember as much as I can of what it was like to be a guest of this country under these unusual circumstances. Someday my journal will be precious.*

Cheerful members of the U.S. Olympic Organizing Committee greeted Sandra and her teammates as they stepped off the tarmac into a vestibule immediately inside the terminal. Standing behind long tables filled with documents and boxes, the committee members checked the athletes' papers and issued individual Olympic credentials that had to be worn at all times other than during competition. They also issued invitations to a presidential reception at the White House on April 28, a 1998 USA Olympic Team watch, and a bag filled with 1998 USA Olympic Team/Nagano Olympics trading pins. Sandra studied the credential hanging on a chain around her neck and thought, *At last, I'm really an Olympic athlete.*

For security reasons, the USOC volunteers directed the travel-weary athletes to pick up their own luggage and hockey bags on the baggage carousel and then proceed with their passports through customs. As they entered the main terminal, the women stopped to speak with the media who had gathered to meet them. American, Japanese, and other news correspondents snapped photographs and asked questions until the players were hustled onto a chartered bus for downtown Osaka. As the bus pulled away from the bustling airport and entered the congested causeway that crosses Osaka Bay, Sandra gazed at the skyline of the City of Water and started to relax.

Forty minutes later the bus stopped at the entrance to the Ana Gate Tower Hotel in the heart of Osaka. Team members hurried to their rooms with their carry-on belongings to try to get some sleep. They were told to meet on the sixth floor of the hotel early the next morning for "team processing."

Sandra ate breakfast with her roommates and then took the elevator to the sixth floor. She was led into a large room where a professional photographer took a formal portrait of her for the official Olympic commemorative book. When he finished, a tailor fitted her for the Olympic black leather jacket. She then moved to a table where a jeweler took measurements for her Olympic ring. Sandra particularly liked the beautiful gold ring, which had the Nagano flower symbol on one side and her name and the five Olympic rings on the other side. She was told that if she won a medal she could have the words OLYMPIC MEDALIST engraved around the center. She marveled at the remarkable gifts each Olympic athlete in the U.S. delegation was given.

Sandra then moved to the next table, where she was invited to order complimentary tickets for specific Olympic events for two of her family members. She ordered tickets for her mother and her aunt Priscilla, who would arrive in time for the Opening Ceremonies, and thanked USOC officials for promising to deliver the tickets to the Metropolitan Hotel in downtown Nagano. The Metropolitan was the site of the AT&T Family Center for American athletes, and the most convenient place for athletes to communicate with their families. When she had finished arranging for the tickets' delivery, Sandra proceeded to the "apparel distribution" room across the hallway.

At the entrance to an enormous ballroom called RICC Hall, Sandra grabbed a shopping cart and pushed it to the first station, where she was handed a navy blue wool cowboy hat. Adjusting the hat on her head, looking every bit like a cowgirl, Sandra realized that at the Olympic Opening Ceremonies, the United States team would march into the stadium wearing these "parade hats." Sandra turned to the attendant and said, "It's perfect. I've always wanted to be a cowgirl."

Sandra looked around the ballroom. Along the periphery of the gigantic space were approximately twenty more stations distributing everything from U.S. Olympic team shoes to U.S. Olympic team underwear. At each station, one or two attendants, most of whom were former Olympic athletes, helped teammates, coaches, and staff members disrobe, try on apparel, and load their shopping carts. Some of the stations had makeshift dressing rooms behind curtains, racks of clothing, or shelves filled with boxes.

Sandra heard laughter ripple through the room as she moved to the next station. Ben Smith, who was shopping with Bob Webster and Tom Mutch, innocently appeared from behind the thermalwear station in his stockinged feet wearing a pair of Olympic spandex tights and a turtleneck. A teammate boldly commented that the coach had nice legs and would make an excellent Peter Pan. As he pranced to the center of the ballroom, clicked his heels, and danced back toward the dressing room he said, "You think so?"

In the back of his mind Smith was thinking of the many old coaches he had known who had become the butt of their players' jokes over time. He told Tom and Bob that he would rather give the players reasons to make fun of him then let them find flaws themselves.

By the time Sandra reached the third station, the environment in the ballroom was like a circus. The excitement of the players who were finishing the Olympic team shop-a-thon was infectious. Giggling and laughing, they pushed their overflowing carts to the final two stations, where they were handed the pièce de résistance, a red-white-and-blue awards-ceremony jacket.

Sandra gulped as she threw the jacket over her shoulders and spun around to display it. Large white and gold stars had been embroidered across the upper chest, back, and sleeves. In her mind's eye she could see the awards ceremony—she and her teammates standing on an elevated platform wearing their stars-and-stripes jacket and waving to an enormous Japanese audience. Behind the platform, spotlights lit three flagpoles. Old Glory waved proudly on the tallest pole as snowflakes, caught in the light, sparkled.

Within two hours Sandra, like the other U.S. Olympic athletes and staff on her team, had collected all of the items that the U.S. Olympic Committee had put on the official checklist—over $4,000 worth of Olympic clothing, shoes, and equipment. She was astonished by the generosity of the USOC organizers. Among other things on the checklist for each athlete and staff member were a parka, a coat, hats, headbands, sets of underwear, gloves, cotton and wool sweaters, a bathrobe, towels, T-shirts, polo shirts, jeans, a jean jacket, corduroys, dress slacks, a blazer, a silk blouse, socks, nylons, slippers, dress boots, hiking boots, ski pants, scarfs, a garment bag, a duffel bag, and a briefcase. When she had collected everything, Sandra moved with the last ten team members into the tailors' section. A small army of seamstresses and tailors—some American, some Japanese—were busily sizing and stitching. While Sandra was being measured for new hems on her dress pants and corduroys, she noticed that almost every piece of clothing and equipment lacked a label. One exception was a red-white-and-blue Dale of Norway sweater designed specifically for the parade outfit. There were no brand names in evidence, only sizes, but every item was top-of-the-line quality and, with alterations, fit well.

When all of her clothing was tailored, Sandra was instructed to pick up a packing carton for the lightweight items she would not be wearing in Nagano. While a USOC volunteer assisted, Sandra reviewed the checklist, sorted out the lightweight summer clothing for the shipping carton, and forwarded the rest of the items to her room at the Olympic Village. The variety of Olympic clothing and accessories was remarkable. The assistant arranged to send the light weight items to Sandra's home in Massachusetts.

As Sandra completed her sorting and packing she marveled at the generosity of the U.S. Olympic Committee and the efficiency of its credentialing and distribution operations. Within one day of their arrival in Osaka, the players had received everything they needed to move on to Nagano. Their last obligation before leaving the USOC's debarkation center for the Olympic Village was the official USOC debriefing.

After lunch the women and their associates joined several other American teams in a hotel conference room set up as a debriefing center. In the first session a group of former Olympic athletes followed an agenda that covered everything an American athlete needed to know about what to expect, whom to go to for help, and how to behave with regard to protocols and etiquette. The athletes were advised to act respectfully toward their Japanese hosts at all times and do nothing that would disgrace the American people. They were also asked to remember that the American flag is a sacred object that should be handled and treated with reverence. They were repeatedly reminded of the honor and responsibility of representing their nation as Olympians.

The second session involved interactions with the media. Olympic officials explained the communication protocols that had been agreed to prior to the games, and what was expected of the athletes in fulfilling them. Sandra listened dispassionately, having assigned herself "LP"—low-profile—status. It was the "HPs," high-profile players, who needed to get their acts together for the media.

The third session was about medical rules. Two USOC doctors explained what to expect with regard to gender and drug testing. Upon arrival in the Village, every player would have to fill out paperwork, have a picture taken, and then submit willingly to a buccal smear conducted by an International Olympic Committee medical officer. The doctor would scrape cells from inside the athlete's cheek with a small instrument. The cells would be placed on a slide, stained, and examined under a microscope to see if the cells showed the presence of Barr bodies, the indicators of the stored X chromosome in a female. The photo and test result would then have to be worn at all times with the athlete's credentials. For many of these Olympians, who had spent their girlhoods passing for boys on hockey teams, this test seemed particularly ironic.

The drug testing seemed more intense than the gender testing. All team members had to undergo a comprehensive drug screening upon arrival at the Village, then one player would be selected at random immediately after each game to be retested. Every player would have to be prepared to participate in the test. Players were warned to consult their trainer and doctor about every substance that might have chemical drug properties, and not to ingest any form of medicine provided by a relative, friend, or acquaintance.

The final session was a highlight film containing footage of each of the 1998 U.S. Winter Olympic Teams. The film contained a clip of

Alana Blahoski's amazing goal in the 1997 world championship game against Canada. The hockey players, biathlon team, and other athletes in the room became pumped up with excitement during the film, which ended with an enthusiastic message from President Bill Clinton. Unfortunately, the presidential scandal involving a White House intern had broken only days before, prompting a few comments from members of the audience.

When the hockey team had finished the official debriefing, they proceeded to the hotel's exercise room for their daily workout. Amie had made prior arrangements to rent out the room for this purpose. The coaches did not want the players' fitness level to drop only days before their first game. Players lifted weights, danced aerobics with Lisa, or joined Alana, the "queen of spin class," for a difficult sequence on the stationary bicycles.

Alana Blahoski was, along with Sandra, one of the most fit athletes on the team. The coach described them as "pound for pound, the strongest players." Neither was large. Alana weighed 127 pounds and was five feet seven inches tall. Sandra was also five foot seven and weighed 130. Their strength gave them tremendous quickness. Consequently, along with other fast and agile forwards like Tricia Dunn, they were tremendously effective defensively. And because they were highly athletic, they also had great stamina. They could kill penalties in an unrelenting fashion. "Real diggers," Ben Smith would say. "The athletes who win you games." Smith saw both women as big-game players whom he could rely upon in games with Finland and Canada.

Alana epitomized what made Team USA successful. She was a superior athlete who took any role her coach assigned that would make the total team more competitive. She did so graciously even though, like so many of her teammates, she was a star in her own right. Alana grew up in St. Paul, Minnesota, admiring her older brother Roman, who loved to play hockey. Like him, she started playing on little boys' teams in St. Paul. Her mother, Olga, supported her indirectly, while her father, Wade, helped to guide and coach her. When she no longer wished to play with the boys, Alana moved to the Minnesota Thoroughbreds girls' teams. In high school she ran cross-country, played soccer, and excelled in softball, winning state and regional honors.

Like six of her teammates, Alana chose Providence College, where she majored in sociology. She co-captained the hockey team and earned ECAC Co-Player of the Year honors in 1995–96. The Friars won three ECAC titles during her time there and lost the fourth in a heartbreaking loss to UNH in five overtimes. Even though Alana accidentally skated into Ben Smith during her first on-ice drill with him in Lake Placid, he chose her for both the 1996 and 1997 national teams.

Alana was one of the women players whose appearance fascinated reporters and sports fans. She was a strikingly beautiful and elegant blue-eyed brunette. A vegetarian, she avoided candy and focused on eating nutritiously. Her good habits were reflected in her good looks. Thin and statuesque, most would guess she was a figure skater. They would scratch their heads when they discovered she was a hockey player.

When Sandra and her teammates had exercised, showered, and enjoyed a delicious dinner, team leader Amie notified the team of the next day's schedule. They would fly to Matsumoto Airport in Nagano Prefecture and then take the one-hour bus ride to the Village. After moving in and completing their medical tests, they could visit the International Zone in the Village and have lunch. Then they would be off to their first practice in a rink called Aqua Wing. Amie said, "Before we break up tonight, Coach wants to talk with all of you. Please meet him in his room at nine P.M."

Sandra and her exhausted teammates grumbled about holding a team meeting at that hour. They had not yet fully adjusted to Japan time and had spent most of the day shopping till they dropped. At nine P.M. they dragged themselves to the hallway outside their coach's hotel room and stood in a group quietly grousing.

Smith intentionally made his team wait until slightly after nine P.M. He had observed certain behaviors during the day that concerned him. Shortly after the designated time, he arrived, checked to see that they were all present, and asked them to step into the room and listen carefully. "*Konichiwa* (hello)," he began. "It's been a fun day. You're all credentialed, dressed, and debriefed. You're ready to be the 'beautiful' rather than the 'ugly' Americans. That's great. But I wanted to get us together to remind everyone of the reason why we're here.

"Today was not about new clothes. Today was not about fancy rings and highlight films. It was about the inner circle and what we came here to do.

"There were a lot of distractions today and you got a good idea of how things can easily get frenetic. I want you to go back to your rooms tonight and fall asleep not thinking about our pretty clothes but about our exhibition game against Japan on Wednesday. It's only one day away. We want to be ready. We want to be sharp.

"Osaka has been great. We've had time to decompress and enjoy being in Japan. But we have to stay focused. Get a good night's sleep and be on time for the shuttle in the morning. Tomorrow's another big day. Good night."

Back in her suite moments later, Sandra wished her roommates *"Oyasumi nasai"* (good night). Then she pulled out her journal and wrote the day's closing entry.

> *So I thought it was great that we can laugh at the sight of Coach wearing tights and still maintain our respect for him.*
>
> *I wish I could follow his advice and think about our exhibition game, but as I jump in bed tonight my thoughts are filled with scenes of the gold medal ceremony. I can't believe how many times my thoughts have wandered to that image today. Now that we are in Japan and have our awards ceremony outfits, it is completely clear in my mind. The game is two weeks from tomorrow, I can hardly wait.*

MONDAY, FEBRUARY 2, 1998

THE OLYMPIC VILLAGE

Early the next morning, as directed by Amie, Sandra dressed in hiking boots, a white polo shirt, a pair of jeans, and a navy blue "delegation parka" for the team's flight from Osaka's Kansai International Airport on the sea to Nagano's Matsumoto Airport on "the roof of Japan." The Japan Air Lines flight contained commercial passengers as well as American teams arriving in Nagano for the first time. Again a bevy of USOC volunteers met the athletes at the airport and assisted with their baggage. The volunteers separated the teams and escorted them onto specific buses bound for the Olympic Village.

When the hockey team's large bus pulled away from the Matsumoto terminal for its one-hour trek to the Village, Sandra had her
first opportunity to study the city that had fought to host a Winter
Olympic Games for over fifty years. Nagano appeared in the distance
nestled in a long, flat, snow-covered valley carved from the Japanese
Alps. The land was said to be enchanted because of the cultural and
religious importance of its ten-thousand-foot mountains and active
volcanoes. One of the seething volcanoes, Mount Asama, had blown
in 1783, killing sixteen hundred poeple. In 1998 the beautiful resort
at its base, Karuizawa, would be the venue for the new Olympic sport
of curling. Sandra had read that the mountains represented religious
deities, Buddhist and Shinto rituals, and sites for meditation. Millions
of religious pilgrims traveled to Nagano yearly to visit Zenkoji, its
thirteen-hundred-year-old Buddhist temple. Millions of tourists
flocked to Nagano's fabulous hot-springs resorts and cultural festivals.

Sandra conjured images of ancient samurai warriors fighting for the
fertile volcanic soil between the mountains as the bus passed small
Buddhist shrines along the road. From elevated sections of the highway she could see open fields, terraced rice paddies, and ancient or-
chards extending up the base of the mountains. A long parade of
telephone and electrical wires crisscrossed the valley and disappeared
in the distance.

When the bus entered the outskirts of Nagano, Sandra realized that
the Olympic city itself was not quite what she expected. While
Nagano was smaller than Osaka, which was a metropolis of over
three million people, it was larger than the hamlet in her imagination.
She was slightly disoriented because cars drive on the left side of the
road in Japan. She marveled at the orderly flow of traffic and pedestrians, guided by Nagano police dressed in banana-yellow uniforms
with light blue trimming. The bus lumbered past small private homes
with pagoda-style roofs built side by side on small lots. Narrow drive-
ways, tiny courtyards, or shallow cement canals (designed to channel
melting snows into distant fields) separated one home from another.
In a mixture of past and present, peaceful Buddhist cemeteries appeared within feet of noisy Nissan showrooms. Bright pink or blue
Olympic banners, designed to welcome athletes and visitors to the
Winter Games, hung from streetlamps, flagpoles, and city signs.

Sandra was surprised by what she saw when the bus rolled to a stop at what appeared to be a checkpoint at the main entrance to the Olympic Village. Nagano police and security guards were stopping every vehicle and very carefully studying each occupant's credentials. If clearance was granted, the guards opened the gates of a high electronic fence and allowed the bus, car, or van to move forward toward either the International Zone or the athletes' entrance to the Village. If clearance was not granted, the vehicle was detained and its occupants questioned further. Some people were being denied entrance and directed to leave the Village.

Sandra could see that the Village security guards were handsome young Japanese officials wearing formal, navy blue regimentals. The Village police wore silver-and-black all-weather uniforms. Every male and female officer acted politely but seriously. When Sandra's bus was approved for entry, the gate was opened quickly and then closed immediately.

Because the women's team was arriving for the first time, the bus drove down a long concourse between seven-story concrete apartment buildings to the front door of the International Zone, rather than to the athletes' general entrance. Different nations' flags flew from the balconies of the apartments. Sandra tried to identify the countries represented by the flags as the bus rolled slowly past the colorful display. She noticed that the United States standard was missing, then recalled that Americans had been asked not to identify their building or rooms. Precautions against terrorist attacks were considered prudent.

As the women's bus meandered toward the cul-de-sac designated for loading and unloading passengers, scores of blue-and-white Toyota vans carrying colorfully dressed athletes and their guests passed to its right. Toyota Motor Corporation, an official Olympic sponsor, donated fifteen hundred vehicles—including electric, natural gas, and hybrid models—to serve as transportation for the Games. Sandra noticed that a long line of Toyota vehicles, marked with the Nagano flower symbol and the five Olympic rings, were lined up at the front door of the International Zone awaiting the travel needs of busy Olympians.

Sandra's first impression of the Olympic Village was disappointment. The "village" was not at all what she expected. After spending months in Lake Placid, she had envisioned a quaint little compound on the outskirts of a small town. The Village instead was an efficiently designed high-rise housing complex in the heart of a city of 360,000 people. Sandra could tell that many of the free-standing facilities surrounding the central apartment buildings were temporary. She recalled that the Japanese Olympic organizers had dedicated themselves to acting responsibly with regard to the environment. Nature conservation and recycling measures had been deemed paramount. Thus, many of the Olympic buildings were destined to be recycled.

One such edifice was the so-called International Zone, a series of linked modules that only athletes, officials, and their guests with security clearance could enter. When the bus pulled onto the rotary at the entrance to the modules, Sandra saw an Olympic official ceremonially raise the stars and stripes to announce the arrival of the first American team to reach the compound, the women's ice hockey team. Very few of the seventy-two flagpoles constructed outside the International Zone as yet flew a banner. In the next forty-eight hours all seventy-two flags would be raised as most of the 2,339 athletes competing in the Games arrived before the Opening Ceremonies. The bus came three-quarters of the way around the rotary and stopped at the front entrance to the International Zone.

Several USOC officials greeted the team as it disembarked. Kirk Milborn, who was in charge of transportation, and Nancy Gonzalez, who oversaw "international games preparations," welcomed the women and invited them inside the large lobby. Nagano schoolchildren presented each person in the American delegation with an origami animal as they entered and Nancy gave each of them a room key for USA House, Team USA's residence. Nancy then escorted the delegation across the lobby to another checkpoint through which only credentialed athletes, staff, Games personnel, and official guests could pass.

By the time she reached the second checkpoint, Sandra was impressed by the security in the Village. To the right of the lobby, behind a long counter decorated with Olympic posters, groups of young multilingual interpreters processed athletes' and visitors' requests to enter the compound. Athletes with proper credentials could approach the checkpoint immediately. Athletes with questionable credentials were automatically detained. All visitors had to stop at the desk for permission to approach the checkpoint. If special arrangements had been made in advance with the IOC or a specific country's delegation, a half-day pass was issued. If no such arrangements had been made, the visitor was told to sit outside the checkpoint at one of a dozen tables set up in the lobby. Unapproved visitors had to settle for a public conversation with the athlete they had come to see, who was paged to come outside the checkpoint to greet them. The lobby was filled with visitors-in-waiting.

Uniformed police and security guards patrolled the lobby and the checkpoint. When Nancy Gonzalez led the women's team to the checkpoint, several guards electronically scanned individual team members' credentials while police searched every bag and package. When everyone was cleared to proceed, the group passed through metal detectors overseen by additional police and security officers.

While the delegation was being processed through security, Amie greeted two Japanese attachés assigned to her as team leader. Miko and Yosiko became Amie's constant resources. Their responsibilities were to meet with her each morning and make arrangements for everything the team needed outside the Village. Miko and Yosiko also escorted the team on buses, translating, directing, and, when necessary, cutting red tape.

When everyone had cleared security, Nancy guided them down the long hallway that was in effect the main street of the International Zone. Sandra was surprised to see a general store, post office, camera shop, international library, chaplaincy, clothing store, beauty parlor, embroidery shop, video game arcade, nightclub, bank, laundry, and a communications center called "The Surf Shack." Decorated in a tropical motif, the "shack" was equipped with top-of-the-line IBM computers and monitors.

At the end of the L-shaped center hallway, the team exited the International Zone and walked under Nancy's supervision across a courtyard, past the athletes' dining hall, and through another checkpoint to the front entry of USA House. The Americans' "house" was a seven-story section of the large concrete apartment complex Sandra had noticed as the bus entered the Village. The team followed Nancy up some concrete steps to the walkways that led to their apartment entries. From the walkways they could gaze into the courtyard below or look into windows on the opposite side of the quadrangle. Team USA had no trouble identifying their cross-courtyard neighbors. Canada House residents had hung scores of red-and-white flags from every foot of exposed walkway banister. It appeared that no one in the Canadian delegation was the least bit worried about terrorists.

While the American coaches groused about the Canadians' audacity, the players unlocked their room doors, hurried inside, and dropped their carry-on bags. Five players were assigned to each suite. Each apartment had a different floor plan that included an efficiency kitchen off a small living room, a full bath, and three bedrooms set up with temporary walls. All of the bedrooms were doubles except for the single rooms assigned to every goalie.

The Nagano Organizing Committee provided very simple furnishings in the athletes' apartments—essentially wooden beds, side tables, and folding chairs. The committee decorated the walls with lovely handmade drawings offered as gifts to their guests. One drawing hung above each bed. To the delight of the residents, a large television, programmed to receive live coverage of every event taking place at the Olympics, stood on a platform in the center of the living room. Players could watch official Olympic coverage of one sport or ceremony, or as many as nine at once. Within minutes Sandra and her teammates had chosen beds, dropped their gear, and dragged their duffel bags into their bedrooms. Then they scattered to have lunch and explore the Village.

Sandra quickly discovered that dining in the Olympic Village was a pleasure. Again the entryway was secured. Only athletes and staff with specific credentials could enter. Once inside, diners were treated to a wide array of international foods served cafeteria-style from different stations. Cordial Japanese chefs and attendants said, "*Konichiwa*," as they served delicious hot and cold meals. Sandra was surprised to find that the dining hall served three soups at every meal, along with deliciously prepared dishes of rice, fish, chicken, and beef. Long lines of colorfully dressed athletes stood before the McDonald's station and fruit pavilion. Sandra quickly learned that anyone who loved fresh produce, including strict vegetarians like Alana, would be well satisfied in the Olympians' dining hall. Enormous Nagano apples, the agricultural symbol of the region, and luscious strawberries were gobbled by hungry, nutrition-conscious competitors. Well-equipped beverage stations provided milk, juices, water, and soft drinks. Cereal stations—the women's favorite—were similarly well stocked.

Team USA filled their food trays and found seats together at long wooden tables. Sunlight poured into the space through large skylights and plate-glass windows. Flags representing the seventy-two nations competing in the Winter Games hung from beams supporting the ceiling, alongside banners bearing the official Nagano Olympics symbols. Brightly hued images of skaters, jumpers, skiers, curlers, and snowboarders fluttered gently above the athletes as they ate and relaxed. The room buzzed with a mix of many languages.

The American women, like members of most of the teams seated around them, stayed together while dining but scanned the crowded tables for familiar faces. Sandra knew that in a matter of hours the room would be filled with the world's finest winter athletes and would be the best place to see future immortals. As she picked up her tray she noticed her bracelet and resolved not to become too distracted in the dining hall. She bowed to the attendants who were taking the trays and said, *"Domo arigato"* (thank you very much). The dining-hall staff returned the bow, then processed the used materials for recycling. All of the Americans were impressed to learn that their plates were made of reconstituted apple pulp and their food containers biodegradable potato starch.

Pondering the technology that turns fruit into dinner plates, Sandra followed her teammates across the courtyard to the Sports Medicine Room for the long-awaited ritual of gender testing. Sue Snouse, a USOC official, organized the procedure for the American teams. The squads appeared in waves on the days they entered the Village. Snouse helped the IOC's Japanese sports medicine officials process them immediately. The sports medicine crew sensed they were in for plenty of excitement when the twenty members of the women's hockey team arrived for testing.

Snouse directed the athletes to fill out paperwork and fall into line in alphabetical order for mandatory photographs. Meanwhile, team ringleaders suggested that everyone make a funny face for what Sandra dubbed the "I Am Woman" photo. The Sports Medicine Room became a comedy club as the team tried to see who could have the funniest face on the official gender card. They knew the cards had to be attached to their credentials, but they didn't care. Each woman was proud to be a "46XX-er" and confident no one would need the picture to illustrate otherwise. Plus, many of them considered gender testing a joke. Innovations in genetics research had shown that the tests could be misleading or inaccurate.

The Sports Medicine Office staff dutifully scraped cells from the inside of each player's mouth, smeared slides with the sample cells, studied chromosomes, and photographed faces while the players roared with laughter at the process and the photos. The formal Japanese medical officials stifled their laughter but Sandra could tell that privately they were enjoying the show.

Sandra chuckled at the way her team's good humor and excitement charmed the medical staff. She had started noticing that everyone her teammates dealt with, including bus drivers, flight attendants, USOC staffers, photographers, reporters, and now these medical officials, enjoyed their company. We never take anything for granted, she thought. Everything we do is an adventure, and people sense it. They know they are part of our adventure and they get pulled in.

By the end of the team's gender testing, Sue Snouse and the Japanese sports medicine staff were certainly part of the adventure. They told each woman that they would send her test result and her gender card as soon as they were processed. The players then hurried off to explore the International Zone or stayed to have a tour of the Sports Medicine Training Room.

Sandra wasn't surprised to see Karyn and Tara, both of whom had been injured in the team's upset victory at Team Canada's Olympic send-off in Calgary, stay to speak with the trainers. Both players had been placed on crutches in Calgary and sent home to Colorado Springs on an early flight to begin physical therapy. Tara had spent several additional days on crutches and been told to limit her skating before the medal games. At one point she was fearful that her sprained ankle and sore left knee would force her out of the Olympics. But Jeanna and the medical staff in Colorado Springs had been extremely effective. Jeanna arranged massages and use of electrical stimulation machines and stationary bicycles in the Village so that Karyn and Tara could immediately continue their therapy. Both hoped for a full recovery in Nagano.

Meanwhile Sandra and her other colleagues investigated what had been advertised as the "technologically advanced Olympic Village." After a quick assessment of what was available, they were impressed. IBM, an official sponsor of the Olympic Games, provided the Village with an outstanding array of technologies. The players were assigned personal and public e-mail accounts and shown how to log on to the powerful personal computers in the Surf Shack. The computer room quickly became a favorite facility. Instantaneously the women connected with loved ones and friends many time zones away and started sending messages about their remarkable adventure. Within minutes they received return e-mail carrying personal news and details about the media coverage leading up to the Opening Ceremonies.

Sandra thought it was exciting that her family and friends could pass along her Nagano e-mail addresses. She also thought it was great that, through a collaboration between Kodak and IBM, she could rent digital cameras and send home digital photos of herself and her teammates in action. Before she logged off her accounts on the first day, she had hits from relatives, friends, and even hometown schoolchildren. IBM's technology allowed individual athletes to start electronic person-to-person conversations with hundreds of well-wishers around the world before the Olympic Games even opened. Sandra, who had become computer literate at Harvard, was thrilled to have free, immediate Internet access.

Late in the day, after researching all of the services the Olympic Village had to offer, the team met for its first on-ice practice in Nagano. The players congregated at a set point in the Village and then boarded their bus together. The bus crossed the city to reach Aqua Wing, the venue where their first five games would be contested. Aqua Wing was one of four skating facilities constructed for the Olympics. Aqua Wing and the larger Big Hat were designed as hockey rinks. White Ring hosted figure skating and M-Wave featured long- and short-track speed skating.

In comparison to Big Hat, where most of the men's hockey games were to be played, Aqua Wing was modest. It was designed to be converted to a swimming pool in the summer. The roof, which let in natural light to conserve energy during the winter, could retract during the summer. The walls and ceiling were painted aqua blue to reflect the building's multiple uses. All of the spectators' seats were positioned high above the ice (or water) surface, giving swimming fans an excellent vantage point and skating fans the impression that they were in a coliseum.

Bob Webster was on-site in Aqua Wing with the equipment that had arrived on cue either from the Village or from Bob's facilities in

Colorado Springs. Bob had packed all of the equipment he and the team would need and delivered it to the airport in Colorado Springs several days earlier. The USOC had transported the team's gear to Japan, along with all of the other supplies and materials the American teams would require during the Games, in two enormous 747s. Trucks had then transported each team's equipment to specific sites in Nagano so that the equipment manager could have everything ready for the team's first practice.

Team USA's locker room was one of six—three on each side of a common hallway. The rooms were assigned by order of pre-Olympic standing. Canada was assigned, therefore, to the first locker room and the United States to the second. Bob had Lady Liberty and all of the gear and uniforms ship-shape when Team USA walked into the silent, aqua-blue stadium.

Sandra enjoyed the peacefulness of the team's first practice. No one was allowed in the building. Olympic officials prohibited media and other spectators from watching and interrupting. The coaches, consequently, could put finishing touches on plays and help the athletes become fully acclimated to their new surroundings. After three days of travel, processing, and testing, the quiet practice time with the inner circle felt special.

Back in the Village later that evening, Sandra tried to recall everything that had happened. The day had started in a hotel in Osaka and ended in a hockey rink in Nagano. She was exhausted. Staring at the Japanese line drawing above her bed, she ended her journal entry with a short, hopeful paragraph.

I'm surprised by the number of times I visualize the gold medal ceremony. I really think we can win the gold. One year with Coach has made the difference. I believe we can do it.

TUESDAY, FEBRUARY 3, 1998

PAGERS

I went to a team breakfast, sent e-mail, practiced, had lunch, and took a nap.

Amie issued everybody on the team an alpha-numeric pager. The pagers are part of the "Info 98 System" designed for the Nagano Olympics following USOC authorities' difficult experience locating athletes after the Atlanta bombing incident. In theory the pagers will enable USOC officials to locate every American athlete quickly in the event of an emergency. Once I punched in my accreditation number, I could automatically communicate with other people on the system, monitor event results, and check my e-mail.

Amie made each of us swear to take care of our pager and return it safely. She half-kiddingly warned, "If I do not get back your pager, you do not get back to the United States."

No surprise, the first beeper message was from K.L.!

WEDNESDAY, FEBRUARY 4, 1998

JIMMY CAPS

After breakfast there was a mad rush to get to the computer room before nine A.M. Everyone was anxious to read their personal e-mail messages from people at home.

We played in an exhibition against Japan. Gretchen and Vicki were hilarious before the game. They were planning to wear their "jimmy caps"—which look like swim caps—under their helmets, so they each put a small strip of tape over their noses and did an imitation of two synchronized swimmers in the locker room.

When the swimmers were finished, Vicki did impressions. The woman is gifted. We laughed till we cried.

THURSDAY, FEBRUARY 5, 1998

CORRELATIONS

We had a big press conference today. The reporters asked foolish questions like, "How do you plan to stop [Canadian] Jayna Hefford?" and "What do you do when you run into the Canadians in an elevator?" We told the press we need to focus on one game at a time.

At our workout today Coach was chasing the forwards around the circles to make us skate faster. He was having fun. It's amazing the correlation between his stress and happiness and ours as a team. When he has fun, we have fun, and when he is happy, we are happy.

Today was Bail's birthday and we gave her a big cake and sang "Happy Birthday" during a break in our practice. She was thrilled to celebrate her birthday in Nagano.

I have loved our practices. There are no media. No one is watching. Just good ol' hockey. No pressure. This whole week our practices have been wonderful because it's just the inner circle and we know our work is done. We're ready.

FRIDAY, FEBRUARY 6, 1998

CAR TOWN

This morning we went as a team to "Car Town," better known as Nike Town, to pick up a gift bag of apparel. Car Town is located in an anonymous building across the street from Big Hat Arena. Behind blackened windows is a nightclub-like environment where athletes can hang out, enjoy snacks, and play air hockey or video games.

My teammates and I were invited to Car Town because USA Hockey purchased Nike-manufactured apparel for its Olympic teams. When we entered the building, Car Town officials checked our credentials and then gave us Nike gift bags filled with a jacket, boots, socks, gloves, T-shirts, sweatshirts, and hats. Cammi, who visited Car Town yesterday to make a special appearance with fifty Japanese children, was given a ride back to the Village in the official Nike Hummer. We rely on Amie to tell us *which corporate sponsors' gifts and services we can and cannot accept under IOC, USOC, and USA Hockey regulations and agreements.*

In the afternoon we spent five hours to get one hour of practice at the Nagano Skate Center. We bused from the Village to Aqua Wing to pick up our equipment and then traveled to the Nagano Skate Center. After practice we had to travel back to Aqua Wing to undress, and then jump back on the bus to go back through traffic to the Village.

SATURDAY, FEBRUARY 7, 1998

OPENING CEREMONIES

Sandra looked out her bedroom window and saw an endless row of buses lining up on the concourse leading to the entrance to the Village. Fully dressed in her parade uniform, she grabbed her hat and beeper and followed her teammates downstairs to the courtyard for boarding. Thousands of athletes and their assistants, dressed to reflect their national colors and heritage, poured out of the complex and into the caravan in an ordered chaos that lifted Sandra's spirits and sense of anticipation.

Sandra had barely slept the night before, waking repeatedly to check her watch and count the hours until her departure. She had seen Nagano's *sakura*, the cherry blossom–shaped stadium, in the distance as she commuted to practices at Aqua Wing. Now it was time to enter the spectacular stadium for the commencement of what Nagano called "Games from the Heart." The organizing committee had set three goals for the XVIII Winter Olympics: promoting the participation of children, respecting the beauty and bounty of nature, and staging a festival of peace in friendship. As she jumped on the bus, Sandra hoped the Opening Ceremonies would be everything Peter Haberl had predicted and she and her teammates had visualized.

The mood on the Team USA bus was jovial as Amie handed everyone a "parade marching card" and told them to clip it to their credentials. She directed the team to stay together as they deboarded and joined the entire U.S. contingent at a fitness center that organizers had rented as a holding area. Sandra's gaze darted from face to face as she searched for old friends from Lake Placid and new friends from the Village. Everywhere athletes were taking photos and exchanging pins. The atmosphere inside the holding area was joyous as members of the full U.S. contingent sat down to watch events in the stadium unfold on large television monitors. They joked, sang, and munched fruit, Oreos, and Pringles while waiting to step into the limelight.

The atmosphere inside the stadium was equally joyous. At eleven A.M. the ancient bronze bell of Zenkoji Temple was rung to purify souls and signal the start of the Opening Ceremonies. When the bell fell silent, one thousand Suwa-region log carriers chanted and cheered while erecting eight two-ton *onbashira* pillars to serve as sacred gateways into the stadium for the athletes. Sandra watched as the crowd of fifty thousand spectators applauded the completion of this dramatic and dangerous religious ritual and the arrival of Emperor Akihito and Empress Michiko. The Japanese royal couple had met and fallen in love in nearby Karuizawa, in the shadow of Mount Asama. The emperor and empress acknowledged the gracious greeting with a bow and happily joined the ovation for Japan's 512-pound *yokozuno,* or sumo grand champion, Akebono, and his fellow sumo wrestlers who, in thirty-four-degree temperatures, were dressed in nothing other than topknots, loincloths, and aprons. Akebono and the other sumos paraded onto the dais of the stadium to perform the *dohyoiri,* a sumo ring-entering ceremony to drive the *jaki,* or evil Earth-dwelling spirits, from the land of the Winter Games.

When Akebono had purified the stadium, the XVIII Olympic Games, the last Olympic Games of the second millennium, were properly blessed and ready for the arrival of 150 *yukinko,* or snow-children, who sang a peace-appeal song, Andrew Lloyd Webber's "When Children Ruled the World." The *yukinko* then ran in pairs to join seventy-two more sumos who lined up to escort each country in the parade of nations. Greece, as always, appeared first, led by a handsome and popular sumo who guided the athletes out of a tunnel and through the sacred pillars.

When Greece appeared on the monitors in the holding area, Sandra and her teammates stood up and got ready to march. They had been advised to walk at the end of the American delegation as it entered the stadium in order to have the best chance of being seen on television. When the Americans were signaled to fall into position, a standoff started between the women skaters and another set of Olympic newcomers, the snowboarders, who also wanted to advertise their presence by going last. Sandra nervously noticed that a gap was starting to form between the back of the U.S. delegation that was approaching the stadium and the two rival teams jockeying for attention. Her teammate Chris Bailey dug in her heels and told her teammates to do likewise. Chris said to the snowboarders, "We're not budging. You can delay all you want, but our team is going last."

Chris's tenacity fired up her teammates and paid off moments later when the snowboarders caved in, leaving the anonymous but excited skaters to march at the back of the procession. They hustled to catch up with the pack and high-fived each other for outlasting the snowboarders. Then Gretchen led the women in a simple little song as the delegation approached the entrance to the stadium.

Chris Bailey's leadership in insisting on a prominent position for the women's team was an important gesture. The women took their role as ambassadors very seriously. They knew that only 217 women had marched in the Opening Ceremonies in Sapporo in 1972, and that only 400 had appeared in Lillehammer in 1994. The introduction of women's ice hockey four years later pushed the number of female Winter Olympians to more than 800 for the Nagano Games. When American children studied the faces coming through the sacred pillars, Chris and her teammates wanted American cowgirls to be just as prominent as their cowboy teammates. They also wanted the world to know their game had arrived.

With American flag bearer Eric Flaim at the front of the delegation and the intrepid women hockey players at the rear, the U.S. contingent, holding small American flags handed out as the athletes exited the holding area, entered the long, dark tunnel leading into the stadium. Beside Eric walked one of the impressive sumos dressed in a black jacket and khaki-colored ceremonial robe. The sumo held the hand of the *yukinko* for the United States, a little girl named Serina Saito. Serina wore white boots, tights, and gloves and a short white skirt with ruffles that made her look like a snowball. She also wore a lovely red-white-and-blue hooded sweater knitted to resemble the American flag.

Sandra could not see what was happening at the beginning of the procession, but she could feel a contagious excitement rolling backward over the slate-blue marching mass. In the semidarkness of the tunnel she could see hundreds of cowboy hats bobbing on the American athletes who were moving excitedly down the ramp. The marchers started hollering, "Yahoo!" as though cowboy lingo had instantly become a shared dialect.

Sandra caught a glimpse of the thousands of spectators seated in the stands opposite the tunnel. They were waving Olympic flags and smiling. When sunshine fell on the American flag as Eric, Serina, and the sumo entered the daylight, the entire American delegation roared. This is the moment, Sandra thought as her heart started to race and the march became a jog. She could hear athletes on all sides of her struggling for words. Most had tears in their eyes as they stepped out of the darkness and into the light. The enormous audience waved a jubilant greeting, which the Americans returned as they moved between the sacred pillars and around the track. The stadium was awash in color and movement as sumos, *yukinkos,* and athletes paraded together in a circle of friendship, solidarity, and peace. The solemnity of the scene was breathtaking.

Sandra smiled when the camera crews, as predicted, started filming the athletes who paraded and then sat at the front and back of the American delegation. She and her teammates mugged for the photographers and tried to describe their emotions, but the moment was difficult to put in words. How does one describe a sensation of world harmony and equality? Sandra thought as the journalists persisted.

As her teammates responded to the cameramen's and journalists' questions, Sandra turned and focused on the highlights of the ceremonies, including Midori Ito's lighting of the Olympic flame. Dressed in a beautiful rose-colored Japanese kimono and accompanied by an aria from Puccini's *Madame Butterfly,* Japan's silver-medal figure skater ascended like a deity above the audience. Sandra thought how wonderful it was for a Japanese woman athlete to be so honored. Moments later Sandra marveled at the release of thousands of dove-shaped balloons above the stadium as orchestra and choral conductor Seiji Ozawa cued five cross-continental choruses and hundreds of millions of television viewers for the start of a global sing-along. For the next eighteen minutes Sandra and the world shared Beethoven's "Ode to Joy" in a spirit of sister- and brotherhood.

When the Opening Ceremonies ended, the athletes marched out of the stadium and then wandered happily back to the buses. Sandra felt inspired by the simplicity and spirituality of her Japanese welcome. There had been a lot of commotion getting into the stadium, but the solemnity of the ceremonies had set a serious tone for the work at hand. Sandra and Sarah Tueting jumped onto one of approximately one hundred IOC buses returning to the Village and talked about the highlights of the Opening Ceremonies with a bunch of equally impressed New Zealand bobsledders.

In the quiet of her bedroom in the Village, later in the evening, Sandra thought of the many times she had visualized the Opening Ceremonies as Peter had recommended. In spite of her best efforts, the real ceremonies had been far greater than she ever could have imagined. Though weary, she briefly summarized what she wanted to remember.

I was sitting near Coach and Bob Allen. Our eyes watered when the Olympic flag was carried around the track and raised. It was magical. I looked at the flag and felt an amazing release of emotion. I have made it, I thought, I have finally made it to the Olympic Games.

SUNDAY, FEBRUARY 8, 1998

USA v. CHINA

We beat China today in our first game 5–0. It felt like just another game to me, although we had too many penalties. It was exciting in the first period when Cammi scored the first goal by an American woman in an Olympic contest. Jenny and Greta assisted. Teeter was in the nets for us and and Guo Hong played for China. We had thirty-one shots on Guo.

After the game Kris Pleimann came into the locker room as always to get people to speak to the media. There were a lot of reporters. Before Kris could even speak, we teasingly yelled, "I need..." She hates that because she

knows we think HPs and LPs are a joke.
I'm definitely an LP.

MONDAY, FEBRUARY 9, 1998

USA v. Sweden

We beat Sweden 7–1 in our second game. I played well
but was pointless. Too much penalty killing! Too much
penalty killing! Our team had forty-seven shots on
Annica Ahlen. We were hot on offense. The defense was
also great and limited Sweden's chances. Sara D. was in
the net.

TUESDAY, FEBRUARY 10, 1998

E-Mail Home

I sent home this e-mail message to Tim, Dad, and the rest
of the family.

Subj: Re: Olympic 2/10
Date: 98–02–06 20:04:31 EST
From: USA9@hotmail.com (Sandra Whyte)

Hi everyone.

Everything is going great so far. We were happy with our two
wins over China and Sweden. Sweden played us tough for a
period but we finally opened the floodgates to win 7–1. We
certainly had to work hard for our goals though.

I have been getting a lot of ice with my regular shifts and a lot
of penalty killing. Last night I felt like I played more shorthanded than five on five. My line didn't put any in last night
but I was very happy with the way we played. We were working hard and had a lot of great chances.

Today is an off day for us. We have practice this afternoon
and then we have some free time tonight. Most of us are
planning to go to the AT&T reception center to meet our families and have a meal. I hear the AT&T center is great—"like a
cruise ship" was the way my mother described the endless
food and drinks.

We are getting psyched up to play Finland tomorrow. As always with them we are expecting a battle.

Thanks for all your messages ... I enjoy hearing what is going on at home and how much you are seeing/hearing of our games.

Keep cheering us on ...

Love,
Sandra

I went to the AT&T Family Center in the Metropolitan Hotel to say hi to Mom and Aunt Priscilla, to pick up my cell phone, and have dinner. I have to admit I was overwhelmed. I took the train that stops near the Village to the hotel. Even though my train was incredibly crowded, a man on the platform shoved ten more people into my car. When I got to the hotel I was processed for another credential to enter the Family Center. The room was huge—like the ballroom in Osaka—and filled with American athletes and their families. There were enormous full-color posters hanging from the ceiling with action photos of great Olympic moments for every sport. There were gigantic screens broadcasting live events, televisions showing other competitions, and banks of free computers and telephones. In the middle of the room there were banquet tables filled with beautiful flower arrangements and gourmet Japanese and American foods. It was unbelievable.

The AT&T managers gave every American athlete a free cell phone and calling card. Vicki was funny. She commented on how we are so important now with our beepers, phones, special clothes, credentials, etc. ... then we will go home and back to being our little old selves. I told her at least she recognizes that this fantasy world won't continue.

I've been feeling obliged to spend time with Mom and

Priscilla and I really wanted to get out of the Village, but I could tell right away that being in the Family Center was straining the inner circle. I started to hear people gossiping and complaining and realized that the parents aren't focused like we are, and that what Peter had warned about was starting to happen. I hated to say good-bye to Mom and Priscilla but decided this isn't what I'm supposed to be doing. I think a lot of my teammates realized the same thing. Something tells me the cell phones and the rest of our communication instruments are going to be a mixed blessing.

WEDNESDAY, FEBRUARY 11, 1998

USA v. Finland

Coach Ben Smith wasn't happy. As a superstitious person he didn't like the fact that the moon was full. As an inner circle member he didn't appreciate players' cell phones ringing on the bus ride to Aqua Wing. And, as a hockey coach, he was furious that his penalty killers were covering far too many unnecessary infractions. The game was enormously important. Team USA had to beat Finland to move into the gold-medal round. This was no time for mistakes and distractions.

Sandra felt pretty much the same way. Along with Vicki, Tricia, Alana, Chris, Colleen, Sue, and the other penalty killers, she was exhausted. The team had beaten Finland in their last meeting at the Three Nations Cup tournament in December. Team USA couldn't let down now. The American fans in the crowd agreed. It was time to quit getting penalties and put Finland out of contention.

Vicki took the first step in that direction by scoring a nice goal on an assist from Katie in the first period. Finnish defender Krisi Haenninen, however, responded quickly and scored on a slap shot from the blue line during a power play. In the second period Karyn broke the tie by beating Finnish goaltender Tuula Katriina Puputti on a rebound from a shot by Jenny. Finland's Riika Nieminen restored the tie with an open-net goal on Sarah Tueting, who slipped clearing a puck from behind the net. Tara scored a tiebreaker ninety seconds later with help from Sue and Karyn and the Finnish team, who had put two players in the penalty box. While the American and Finnish men's Olympic teams looked on from reserved seats, Gretchen scored Team USA's fourth goal with three minutes left in the period. But everyone knew that a two-goal lead might not be enough to win. The American squad had to play tighter, smarter hockey.

Frustratingly, that was not what happened. In the third period the referees again called lots of penalties on both teams. Sarah and the penalty killers nevertheless made the difference. While Finnish Coach Rauno Korpi watched with disappointment, Teeter stopped two breakaways. She then shuffled between her posts nervously as more penalties were called on both sides and both teams lost their line rotations and rhythm. Sarah's brother Jonathan, Chris Bye, and other brothers were sitting behind Sarah's net wearing Dr. Seuss hats and cheese heads. They screamed to her to hang tough. But Sarah wasn't listening. She was in goalie world, telling herself, No mistakes. Just protect the lead.

In spite of many close calls, Sarah did. She stopped twenty shots to earn her second victory in a wild and physical game. The 4–2 win didn't come easy. She and the designated penalty killers had preserved the win but learned that medal contenders weren't going to play passively. China and Sweden had not been in contention. Finland wanted to win the gold.

After the game, Coach Smith was relieved but not happy. As usual, he shook hands with every player. They could see, however, that he was agitated. Smith was worried that his team was losing their energy and focus. He decided to give a stern postgame soliloquy. "Okay, we won. You did some good work around the net, Sarah stood on her head, and the penalty killers saved the third period," he said in an officious tone that matched the brevity of his summations. "But there were lapses when players lost their focus. We can't have that. We can't lose our focus when we only have two more contests before the gold-medal game."

As Smith prepared to speak again, Sandra couldn't tell if he was infuriated, fired up, or simply disappointed. He paced in front of her stall collecting his thoughts and trying to find words to express them. Then he put the palms of his hands on the training tables in the center of the Aqua Wing locker room and stared at his sweaty, attentive players. "Look," he exclaimed, "you need to stay focused. *That's why you have these Peter-ass bracelets!* You have to shut off the damn phones and remember who's in the inner circle."

Smith paused, sucked in air, and began again. "And, you have to stay strong. You must drink that mother's-milk shit that Jeanna gave you—that gator-load stuff or whatever she calls it—to maintain your strength and endurance. Every game has been very physical and the rest of them will probably be worse."

Calming down and dropping his voice, Smith asked, "Do you see this table? There's a crack down the middle because it's actually two tables. That's us. We're either one team or we're twenty-six separate individuals. We can stay together, or"—pushing the tables apart—"we can come apart. You decide." He pulled the tables back together again and walked out.

He's fired up, Sandra decided, but he's also pissed. He doesn't like the phones and beepers, or, for that matter, the parents and friends who are distracting us. She turned to Tricia in the next stall and said, "He's reining us back in."

"You've got that straight," Tricia agreed.

"I bet he'd eliminate the beepers, phones, and media if he could," Sandra added.

"Ya, well, it's too late for that," Tricia pointed out, nodding toward the doorway where Kris Pleimann stood ready to make her traditional postgame announcement.

"I need Karyn, Gretchen, Tara, Sarah Tueting, Vicki, and Colleen," she said in a harried tone. "Right away."

"Whoa, Colleen and Vicki!" their sister LPs teased. "It's your turn. Go for it!"

"Remember, you guys, 'It's teams, not individuals, who win hockey games,'" Sandra teased.

"Yes, ma'am," Vicki quipped. "That's why we have our 'Peter-ass bracelets.' Right, Colleen?"

They all laughed—HPs and LPs alike—knowing that women athletes of any status were basically low profile when it came to the media.

It was very late when the bus arrived back at the Village. As she walked to USA House, Sandra noticed the light of the full moon reflected off the snow, giving everything in the compound an eerie silver glow. She was tired. While some of her roommates went to the

International Zone to relax, she went to the apartment to retire and write in her journal.

> *I'm glad I took a game-day nap. This afternoon we watched Canada play Sweden and the whole team cheered for Sweden. Unfortunately Canada won 5–3.*
>
> *We beat Finland tonight 4–2, but our game was exhausting. Finland tried to make a comeback in the third, but there was not enough time and maybe enough depth. I thought we really dominated until we got into penalty trouble. I felt like I spent the whole game killing. I think I only had two shifts with Cammi in the second. Brutal. I don't mind killing penalties but ten is a few too many.*
>
> *Coach got riled up at the end of the game and referred to our "Peter-ass bracelets" and "mother's milk" carbo drink. I'm not sure if it was our overall performance or the full moon that got to him.*
>
> *Japan tomorrow.*

THURSDAY, FEBRUARY 12, 1998

USA v. Japan

> *We had the strangest weather today. After a balmy start we had heavy snow, then a hard rain with thunder and lightning. I sent Tim this e-mail message from the Surf Shack.*

Subj: Re: Olympics 2/12
Date: 98–02–12
From: USA9@hotmail.com (Sandra Whyte)

Hi Tim.

We are now officially in the Gold Medal Game! Canada beat Finland 4–2, so Finland and China will meet in the bronze.

The Japan game, which we won 10–0, was horrible. It is very difficult to play like we know how when the puck stays in their end. They crowd around the net. Coach hates when we force the puck, so we end up cycling on the outside trying to find ways to penetrate ... Yuck! At least I got a goal, which I hope will make everyone at home happy. Unfortunately I tweaked my knee in the third period so I will spend the day tomorrow in the training room.

Okay, I'm out of here. I hope everything is going well at home.

Love,
Sandra

Other than our game with Japan, which was a blowout, today was a big day for the Japanese people. They celebrated Foundation Day, a national holiday, and twenty-one-year-old mogul skier Tae Satoya's first gold medal for a Japanese woman in the Winter Olympics.

FRIDAY, FEBRUARY 13, 1998

THE CHILDREN OF NAGANO

It's Friday the 13th.

The U.S. men played their first game today, against Sweden, and lost 4–2. There are fourteen men's Olympic ice hockey teams with a total of 322 athletes. Nine teams have NHL players. I think all of them are staying in the Village.

Our team had a practice in the Nagano Skate Center near Car Town because men's games were going on in Aqua Wing and Big Hat. I had a chance to look at Nagano as the bus moved slowly through the city.

I saw people on dented bicycles navigating beside narrow sidewalks filled with pedestrians. Small family shops sit beside large department stores featuring expensive clothing from Tokyo, New York, and London. Burberry raincoats appeared in storefront windows beside gorgeous Japanese kimonos.

Nagano always seems to be filled with children, maybe because there are a lot of schools here, or maybe because teachers and parents are bringing kids into the city to see Olympic events. The Olympic organizers focused on involving children in the Games, so that may be the reason.

Schoolchildren can be seen everywhere, congregating in little clusters. Teenage girls, hurrying home from school, wear traditional loden coats in a vast array of colors, every hue from burnt orange to lime green and black. Around their necks the girls wrap wool plaid scarves or fleece neck warmers. In spite of the slush on city sidewalks, they prefer penny loafers with white ankle socks to boots. Many girls offset the conservative look of their school uniforms with hot-pink lipstick, bright blue eye shadow, and silver-speckled nail polish. Schoolboys throw multicolored ski parkas over white shirts and navy blazers. The girls like earmuffs and the boys like baseball hats. And everyone wears pins, lots of them, on hats, scarves, and overcoats. Pin trading, an Olympic tradition, seems to have arrived in Nagano long before the start of our sixteen-day festival.

The younger children are dressed in brightly colored snowsuits and boots. Their parents bundle them up in hats and hoods and take them everywhere. The children are gorgeous. They have the rosiest cheeks I have ever seen. The children wave at our bus when they see us looking out the windows. Everyone is incredibly friendly.

"Gold medal preview game" with Canada tomorrow.

SATURDAY, FEBRUARY 14, 1998

VALENTINE'S DAY

Sandra went to the team's pregame skate in a good mood. After treating and resting her knee, she felt better. Before jumping on the bus for practice she dropped into the Surf Shack to check e-mail and discovered that the Japanese enjoy St. Valentine's Day as much as Americans. The Village attendants had hung a "Love Shack" sign and decorated the room with balloon hearts and red and white ribbons.

She learned that the Japanese custom is for women to give their male friends and lovers traditional chocolate candy on Valentine's Day and for the men to reciprocate, with white chocolate, one month later on a holiday called "White Day."

Sandra thought of her boyfriend, John Sweeney, who had arrived in Nagano to see the medal games, and regretted not being able to spend time with him. She knew John would initially be disappointed, but would eventually understand. John knew how much Sandra had sacrificed to be in Nagano and how much winning a gold medal meant to her. She and John could celebrate their own private Valentine's Day and "Whyte Day" when the Games ended. Until then she needed to focus on the inner circle.

The Valentine's Day practice was going to be a light one. The team had to be ready to play Canada at eight P.M. Instead of a full session, Coach Smith asked everyone to wear their sweats, skates, gloves, and helmets. The Nagano Skate Center was deserted. Bob, Amie, and Jeanna watched nonchalantly while the coaches put the players through ten minutes of light skating drills. They and the players were surprised when Smith suddenly ended the session and asked everyone to join him in the locker room.

What happened next shocked everybody. Ben Smith wasn't the type of guy to express his emotions. He had worked hard since accepting his USA Hockey appointment not to let players or personnel into his private world. He chose not to share information about his family background, social circle, or professional career. The inner circle caught very few glimpses of the private person—a man unusually close to his family and a small but loyal circle of friends. He had always been Coach with a capital C—not a friend and certainly not a father figure. You went to Smith for coaching, not counseling. Smith communicated so few specific words of personal praise or criticism and so few anecdotes about his life off-ice that there was no window into his psyche or soul. He remained essentially a mystery to everyone around him, including the people he spent the most time with, the inner circle.

Until Valentine's Day. For some unfathomable reason, Smith decided to open up. When everyone had settled down in the locker room, he picked up a bag of small chocolate hearts he had hidden in his briefcase and handed one to each person in the room. Then he put down the bag and cleared his throat. Sandra realized that something other than chalk-talk was about to happen when Smith's eyes began to water and he said, "As you know, I'm a quiet person. I keep to myself. But there are some things that I need to say and I thought this would be a good time to say them. It will only take a few minutes."

Sandra quietly placed her chocolate heart on the bench and, like the rest of the listeners, fell silent. She and the inner circle members then held their collective breath as the man of few words welled up further, knowing what he wanted to say next and struggling to express himself clearly.

"Before this experience is over," he began, looking around the room and making eye contact with every person, "I want you to know what you mean to me." Then, looking directly at his players, he said, "You players are the best people I have ever coached, and I can assure you I have coached many wonderful people. I have enjoyed every single day I have worked with you. This experience has been extremely rewarding for me."

Smith stopped and, searching for the proper expression of affection, started to stutter, "I ... um ... well, I have come to care about each of you individually—that is, I am concerned about what happens to you now and in the future. I will be available to support you if you need me. I mean it sincerely when I say it has been an honor for me to be your coach. My affection for all of you is unconditional. It will last forever. I don't know how else to say it."

Sandra could hear sniffing as Smith paused again, looked at the floor, and then threw back his shoulders and continued, "I think you all realize that this would not have been such a positive experience without Amie, Bob, Jeanna, and Tommy. I want you four to know how much you mean to me also." Smith turned toward Amie and Bob, who were standing behind the players, and said, "Simply stated, I wouldn't have done this job without you two. You are both the absolute best at what you do. You are class acts. I appreciate the hundreds of ways you have supported me and the players." Sandra could tell by Bob's facial expression that he was deeply touched. Amie's tears gave away her response.

Smith then focused his gaze on Jeanna, who appeared stunned by his uncharacteristic candor. "And you, Jeanna, have been a great trainer, always around and attentive when we needed you. You're a terrific professional and super role model." A naturally shy person who spoke even less than Smith, Jeanna blanched. Smith's positive, public feedback brought her to tears as well.

"Finally, Mutchy," Smith began, facing his assistant, who tightened his jaw. "Very few people here realize how long and well I've known you and your family, Tom. We go way back. I had the pleasure of coaching your brother Kevin at BU. He was a great guy, and I know how much he meant to you. Kevin died in a tragic accident on Cape Cod a few years ago and we both lost someone important. I can't tell you, Tom, how great it has been to have you here—someone so loyal, so dedicated, so nuts that he'll do anything for the players, the staff, and me personally. You're someone special, Tom. It's been fun." Tom nodded and then looked at the floor. He was confident that everyone in the room would understand that it was Smith's loyalty as well as his own that was noteworthy.

"That's it," Smith said in closing, appearing somewhat surprised to have generated so much collective emotion. "I've been wanting to say this for a long time but today seemed like the best day. Tonight, and Tuesday, win or lose, I want you to know how proud I am of all of you.

"This practice is over. Let's get back to the Village and get ready. And tonight, when we once again face the Canadians, as Tom likes to say, 'Surprise me. Show me something special.'

"Oh, and . . . Happy St. Valentine's Day."

While the players and staff composed themselves, Smith slipped out of the room. No one quite knew what to say. Smith had offered a pledge of support. What did it mean? Sandra felt he was expressing his admiration for their sacrifices. He was acknowledging that he "got it"—the fact that his players were passionate about the game even though it probably held no future for them. He had coached scores of NHL hopefuls. He understood the motivations for the men's achievement. But what motivated the women athletes? When he started coaching the women Smith wasn't quite sure, but by the time they reached the Olympic Games together, the answers were perfectly clear: A pure love of the game. A desire to end discrimination. A wish to give others the opportunity to play. Smith respected these motivations and realized that he was part of something special, something bigger than himself—something that would have lasting cultural implications. And so he decided he wanted to become more than just the women's "coach." He commited himself to being their ally. He wanted to help them collectively and individually. He wanted to be an agent of change in a sport where too few leaders "got it." He wanted hockey to be democratic.

Sandra sensed that Smith's expression of affection and commitment had forever changed his interpersonal relationships with his players. Too few people had ever been so generous. In a world obsessed with personal gain, he was giving something back. He was saying thank you and articulating his respect. Sandra was both shocked and grateful. Judging from her teammates' emotional response, she knew they were also. Coach is a very complicated but wonderful guy, Sandra thought. In that sense he's a lot like me—quiet and intense. She wiped a tear, unwrapped her chocolate heart, and ate it with pleasure.

Between the candy and the timely release of pent-up emotions, Sandra and the other members of Team USA were on a personal St. Valentine's Day high by game time at eight P.M. During warm-ups, the players could tell that much of the audience was also. Aqua Wing was packed. American and Canadian fans were seated so close together that their flags literally flew in each others' faces. Not a single press seat was vacant. The atmosphere was like a carnival, with many of the spectators in costumes: Santa suits, cowboy outfits, kimonos with American or Canadian flags for sashes. A.J. Mleczko's mother, Bambi, wore a heart decal on her cheek. Hundreds of other fans wore face paint. One young fan dyed her blond hair red, white, and blue. An older one wore multicolored dreadlocks. David Letterman's mother, Dorothy, sporting an official Team USA jersey, came in and sat down between two enormous American guys dressed like Uncle Sam. For every Canadian fan wearing a karate headband decorated with a maple leaf, there was an American fan wearing a ten-gallon hat decorated with Old Glory.

Most of the Japanese fans took sides and carried colorful signs and flags. Many also carried plastic tooters. Whereas the Lillehammer Olympic Games were filled with the ringing of Norwegian cowbells, the Japanese fans preferred what they called "mini cheer horns." Some were regular little trumpets, others were four connected windpipes. When hundreds of cheer horns sounded, the venues were really noisy.

No fan hesitated to show his or her allegiance. The match wasn't for points or medals; the United States and Canada had both qualified for the gold-medal game on Tuesday. In a practical sense the contest was to complete the Olympic round-robin, giving one team a two-day psychological advantage and their fans temporary bragging rights. In a less practical sense the contest was to showcase the world's two best women's ice hockey teams and demonstrate how intense their competition had become. In an Olympic schedule that lacked many old-fashioned head-to-head rivalries, the USA–Canada standoff was a crowd-pleaser. After thirteen games, the Canadians boasted seven wins to the Americans' six. Team USA preferred a 7–7 tie heading into the gold-medal contest. The match was about competition and pride.

Coach Smith told his goalies he wanted Tueting to start and DeCosta to finish—an even split. DeCosta would come in cold in the middle of the second period so that he could watch how she and the Canadians responded. Smith wondered if he had seen all of Canada's cards or whether Shannon Miller had a few left to play. If Team USA skated well and won they would earn a better seeding, an earlier practice time, and the last line change in the gold-medal game on Tuesday. If they played well their coach would discover what tricks, if any, Miller still had up her sleeve.

By the end of the opening period all Smith had actually learned was that two Canadian players, Karen Nystrom and Fiona Smith, were sitting out the game and that the style of play was once again going to be physical. After Sue got the gate for interference, Tara, Tricia, Karyn, Sandra, Lisa, and Shelley killed off the Americans' first penalty. They had no idea what was coming. First Lori Dupuis scored for Canada. Then there were penalties against Tricia for tripping and A.J. for body checking. When A.J. went to the box, Shannon Miller yelled, "Make it count, make it hurt, make them pay!" Instead Lori Dupuis was called for body-checking and Judy Diduck for holding. With twenty-eight seconds left in the period, Cammi tied the score on a spectacular, tic-tac-toe power-play goal that impressed everybody in the building.

The second period opened with a penalty against Angela for checking from behind. Gretchen had a breakaway but missed to Lesley Reddon's left. Danielle Goyette followed Angela into the box for roughing, followed by Cassie Campbell for holding. About a minute later Therese Brisson got the gate for body-checking, giving Team USA a five-on-three advantage. Ben Smith crossed his arms and put out two sets of play makers. Tom put one foot on the boards and the other on the bench to watch more closely. But, amazingly, no Americans scored. With ten minutes gone in the period, Smith signaled Tueting to switch with DeCosta. Lesley Reddon remained in the Canadian net.

In a quick and dramatic turnaround, Chris was called for a body check with three minutes left in the period. While the American penalty killers struggled to prevent a goal, Vicki was called for high-sticking Danielle Goyette as the period neared its end. Goyette, Canada's leading scorer, skated to the Canadian bench clutching her neck as Vicki stepped dejectedly into the penalty box. Like the rest of the American defenders, Vicki was hustling. The high stick was unintentional.

Shannon Miller didn't seem to agree. She screamed at the American team and coaches over the glass between the two benches to protest what she felt was unnecessary physical contact. Meanwhile, Sara DeCosta, minus a warm-up, kept the score even. Smith ignored Miller's offensive remarks and watched Sara flip and flop, poke and push to keep players and pucks away from her net. Sandra helped her out by sprawling in front of a blistering slap shot. When the period ended, Smith avoided Miller in the hallway and congratulated his heavily perspiring goaltender as she breathlessly made her way to the locker room.

Moments later, while the enormous crowd enthusiastically performed the wave from two different directions at once in the stands above his head, Ben Smith cautioned his team about the large number of penalties. "This is a great game, we're right in the middle of it," he said, "but let's not beat ourselves. We've only played two periods and there are thirty-six penalty minutes between us. Let's keep cool and play smart."

Vicki was frustrated that in trying to kill a penalty she had been called for one that now spilled over into the start of the final period. She knew how hard it was to play shorthanded at this stage in the game with such a highly skilled opponent.

Sitting in her stall feeling stressed, Vicki closed her eyes and tried to use Peter's advice to create a happy place in her mind where she could refocus and relax. "Wicki," Peter would say in his Austrian accent, "you must wisualize a special place with everything that makes you joyful." Vicki thought of her boyfriend, Chris Lamoriello, and happy times skating together just for fun. She also visualized sitting with Chris in the stands at the NHL's New Jersey Devils games. Chris's father was the general manager of the Devils as well as the general manager of the U.S. men's ice hockey team in Nagano. He enjoyed having Vicki attend Devils' games. Chris was a hockey player and understood her pressure. Vicki knew Chris was in the stands in Aqua Wing and wondered what he was thinking.

Vicki Movsessian had felt plenty of pressure in the past. To relieve it she liked to laugh. Her teammates could count on her for a funny comment or comic impersonation that would get the whole team chuckling. She inherited some of her sense of humor from her father, Lawrence, who had always been supportive of his youngest child. He had inspired her to love the game and follow her dreams. Her mother, Frances, had done likewise and, when her husband passed away in 1994 after an extended illness, encouraged Vicki to continue her goal of making the Olympic team. After Vicki was selected for the 1994 national team, her mother hoped she would continue to achieve and eventually qualify for the Olympics.

Vicki had a long record of achievement. She had played hockey with boys' teams in Lexington, Massachusetts, for eight years as well as with the Assabet Valley girls' regional team for twelve. She played soccer and softball at Arlington Catholic High School before enrolling at Providence College and concentrating on hockey. Vicki earned several ECAC honors at Providence and graduated magna cum laude in her major, marketing and business administration. To support herself she worked as an account representative before joining the national team. Vicki had, like so many other teammates, deferred her career in order to compete in the Olympics.

As the players returned to the bench at the start of the third period, Vicki skated back to the penalty box. She thought that Shannon Miller's comments to Ben Smith might be worthy of a comical remark, but decided not to say anything. Meanwhile Smith caught Tom Mutch's eye and said, "Hang on, buddy. This could be a wild one."

"Are you kidding?" Tom replied. "This already *is* a wild one!"

With Vicki still serving her penalty, Sandra and the other penalty killers jumped over the boards to try to stop the power play. Sandra glanced at the players standing at the end of the bench and felt sorry for them. She knew how hard it was to be "taken out of your game" and forced to wait. Neither your mind nor your legs remain sharp. You have to bear down mentally to restore any kind of rhythm to your performance. Sandra thought, Please don't tune out now. Your penalty killers are wiped out. When things calm down we're going to need you to win this one.

The wear and tear on the special team started to show when they couldn't stop Lori Dupuis's power-play, go-ahead goal at 1:24 of the third period. The American penalty killers skated despondently to the bench while the Canadian fans celebrated wildly. The penalty killers' rest was short-lived. Laurie was whistled for upending Vicky Sunohara and Angela was given the gate for body-checking and boarding. Once again the special team was sent to defend against a Canadian power play.

Canada quickly took control of the game with a five-on-three advantage. Jayna Hefford scored at 5:28 to make the score 3–1 and Therese Brisson beat Sara between her pads forty-five seconds later to make it 4–1. The Canadian fans assumed that the American team was collapsing. The maple leaf–clad fanatics waved and screamed, clanged and tooted until the rafters of Aqua Wing shook with the cacophony.

Ben Smith called a time-out and repeated his concern about penalties. "You can win this if you can stay out of the box. You know how to come from behind. You know how to put the puck in the net. You've got plenty of time. We have too many people getting tired killing penalties. Let's tighten up."

When the time-out ended and the players took their positions, Sandra could see multiple rows of American skiers, jumpers, and sledders standing behind the glass in back of Lesley Reddon imploring their USA teammates to dig deep and pull out a win. Above and beside them, the American players' parents, relatives, and friends called for a comeback. Mat DeCosta, Jason Mleczko, and A.J.'s boyfriend, Jason Griswold, led the cheers. Jonathan Tueting and John Miller followed suit. The entire Granato family, including Tony and Linda, stood in one long row directly above the glass and waved an enormous American flag from their balcony. Colleen Coyne's family members stood and screamed for a comeback. A few days earlier the Coynes had all appeared on Oprah Winfrey's show to discuss Colleen's heroic struggle to make the Olympic team following the family's tragic house fire. On the opposite side of the ice Shannon Miller, no longer upset, smiled and gestured confidently. Sandra looked at the clock. We've got fourteen minutes left, she thought. Anything can happen.

The referee dropped the puck and, with both teams at even strength with 12:30 left in the period, Laurie scored with help from Katie and Alana. The score was 4–2 and the American fans were rejoicing. But their celebration was shortlived. Karyn was penalized for high-sticking and the Canadians attacked Sara's net. Stacy Wilson capitalized on an odd-man break and Lori Dupuis followed her, forcing Sara to make another incredible save. Sara got a break when Jayna Hefford boarded Lisa. With the power-play unit on the ice, Sandra fired on Reddon and Tara blasted a slap shot, but to no avail. Moments later the referee charged Vicky Sunohara for slashing Jenny, giving Team USA a five-on-three advantage with less than ten minutes to go in the game.

Ben Smith took a deep breath. He had seen teams come from behind to win a thousand times but knew it required total team effort. His memory of Canada's stunning comeback win in Burlington still reverberated. That comeback was completely about team confidence, he thought. Total, uncompromised confidence. Let's see if we've learned that lesson since then. Let's see if we can do it.

Five American players controlled the face-off and started passing with complete finesse in front of Lesley Reddon. Each American woman touched the puck on its way to Cammi, who, having fought for position, slammed the final pass behind Lesley for a score. Cammi's second goal shaved the lead to one.

The Americans in the audience erupted. Team USA looked inspired. Their passing and execution were textbook perfection. Their speed was amazing. Everyone was clicking. Everyone was in the moment. Then Jenny fired a beautiful shot past Reddon, erasing Canada's lead and sending the American fans into a frenzy.

Ben Smith looked at his bench and felt optimistic. His team was in sync and had taken complete control of the game. The next goal was likely to be the game winner.

Smith's instincts were correct. Twenty-three seconds after Jenny scored, A.J. made a neat pass from behind the net to Tricia, who shoveled the tie-breaking goal past Reddon. The roof in Aqua Wing nearly retracted as Tricia became airborne and the audience went berserk. The American fans hugged, kissed, and danced on their seats while Tricia's teammates jumped on her, knocking her backward onto the ice. The hardworking digger, a scrappy, no-nonsense forward who had played her heart out in every game, had put the Americans in front 5–4.

The fact that Tricia had scored was impressive. For most of the game she had knocked herself out with the rest of the special team players killing penalties. She was nearly physically spent when she scooped A.J.'s perfect pass behind Reddon. Her teammates acknowledged her outstanding all-around effort and go-ahead goal by burying her under a pigpile on the ice.

Tricia had been in a few pigpiles before. She had been a successful athlete at Pinkerton Academy in her hometown of Derry, New Hampshire, before attending the University of New Hampshire and playing on the UNH women's hockey team that beat Providence for the 1996 ECAC championship. The championship game, which resulted in five overtime periods, was the longest college hockey game, male or female, in the record books. When it was over Tricia was in the middle of a pigpile of truly exhausted athletes.

Tricia had never made a national team before and was excited to be part of the historic Olympic debut squad. She had graduated from UNH with a degree in psychology in 1996 and immediately started training for the national team tryouts. When she made the team, the other players discovered she had a serious crush on an NHL player. They teased her unmercifully, particularly when the team attended the NHL all-star game in Canada. Bob Allen was among the worst offenders. He liked to see Tricia blush. Unfortunately, the Canadian heartthrob was sitting across the ice tonight dressed in his red-and-white Team Canada uniform and rooting for Tricia's adversary. No problem, she thought. This is about performance, not romance.

As Tricia and her elated teammates got up from their pigpile and returned to their bench, Shannon Miller's confident smile was replaced by a dark expression that deepened when Judy Diduck was penalized for body-checking. Ben Smith's calm demeanor never changed. He merely licked his lips while his team played excellent offense, passing like pros and working the seams to try to sneak another point past Reddon. The Diduck penalty ended without a score, but Team USA was fired up. With the teams even-up, they pressured Lesley Reddon from every side. The Canadian defense, disorganized and collapsing, left Reddon exposed and unprotected. Once again A.J. saw a window. She fed a perfect pass to Lisa, who had found a spot directly in front of the net. Lisa slammed the puck home, giving the Americans five unanswered tallies and a 6–4 lead.

Lisa's goal caused another eruption on the American bench and explosion in the stands. American spectators and Japanese fans pounded their feet, waved their flags, and tooted. The clock was bleeding down quickly.

Sandra jumped over the boards to help protect the lead. The Canadian team, shocked and frustrated, was preparing to pull out all stops to make a comeback. Hayley Wickenheiser fired a sizzling wrist shot on Sara, which the American netminder deflected beautifully. The crowd gasped. Sandra watched to see when Miller would pull her goalie. She could sense Danielle Goyette's presence behind her on the ice. Suddenly Sandra winced in pain. Danielle had slashed her across the ankle, a virtually unprotected body part, with her stick. Sandra didn't retaliate, but struggled to the bench in excruciating pain. "Mutchie, did you see that slash?" she asked, grimmacing.

"I missed it, Whytie," Tom responded, opening the gate. "The ref must have, too. Are you okay?"

"I'm not okay, but I will be. What a cheap hack! I didn't even have the puck. I guess it was punishment. The Canadians are frustrated."

As Sandra spoke, Shannon Miller pulled Lesley Reddon and sent six Canadian snipers to attack Sara. The Canadian stars fought desperately to keep the puck in Sara's end and force a tie. But Sara was steadfast and her teammates defended their goal with passion. Eventually Team Canada coughed up the puck and Laurie grabbed it. She skated calmly along the right-side boards, aimed, and shot a bullet into the empty Canadian net.

Aqua Wing again erupted. Laurie's second goal, a back-breaker, made the score 7–4. The American fans screamed, "Na-na-na-na, na-na-na-na, hey-hey, good-bye!" as the entire Aqua Wing audience stood to give Laurie and her teammates a standing ovation. Team USA had scored six unanswered goals in eleven minutes and fifty-three seconds. As time ran out, Tony Granato turned to his parents and said, "The Americans just beat Canada physically, psychologically, and emotionally. That was as exciting a hockey game as I have ever seen."

The two teams surrounded their goalies and then gathered at center ice for the traditional handshake. When Sandra stood face-to-face in line with Danielle Goyette, she raised her finger, pointed it at her, and told her what she thought of the late-game slash. Danielle, who speaks English as a second language, listened and then finished moving through the line. When the handshakes ended, Team USA gathered at center ice to salute their fans, who were still on their feet clapping. As Sandra stood in the happy circle, Danielle approached her and responded to Sandra's earlier remarks. Shelley listened. When Danielle finished saying her piece, she skated to the gate, smashed her stick over the boards, and ran to the Canadians' locker room in tears.

Shannon Miller, who was angrily berating the officials for letting the game get "out of control," noticed Danielle's emotional departure. She asked several Canadian players what they thought was going on and then pulled Cammi aside. Miller did not consult Danielle to get the facts. Nevertheless, she told the Team USA captain that a remark had been made in the line about Danielle's father, who had died of Alzheimer's disease on the day before the Opening Ceremonies.

Cammi listened, astonished by the allegation. When Miller finished, Cammi skated away, concerned that Danielle was in an emotional state but convinced that the coach's accusation was a misunderstanding. She conveyed Miller's allegation to her own coach so that Ben Smith would be prepared if he needed to confront it.

When Smith entered his locker room he was jubilant. He congratulated his players and thanked them for a game that was truly something special—a stunning comeback that showed their talent, tenacity, and team confidence. Then he shook each player's hand and commented on her performance. Sandra's stall was at the end of the room. When the coach reached Sandra he thanked her for an outstanding job killing the penalties.

After commending each player personally Ben Smith spoke once again to the entire team. "By the way," Smith added, "I should let you know that the Canadians are saying someone said something in line to Danielle Goyette, something about her father."

"I said something to her in line, Coach," Sandra confessed, "but nothing about her father."

"Okay, Whytie. No problem," Smith said. "Obviously no one on our team would say anything about her father, but I wanted to give everyone a heads-up. If Miller brings it up again, we'll deal with it. Great game!"

Sandra felt a burning sensation in her chest. What a terrible accusation! She appreciated Smith's trust but felt terrible she had said anything at all. I'm famous for being the quiet one, she thought, and now here I am accused of saying something awful. She chastised herself. Why did I open my mouth? I never talk trash. What a mistake! Why did I say anything at all? Shaking her head, Sandra threw her equipment on the floor and headed for the shower. Watching an excited teammate give Bob and Amie a high-five, she thought, I really hope this is the end of it.

But it wasn't the end; it was only the beginning. Fifteen minutes later, when Shannon Miller stepped out of the Canadian locker room to speak with the press about her team's embarrassing loss, she led with two complaints. The first was for what she described as the Americans' (i.e., Ben Smith's) use of unnecessary physical contact. The second was for Sandra Whyte's alleged remark to Danielle Goyette about her deceased father. Miller avoided discussion of Team Canada's complete meltdown—on defense, offense, and in goal. She also ignored Team USA's remarkable comeback. Miller created an excuse and a deflection. Ben Smith's coaching became her excuse. Sandra Whyte's remark became her deflection. Miller told the sportswriters, "This is only going to add to the intensity of the final. They [the Americans] have been saying things since the Three Nations Cup tournament. Those types of comments just stir us up and piss us off. They are going to pay for it—big time."

The press took down every word. They found the martial-arts instructor and former Calgary policewoman eminently quotable. She had once told the media that the best six months of her life were spent working in her department's undercover armed-robbery unit. "You're taking people down at gunpoint all the time," she said. "I love it."

She portrayed the two teams' rivalry going into the gold-medal contest as bitter and hateful, and characterized the American team as brawling and out of control.

Ben Smith had no interest in embarrassing Shannon Miller for her team's poor performance in the previous game or villifying her personally, even though she had screamed at the American bench during the game. He took the high road, telling reporters that he had thought the game would be a "waltz" for both teams because it didn't mean "a hill of beans." He dismissed the allegation that a remark had been made about Goyette's father, noting that the entire American team had immediately signed and sent a sympathy card to Danielle upon hearing of her father's death. He said his players denied Miller's accusation, "And I trust my players." Smith told the media, "I thought the winner [of this game] would just get a box of donuts and go home." He did not want either the media or Shannon Miller to spin a positive into a negative.

It was too late. Sandra Whyte—the quiet, serious, and cerebral American skater—was no longer low profile: In fact, she was now decidedly quite the opposite.

The hour was late when the bus returned from Aqua Wing. While most of her teammates celebrated their come-from-behind victory elsewhere in the Village, Sandra retired to her bedroom. She was exhausted, shocked, and confused. She wondered how a simple remark about a slash had turned into an incident.

Sandra lay down on her bed, closed her eyes, and wished Peter Haberl had come with the team to Nagano. He was the only member of the inner circle who was missing and she desperately wanted to talk to him. Peter had warned that things would go wrong at the Olympics, that excellent athletes would make mistakes, and that when bad things happened it would be important to call upon personal strengths and prior psychological preparation to handle the stress. As Sandra pulled out her journal, a profound sense of sadness overwhelmed her. She whispered a brief but fervent prayer and wrote one line.

Tonight has been a nightmare.

SUNDAY, FEBRUARY 15, 1998

HIGH PROFILE

Sandra could barely sleep. She awoke early and showered, hoping that the warm, clear torrents would comfort and console her. They did not.

She felt falsely accused and unfairly disgraced. She had said nothing like what Miller alleged, and late reports were that Danielle had refused to validate Miller's accusation. Would it still be an issue? she wondered. If so, what is the point? Women athletes exchange harsh words on the playing field all the time, just like male athletes. Why would the press wish to dwell on the exchange between two women athletes? Why would it be newsworthy? Did the press have a double standard for women? And, worst of all, would the story be used to disgrace her and her teammates as they approached the most important game of their lives? Would a coach do such an unfair thing? Would the press be complicit? Sandra was heartsick.

Sandra stepped out of the shower, dressed quickly, and turned on her hair dryer. In the next room she could hear the doorbell ring and one of her roommates get up to answer it. Feeling self-conscious and ashamed, she dreaded the thought of having to interact with anyone. To her utter amazement, she saw that it was Peter. God had answered her prayer.

Ben Smith had sent for Peter two days earlier when Bob Webster was asked by USA Hockey executive director Dave Ogrean if there was anything else the women's team needed. Dave may have been thinking about equipment, but Bob immediately suggested Peter Haberl. Ogrean spoke with Smith, who concurred. Haberl had just arrived after a seventeen-hour flight from Boston. Sandra arranged to spend time with him right after practice. For the first time Sandra was sensing that somehow things would get better.

But before things would get better, they would get worse. Later that morning Kris Pleimann told Sandra the pool of international reporters wanted to question her about what had actually happened with Danielle Goyette. Kris said that she had set up a press conference for immediately after the team's practice and asked Ben, Sandra, Cammi, and several other players to be ready as well.

Shannon Miller's excuse and deflection had worked perfectly. The media accounts of the Americans' dramatic victory over the Canadians included a side story concerning the alleged remark to Danielle Goyette about her father. Most of the news stories mentioned Sandra, but a few also implicated Shelley. As soon as the reporters' stories about the allegations hit the Internet, Sandra and Shelley both started receiving insulting and even threatening e-mail on their fan-mail accounts. Amie contacted the FBI and Village security. Sandra skated through the practice dismayed by the course of events but resolved to set the record straight.

At the end of the team's practice, Sandra showered and dressed and then went out into the hallway to wait for the press conference. Peter saw Sandra waiting and went over to speak with her. In a quiet section of the hall Sandra quickly summarized what had happened.

Peter processed Sandra's story. He felt that he knew Sandra Whyte as well as any member of the team. She was an exceptional person, someone above reproach. He could see that she was hurt and angry, but she was also forthright, intelligent, and articulate in her brief explanation of the facts. Peter was quite sure Sandra could handle the pressure and scrutiny of the press conference. When Kris called to Sandra to come and speak with the reporters, Peter encouraged Sandra not to worry and to be true to herself.

Sandra lifted her chin, threw back her shoulders, and walked down the Aqua Wing locker-room hallway to answer media questions with her colleagues. There were scores of reporters holding microphones and small pads of paper. She stood before them stoically and waited for their queries. One immediately asked if Sandra had made a remark to Danielle. Sandra admitted making a comment to Danielle in the handshake line but denied that the remark was about Danielle's father. "We have the deepest sympathy for her," she told her inquisitors.

The press asked what, in fact, Sandra did say.

"It is not appropriate for me to repeat what I said," Sandra began. "Some words were exchanged and, of course, I now regret them. But anytime something is said, it is said in the heat of the game, and afterward it is regrettable. But it happens. That's hockey. Heated exchanges go on all over the ice. For one to be singled out is absurd." She took a deep breath and continued, "I don't know why everyone is making such a big deal about us exchanging a few words on the ice when men go out there and pummel each other all the time."

Peter was impressed, but Sandra was only getting started. A reporter asked why the Canadians would suggest that she had made such a remark. Without missing a beat she responded, "Obviously it is a new psychological tactic for them." It was Sandra's honest opinion.

The reporters scribbled quickly. Sandra had given them a whole new twist on the story. Maybe a Canadian had made up the allegation? Could that be possible? Would anyone actually use a player's grief to try to motivate a team? The reporters turned to the other American players for insights.

Sandra's teammates were ready to get back to the facts. Alana reminded the press that the Canadians had failed under pressure: "We've learned that you just have to go after them hard and you have to pressure them. We've also learned that just like any other team, they're going to cough up the puck, they're going to get nervous, and they're not going to know what to do with it." The reporters listened carefully. Lisa added, "Because we have been able to play them so many times, we've gained a lot of confidence against them. Now we've played enough times to put us on an even playing field. There is no such thing as a gap anymore. Both of these teams are very, very good. On any given night, either team can win."

Lisa and Alana were right on target. The record now stood at seven wins and seven losses for both teams after fourteen games. As Ben Smith had pointed out at the Valentine's Day press conference, this game in reality meant a hill of beans. The next game, on the other hand, meant everything.

When the press conference ended, Sandra returned to the Village. She had lunch with Gretchen and Sarah and then met with Peter. "You handled yourself well," he said.

"I felt like I did," she said with relief. "I said what I wanted to say and I got through it. But something is wrong, Peter. I really feel like our competition with the Canadians is no fun anymore. It's too negative. I don't like competition when it brings out the worst in you, not the best. I can't compete because I want to hate the other team.

"Why," she asked, "does one coach always represent the rival team as a noble opponent, so excellent that you must play your very best to defeat it, and the other coach represent the rival team and its coach as sinister and unworthy?"

For Sandra, not liking another team was not what motivated her to win. As she confided to Peter, "I can't find the will and energy within myself to achieve if I have a negative motivation. I want to believe that my opponent is competing for the love of the game and struggling to reach her highest level of achievement. I want to struggle to play better than she does to win the game. On the way, I want to bring out the best in her and she in me. Isn't that what the Olympics are all about?"

Peter reminded Sandra of the teachings from the circle of control. "You cannot control the Canadians or the media. You can only control yourself and how you respond to these attitudes and behaviors." He went on, "Your accusers are testing you for a reason. They want to distract you. Your coaches and teammates have dismissed the accusation. They know you. They respect you. They are supporting you. They are also relying on you. Focus on them and yourself."

Later that day during a team photo session and taping of a spot with Dorothy Letterman in the locker room, Sandra thought about her conversation with Peter. She had made a mistake by commenting on the slash. Okay, she told herself, I'm not perfect. She was ashamed for talking trash to Danielle and upset that Shelley had been inaccurately implicated, but she had taken responsibility and was ready to move on. She had learned a lot about competition, namely that people compete for different reasons and react differently under intense pressure. Sandra could see more clearly how small incidents can become exaggerated or misconstrued in the Olympics. And, finally, she had learned about her own motivation. This is not about me personally, she concluded. This is about the inner circle succeeding for a higher purpose.

Thinking about the team's ultimate goals, Sandra recalled what Peter had taught her about Muhammad Ali. He had been fearful, made mistakes, and been criticized for speaking what he believed. He had endured unfair criticism while struggling for a noble cause. She could not compare herself to him, but she could learn from his experience. Ali had endured and prevailed.

Peter, of course, wasn't the only one helping her through this incident. Back home her family, and in particular her father and brother, were thinking about her. She printed Tim's e-mail message for February fifteenth and placed it in her journal to mark the day.

To: SWhyte
From: TWhyte

Hi Sandra, I know why now!!

I was in bed watching the video a dozen times, thinking why you? Well, now I know. This is to get you off your game. Why you? You are a leading penalty killer. When there is a penalty, who does Coach Smith call? YOU! Canada's only goals came on the power play. Their only hope is to score more on the power play, and they have to do something about you.

Don't let them get to you with this. That is exactly what they are trying to do. Turn it around and use it. We are all behind you, but we wish we were standing next to you.

Love, Tim

MONDAY, FEBRUARY 16, 1998

GOOD-BYE AQUA WING

Today we moved from Aqua Wing to Big Hat Arena for the big game tomorrow. It was sad to leave. Since arriving from Osaka fifteen days ago, Aqua Wing has come to feel like our home. Everything is so comfortable—from the locker room to the feel of the ice.

I couldn't leave Aqua Wing without taking pictures. I walked around and took pictures of this important place where I have learned so much about who I am and what is important to me. I shall never forget this place. Good-bye Aqua Wing.

Gold-medal game tomorrow!

6

GOLD-MEDAL CONTENDERS

"Surprise Me. Show Me Something Special."

NAGANO, JAPAN ~ FEBRUARY 17, 1998

Sara DeCosta stared out her window at a dark sky heavy with snow. She wanted to nap, but her brain wouldn't cooperate. Her mind kept racing over the basic facts: She was twenty years old and in two hours would be competing for an Olympic gold medal.

Outside the bedroom door Sara could hear three of her roommates talking quietly in the common room. Sue, Shelley, and Angela were discussing the terrible e-mail messages Shelley was receiving from Canadian hockey fans. The e-mail was prompted by the inaccurate stories in the press and on the Internet alleging that both Sandra Whyte and Shelley Looney had made unkind remarks to Danielle Goyette.

"Don't worry about it," Sue advised. "There's nothing you can do."

"But it's unfair," Shelley complained. "Sandra and I don't deserve this."

"Of course you don't," Sue conceded. "But we know you didn't do it, you know you didn't do it, and Sandra knows she didn't do it. We just have to roll with it and ignore it."

"Okay," Shelley agreed. "You're right."

"Of course she's right," Angela added. "Those people on the Internet are just trying to make you lose your focus. But you're gonna have a great game today, Shelley. You're gonna show 'em."

"Let's hope so," Shelley said. "The last time I played the Canadians in a championship game one of them fractured my cheekbone."

The three laughed. "Sh-h-h," Angela said. "Don't wake up Jenny. She likes her pregame rest just as much as Sara."

Jenny Lynn Schmidgall was an early riser. As a child back home in Minnesota she was up by four A.M. so that she could complete her paper-route deliveries before school started. Jenny's paper route included three hundred daily deliveries, sometimes on foot, other times on in-line skates.

Just nineteen, Jenny was among the youngest players on the Olympic team. She hadn't started playing hockey until eighth grade, preferring instead to swim and play football, another "boys only" sport. With only three years of ice hockey experience, Jenny showed up in a junior development camp attended by Ben Smith and impressed him immediately. At five feet three inches, she was in what he called the Smurf category, but he liked her "nose for the puck" and ability to bring out the best in her linemates. He noticed that as a left-shot player Jenny could cleverly move the puck to a right wing in scoring position. Because of her talent and versatility she could skate with strong, experienced players like Karyn Bye and hold her own.

During one year of high school in Edina, Minnesota, Jenny played on the boys' senior varsity team. Unfortunately, her experience was different from that of other women like Tara and Karyn, who also played with high school peers. A few of her teammates and their families resented the fact that a girl had taken a place on the roster. Minnesota is hockey country, and a strong high school performance can lead to a college scholarship. Jenny looked to the older guys on the team to be her allies, but this never happened. Occasionally she was even excluded from team activities.

During that year in high school, sometimes Jenny would feel down, especially when she felt her performance wasn't strong. But she never gave up her conviction that her teammates were essentially good guys and that one day they would "get it." Someday her teammates would understand why progressive Minnesota lawmakers, many of them former male hockey players, had fought to give girls in Minnesota equal opportunity under Title IX. Equal treatment included new hockey rinks, high school teams, and college scholarships at the state university.

When she became one of the first girls to receive a college scholarship to play women's ice hockey at the University of Minnesota, Jenny became a living example of the expanding social justice for girls in the state. She was proud to become a Minnesota Gopher. Her mother and father, Terri and Dwayne, and her older sisters, Stephanie and Amber, were also proud. They encouraged Jenny to defer entrance to college for one year to try out for the U.S. national team. When the blue-eyed blonde earned a place on the first U.S. Women's Olympic Ice Hockey Team, they knew that she was going places.

Jenny's Olympic teammates nicknamed her "Schmiggy" and teased her about being "so Minnesota"—that is, so sweet and naive, like a radio character on Garrison Keillor's *Prairie Home Companion*. Schmiggy just laughed. She knew she was in fact two things, a naive rookie and a gifted athlete. She also knew that her Olympic coaches and teammates highly respected her. Unlike in high school, the older players enjoyed having a newcomer and happily took her under their wings.

When Cammi sat down with Amie to put together rooming assignments in the Olympic Village, she placed rookies Jenny and Sara with the team's youngest player, Angela Ruggiero. Angela was the youngest athlete on the team, having just turned eighteen on January 3, but she was hardly a rookie. Angela had made the national team when she was fifteen years old and immediately become a standout.

Although she didn't have a driver's license or high school diploma, Angela had earned a reputation for being the most physically intimidating player on the American team. Ben Smith described her as tough and responsible. Her excellent skills controlling the puck in the Americans' own end made her an invaluable player in the later stages of a rough game. Her style drew lots of penalties, but her ability made her a budding superstar.

Angela Maria Ruggiero was born in Los Angeles, California, in 1980. Family lore has it that she broke her tibia in a "baby wrestling championship" with her older sister Pam and younger brother Billy. Although she had never skated when her father, Bill, signed her up for her first youth hockey program in Coneyo Valley, after a few weeks she loved it so much that she wore her hockey uniform as her Halloween costume. The next year, Bill registered his daughter for the Pasadena Maple Leafs, from which she was chosen for the United States Select Team. Prep school coaches noticed Angela and offered her applications. Bill and Karen Ruggiero hesitantly investigated Angela's options.

Six months later the Ruggieros sent their talented daughter to Choate-Rosemary Hall prep school in Wallingford, Connecticut. It was a difficult but important decision. At Choate, Angela blossomed academically, athletically, and socially. She became a serious student, president of her class (three times), and member of two junior national and three national ice hockey teams. She also competed recreationally for the Connecticut Polar Bears.

Bill and Karen missed their daughter and insisted that she call home every evening. When her parents moved from California to Michigan to support their other children's aspirations, the Choate decision became a blessing for Angela. Not only was she happy to have a stable high school experience, but her academic advisors at Choate helped her devise a plan to accommodate her Olympic training schedule. Today, in less than two hours, the entire Choate student body would be gathering in a large auditorium to watch Angela and her teammates make Olympic history.

Angela's Olympic goal was to win gold. Her role was to play aggressive defense, and she took it seriously. Her nickname was "Rugger," her stick was her weapon, and her style was "rough, tough, know your stuff." Angela led the team in penalty minutes. At five feet nine inches and 175 pounds, she was not your typical "Valley Girl."

Lying in bed, Sara heard Angela, Sue, and Shelley talking, but opted for a few more minutes of rest. She rolled over, turned up her Walkman, and thought about the morning's pregame practice.

The practice had been very meaningful, not only because it was the team's last, but also because it was the prelude to the gold-medal game. Walking toward their Big Hat Arena locker room, the women had passed the U.S. men's team locker room. Jerseys exactly like their own, labeled with the biggest names in men's professional ice hockey, hung in the stalls. Every piece of equipment was in perfect order.

Sara knew her teammates thought it was cool to see the men's locker room, but cooler still to walk thirty feet down the hallway and find that Bob Webster had given all of them the same treatment. The women's locker room was a mirror image of the men's, except for Lady Liberty on the training table. Everything was in its place. God bless Webby, Sara thought. He makes us feel so "big time." This locker room screams out, *"You are the U.S. Olympic team! You are something special!"*

Sara watched her teammates put good-luck Beanie Babies and teddy bears in their stalls along with apples, bananas, and energy bars. Now you can tell it's not the men's locker room, she thought with a smile. She wondered what Brett Hull, Mike Richter, Matt Schneider, and her friend Bryan Berard relied on for good luck.

When all the players were dressed for the pregame practice, they joined their coaches at center ice in the hauntingly quiet, empty arena. Twelve forwards in red, blue, green, or black jerseys, two goaltenders in gray, and five defenders in yellow created a splash of color reminiscent of Nagano's official Olympic symbol. Tara wasn't practicing. She was resting her injured leg for the final contest.

"Okay, everybody, relax," Coach Smith said.

"Yeah, right, Coach," Karyn said kiddingly, and her teammates chuckled in agreement.

"Well, at least try to relax," Smith said. "I've got a little story."

Sara enjoyed Coach's stories. Each one was a parable and all were better than chalk-talk. She knelt on her knee pads and listened.

"I was talking with a golf buddy of mine one day about competition," Smith started. "My buddy said, 'When I'm standing on the putting green at the end of a match, and I'm watching my opponent line up his final putt, I hope he'll put his putt right in the middle of the hole. Then I want to step up, take my putt, and drop my ball right on top of his to win.'

"I always remembered that simple philosophy. You want your competition to be on top of their game, forcing you to play your best, and then you want to beat them.

"The best thing that could happen today is for you and Canada both to play great and show the world that women's ice hockey is a super game. I want Team Canada to show why they've won four world championships, and then I want Team USA to beat them.

"You can do it. You have the skills and training. You know the mechanics of this game so well that your body will take over if you get nervous. You know exactly what to do. Remember, it's the same routine, just another game.

"We're going to have a light practice this morning, then Amie and Kris are going to fill you in on details regarding what's expected of us after the game, depending upon what happens.

"I want the rest of the day to be just like any other. Have a nutritious lunch and a good rest, and drink lots of water. That's it."

When the practice was over and the players had showered and dressed for the ride back to the Village, Sara heard the coaches and Bob Webster invite Amie to bring the team's Japanese attachés to the locker room. The two shy, soft-spoken women slipped sheepishly into the room, fearful that something had gone wrong. They were delightfully surprised when, instead of a reprimand, they were each presented with a stack of official Team USA Olympic clothing—hats, sweat suits, and T-shirts—for their families. The attachés' eyes filled with tears as Amie and the coaches thanked them for their support on behalf of the entire team. *"Domo arigato! Domo arigato!"* the women said, bowing. *"Domo arigato gozaimasu!"*

"It's nothing. We really want to thank you," Amie said, giving her Japanese friends a big American hug.

When Sara returned to the Village for her training meal, a huge bowl of spaghetti, she told Sarah Tueting she liked Smith's story about the golfer. "He always wants to bring out the best in everyone," she said. "Even the Canadians."

"I agree," Teeter said, "but I think he does it best with his own players. He sees each of us for who we want to be. He also sees the best and worst in us and then somehow—not with words, but with gestures—helps us stretch to be our very best. He gets you to think about the person you want to be, and then become her."

Sara DeCosta was delighted that her teammate was in good spirits. During the previous day's practice Ben Smith had asked Sarah Tueting to be the gold-medal game's starting goalie, even though it was Sara DeCosta's turn in the rotation. Smith had called DeCosta aside and said, "Sara, I've decided to put Sarah Tueting in the net for tomorrow's game. You're both equally outstanding goalies, but I think you are better out of the bullpen. It takes Teeter longer to prepare mentally. I think the team will feel confident if she starts and you're there to relieve her if necessary."

Sara was proud of her response. "That's fine, Coach. Whatever you think is best for the team. I'll be ready to come in if you need me."

Sara considered Smith's reaction as she relived the moment from memory. Smith had searched her dark brown eyes for a hint of disappointment or resentment and then smiled appreciatively. "Thanks, Sara," he said, patting her on the back. "We need you in the backup role to win."

"Coach, I'm so happy to be here. I've won three games and I know I can come off the bench to beat them," Sara said. "I'll be ready."

Smith looked at her again and nodded. She could tell he would have stuck a gold star on her forehead if he had one.

Sara could hear the noise in the next room increase when Jenny joined her roommates in the common room. Time to get up and get going, Sara decided. During the postpractice debriefing that morning, Amie had told everyone to wear the awards ceremony uniform with the star-spangled jacket on the bus ride to Big Hat. Sara had prepared the jacket and everything else she would need many hours before. She grabbed her stuff on the way to the dining hall for a snack.

The atmosphere was upbeat. Everyone was rested. As the players grabbed handfuls of apples and bananas, Amie announced that she had received a special delivery from the USOC of sweet, American-style peanut butter. People went crazy. Some put the peanut butter on their bananas and apples. Sue, Karyn, and Teeter smeared it on enormous pieces of toast. Amie told Ben Smith, "This could do it. The peanut butter could put you over the top."

When Smith laughed, Amie asked about the tie he had chosen to wear to the game. "Art Berglund gave it to me. It's my favorite," Smith said. "All these little things are lighthouses. They remind me of my mother, whose home sits beside a lighthouse in Gloucester. My whole family will be there in about an hour to see the broadcast."

"It's red, white, and blue. I think it's perfect," Amie observed.

Smith wondered how his team leader was doing. Amie was handling hundreds of additional details associated with the gold-medal game. "Are you overwhelmed yet, Amie?" he asked.

"No, Ben," she said honestly. "I feel like Cinderella on her way to the ball. I'm excited and honored to be part of the whole thing."

"We'll see if we can find you a glass slipper," he said seriously. "You deserve one."

Sara and her teammates were waiting at the front door of the International Zone to board the bus for the thirty-minute drive to Big Hat Arena. Together with their coaches and other members of their entourage, including Dr. Sandy Glasson, Jeanna, and Peter, they were driven down the concourse, through the security gates of the Village, and into the busy streets of Nagano. The players put on their Walkmans to listen to pregame tapes of choice. Tara picked the soundtrack from *Titanic*. Colleen selected Enya and her favorite song, "Only If." It had inspired Colleen throughout her challenging, remarkable year.

But Coach Smith wasn't interested in music. Five minutes into the ride he slid a video into the VCR. The players were astonished. They looked at each other as if to say, What is he thinking? A video? We're on our way to the biggest game of our lives!

No one was more surprised than Peter. He had put this particular video together using game films produced by the team's volunteer filmmaker, Bob O'Connor, during the pre-Olympic tour. Peter had given the video to Ben early in February, hoping that it would be shown before the final game, but that had not happened.

Peter had designed the film as a teaching tool to remind the women of what they had been through. The film's messages were simple: Believe in yourself. Face your fears. Remember your goal. Like the rope and bracelets in San Jose, he believed the video would affirm the power of the inner circle.

Sara looked at the video screen on the bus and saw great plays, spectacular saves, and intelligent decisions. One highlight followed another. Soon everyone was watching as Olympic clips and interviews flashed in front of them. The video included vignettes illustrating the players' strengths as individuals and as a team. Near the end, in association with a reference to Muhammad Ali, Peter placed a single photo of Sandra Whyte. Peter associated Sandra with the "woman with a trembling hand," the special woman Ali's witch doctor told him would help him beat Foreman.

Sara heard one teammate after another gasp at the images on the screen. Oh my God, Sara thought, looking around at her teammates' misty eyes. This is so powerful. We can win this game.

The video ended as the bus reached the entrance to Big Hat. As the police cleared away the crowd waiting at the door, the women hurried inside, still thinking about the video. Their locker room was under the stands behind the goal, the farthest distance from the runway onto the ice. Canada's locker room was at the entrance to the runway, close to the media and Olympic officials. Ben Smith wanted his team as far away from that spot as possible.

Everything was normal in the locker room. Webby was sharpening skates. Fruit, water, Gatorade, and Jeanna's "mother's milk" sat on the training table beside Lady Liberty and rolls of tape. Just another game, Sara thought, just another game.

As the players changed for warm-ups, Sara noticed that several of them—including Teeter, Colleen, and Gretchen—were wearing T-shirts with a little sheep on them. The shirts had been sent to them by the mother of Sarah Devens, a close friend who had died young. An outstanding three-sport athlete at Dartmouth, Devens might possibly have made the Olympic team. Today, she was with her friends in spirit. They posed for a picture to send to Devens's mother.

The players moved into the unoccupied American men's locker room and jumped on the stationary bicycles. Tara looked at Sara and said, "Check that out. There's Brian Leech's stall."

"Here's Mike Richter's," Sara responded. "He's using his famous helmet. It must be lucky."

"This is so cool," Tara said, looking at the men's gear and trying not to think about her injury.

Tara was waging a psychological battle with stress. As she stared at her injured leg and hoped the cortisone shot Jeanna had given would last through the contest, she started feeling nervous.

All the years of impairment and rehabilitation flashed in front of Tara as she pedaled. Can I stay healthy through this game? Can I play well? she wondered. She thought about her family and pedaled faster. Her mother and father, Sue and Mike, and grandfather would soon be in the stands. They had just learned that Tara's maternal grandmother had been rushed to a hospital in New Hampshire. Tara's great-grandmother was looking after her grandmother in her parents' absence. Tara's parents and grandfather were scheduled to fly to New Hampshire a few hours after the game ended.

I do not want to lose this game, she told herself. I do not want to make mistakes. I do not want to hear "O Canada" at the end of this thing. I just couldn't stand it.

"Five minutes to team stretch," Karyn announced. Tara jumped off the bicycle, wiped her neck with a towel, and left the men's locker room.

Dance music blared from the speakers as the players gathered in a large circle in the women's locker room. Cammi said she'd like to lead the warm-up exercises, the team's last. In a few hours Team USA would be history, a realization that gave each ritual special poignancy.

For ten minutes Team USA stretched, lunged, and laughed to warm their muscles and ease their nerves.

Sara grabbed her water bottle and sat on one of the wooden benches to catch her breath. As she took a long drink she noticed Sarah Tueting pulling her goalie equipment out of her stall and starting to get dressed. Suddenly Sara DeCosta had an idea: This is the biggest game of Teeter's life. I could give her something special for good luck.

Sara dropped her water bottle, jumped up, and pulled her shoulder pads out of her locker. Buried between two layers of foam was a pin, a tiny golden angel holding a hockey stick. Her father had given it to her for good luck when she entered Providence College and she had had a great year playing for the Friars, followed by the good fortune of making the national and Olympic teams. The precious pin had helped her recover from her fractured pelvis and shut out the Canadians in the Three Nations Cup tournament. She thought, This is perfect.

Sara hesitated for a moment, knowing that Sarah Tueting did not welcome interruptions when she was entering goalie world. But she walked over and said, "I've had this angel pin on my shoulder pads for a long time, Teeter, and it has been looking over me. But I want you to have it. I want the angel to watch over you in this game as it has watched over me."

"I can't take that," Teeter said. "It's too important."

"I want you to have it," Sara replied. "Let's find a good place for it." Sara lifted the pad behind Teeter's right arm and clipped it there. Sarah Tueting was speechless.

"Good luck, Teeter," Sara said. Then she hugged her and smiled.

Returning to goalie world, Sarah Tueting thought, This is such a good sign. Sara's given me so much confidence. I have an overwhelmingly positive feeling. It's just what I need. She stepped into her girdle and buckled on her hockey socks. On the other side of the room her backup did likewise.

Sarah Tueting was dressing for the most important and stressful game of her life, but she felt confident. Her Grandma Tueting's advice was echoing in her head. "You can do anything you put your mind to, Sarah," Grandma T. would say. "You can do it!" Sarah believed this simple adage. Her favorite book was *The Power of One* by Bryce Courtenay. She liked many of the book's messages, including believing in yourself and having "the courage ... to think through to the truth." Courtenay wrote: "The mind is the athlete; the body is simply the means it uses to run faster or longer, jump higher, shoot straighter, kick better, swim harder, hit further, or box better." Sarah liked "Hoppie's dictum," which was, "First with the head and then with the heart."* The point was "thinking well beyond the powers of normal concentration and then daring your courage to follow your thoughts."

Today Sarah felt her own personal power and the power of Sara DeCosta as well. The two fine goalies had become completely confident in each other and totally unselfish in sharing their responsibilities. If Coach Smith had asked Sara DeCosta to start, Teeter would have been happy to be her backup.

The locker room was starting to get noisy. Bob Allen entered beaming with excitement. He hadn't been involved in a gold-medal game since the "miracle on ice" in 1980. Dressed in his delegation parka and a blue-and-green-plaid hat, he looked ready for action. "I'll kiss as many sticks as you want me to tonight," he announced to A.J. and her teammates. "Let's win the big one!"

USA Hockey's Art Berglund, who had been hit by the influenza that was racing through Nagano but luckily had not affected the women's team, was quieter than Bob but just as excited. He shook hands with Ben Smith and said, "This is a wonderful moment for you, my friend. You've done a great job. I wish you all the luck in the world."

Smith looked at his close friend and said, "Thanks for believing in me, Art. This is a great opportunity."

As Smith turned to send his players onto the ice for pregame warmups, he shook Bob Allen's hand and said jokingly, "Remember, Bob,

*Bryce Courtenay, *The Power of One*, New York, Ballantine Books, 1989.

this is all your fault." Bob laughed. Two things he loved—women's hockey and Coach Ben Smith—had finally arrived.

Cammi immediately escorted her teammates to the runway. Team Canada entered the ice ahead of them, then the Americans joined the Canadians for the skate-around.

Big Hat Arena was filling quickly and buzzing with excitement. The women's gold-medal game was one of the hottest tickets in Nagano. Japanese families and foreign spectators were pouring into the arena past live performances by Kodo drummers.

The relatives and friends of the American players had gathered in the AT&T Family Center in the Metropolitan Hotel early in the day to prepare for the six P.M. start time. First they dined as guests of Xerox Corporation at a "Breakfast of Champions" featuring gold medalist and sports-medicine physician Eric Heiden, M.D. Nagano's award-winning children's chorus entertained at the breakfast by singing "The Olympic Hymn," "My Old Kentucky Home," and the "Nagano Olympic Spirit Song." At midday the families gathered in the lobby of the hotel and started drawing banners and decorating each other with face paint. Karen Ruggiero helped organize the production of large banners for every woman player on the team. Somebody handed out Olympic flags, but most of the American fans preferred Old Glory.

During the early afternoon many relatives who were scheduled to fly out of Tokyo at four A.M. finished souvenir shopping in the department stores near the hotel. Others hurried up Nagano's main street, Chuo-dori, to the Zenkoji Temple to rub a famous wooden image of the Buddha. Legend has it that if you rub a particular spot on the Buddha image you receive a special blessing for that section of the body. Young folks rubbed the eyes. Old folks rubbed the belly.

After touching the Buddha statue, A.J.'s boyfriend, Jason Griswold, bought an image of the head of the meditation master Bodhidharma— a Monk who spent nine years gazing at a wall and cut off his eyelids to prevent his attention from lapsing—at a nearby shop. The figure had no eyes. The Japanese custom is to make a wish and draw one eye on Bodhidharma. If the wish is granted, the wish-maker can draw a second eye and keep the head as a good-luck charm. Jason made his wish, drew one eye, and put the Bodhidharma figure in his backpack.

By four-thirty, the players' relatives and friends could no longer wait.

They walked, bused, or taxied to Big Hat to watch the women's warm-up. Covered with American flags and face paint and sitting together in the stands above the women's locker room, they loaded their cameras and bit their nails as the clock slowly approached the face-off.

While the players completed their skate-around, they searched for the faces of family and friends in the audience. Sara could see her older brother Frank taking videos while her younger brother Mat unraveled his flag. Both wore USA jerseys bearing her name. A.J.'s younger brother Jason, who had an American flag painted across his face, joined the DeCosta brothers and Jonathan Tueting.

Jonathan looked relaxed in a huge red-and-white "Cat in the Hat" cap he had picked up while visiting the Alamo, but his parents looked nervous. Pat Tueting told her husband, Bill, that if Sarah lost the gold-medal game, he was not to worry. "Everything will be okay in five years," she said calmly.

The Granatos—minus Tony, who had had to return to San Jose to rejoin the Sharks—filled the front row behind the Americans' net, with Don looking pensive and Natalie looking hopeful. Both wore clothing with an American flag displayed on it proudly. Christina, Robby, and Robby's wife were excited. Joey Granato, Cammi's younger brother, was cool and collected. Joey told the press he couldn't wait to see Cammi wear a medal. Like his sister Christina, Joey had interests other than hockey. He attended a high school for the performing arts and was an aspiring actor and director. When he had arrived in Nagano he studied cultural and administrative details. He organized the purchase of an artist's rendering of the women's games, introduced himself to the security police who protected the athletes and Family Center, and entertained the women's families with his humor. Joey would prefer to organize and run the Olympic Games rather than compete in them.

Like Don Granato, many of the fathers were fretful. The Olympic gold medal was one thing each father desperately wanted for his daughter, particularly since many of these fathers had painfully watched the same daughters lose four world championships to the Canadians, the last one in overtime in March 1997.

The mothers wanted the win even more. They wanted their daughters to play well, to achieve, to inspire. They thought about all of the sacrifices these girls had made—joining boys' teams, changing their names, enduring ridicule and insult, and still succeeding. As Bambi, A.J.'s mother, would say, "These girls *are* the message."

When the skate-around ended, the players returned to their locker room, removed their helmets and gloves, and took long drinks from their water bottles. While they relaxed, Ben Smith stepped to the front of the room. "I don't have much to say. Just go out and play your very best. Give a hundred and ten percent and have fun."

Holding one glove under her arm, Cammi stepped forward and put her hand on Lady Liberty. Her teammates did likewise. When they were all crowded around the training table leaning so close to each other that they could feel each others' racing heartbeats, Cammi said, "This is the final stop on our journey, but it's just another game. Let's go! Let's make it a great one!"

Sarah Tueting walked to the locker-room exit and Sara DeCosta fell in behind her. Tara, Lisa, and Angela lined up next while everyone else moved into numerical order behind them. Many of the USA Hockey guys were waiting in the hallway. USA Hockey president Walter Bush, Jr., vice president Ron DeGregorio, and executive director Dave Ogrean wished the women and their coaches good luck.

Walter Bush, who had fought for the women's program for years, inspired by his daughter Ann and hundreds of younger girls he had watched and admired, was moved by the spectacle. A longtime leader of the U.S. men's program, Bush had helped to organize the first women's world championship in 1990 in Ottawa, and had argued for women's ice hockey as an Olympic medal sport in 1998 in Nagano. He was a visionary of the sport and an advocate for the women long before other men in power saw the light. A tireless ally, Bush realized he was watching a decade of work come to fruition as the players waddled down the hallway to meet their opponents. He was particularly excited for Sarah Tueting and Gretchen Ulion, who had attended his alma mater, Dartmouth. With a sparkle in his eye, he slapped the players' extended gloves and wished each one good luck. Then he turned to a colleague and said, "We had a dream, but these girls had a bigger dream."

When the players reached the gate, they exploded onto the ice, cheered by thousands of fans. The Canadian and American players skated their laps side by side while their coaches, trainers, doctors, and equipment managers slid onto their adjacent benches.

The Americans completed their laps, skated to their net, and wrapped themselves around Teeter. Looking through her face mask into the team's anxious eyes, Cammi smiled and said, "Let's play it like a regular game. We know the systems. We're ready. Let's help each other out. You don't have to have the game of your life tonight. We just have to play well as a team." Cammi paused. Her smile widened. "So this is it. This is *our* moment. Let's have fun! Let's go USA!"

"USA!" her teammates cheered. "Let's go! Let's do it!" Peeling away from the huddle, they slapped Teeter's pads with their sticks and skated to the bench.

Sara kissed Cammi's stick for good luck. Then she patted Teeter on the mask. "Let's go, Teeter, you've got it here." Teeter tapped her backup on the shoulder and nodded.

Sarah Tueting adjusted her braided ponytail and shaved the ice in her crease with the blade of her stick. There's no point in getting anxious, she thought. I have a great team in front of me and a super backup. This is the time to turn on the switch and get truly focused. I'll feel better when I touch the puck and make my first save. Then I'll be "in the zone." She swept the shavings into the goal mouth and turned to face Manon Rhéaume, Canada's excellent goalie.

Sara squeezed onto the left side of the bench to manage the gate. She knew her doorkeeper's role would help her concentration. The last thing her team needed was a slow change-up or a penalty for too many players on the ice.

Japanese rock music blared while referee Marina Zenk waited. She stood at center ice, where the middle ring of the Olympic symbol, painted on the surface beneath the ice, represented the face-off circle. Zenk, a Canadian, had not been scheduled to officiate. Olympic organizers requested her when German Manuela Groger became bedridden with the flu. The linesmen—Isabelle Giguere, a Canadian, and Debra Parece, an American—joined her.

The rock music faded into a loud, repeated refrain which sounded like a command. "Face-off! Face-off! Face-off!" the sound system screamed as the JumboTron flashed the same decree in capital letters. Many Japanese fans picked up the refrain and chanted, "Face-off! Face-off! Face-off!"

The players obeyed. Their two captains glided to center ice, greeted each other and the referee, and leaned forward for the historic encounter. The crowd roared as Zenk threw down the puck.

Every player felt tight, afraid to make a mistake. For the first few minutes the finest women skaters in the world played it safe. They needed to touch the puck to dissolve their nervousness. They needed to realize it was the same old game with their far-too-familiar rival. Sure, there were millions of people watching. So what, Karyn told herself as she changed on the fly, jumping over the boards so that the next line could hurry onto the ice. It's just a bigger audience.

Everyone started to lose the jitters after skating a few shifts. Passes started to click. Tension started to fade. Angela fired a hard shot at the Canadian goaltender. Jenny made a spectacular rush. Tara hustled and dove. Lisa attacked. Tricia crashed with confidence and launched a terrific backhander.

Everyone became less tense except, of course, for Sara. Unable to leave the bench and forced to remain focused, she became increasingly nervous. With each shift, she felt pressure building in her chest, tension growing in her neck. My teammates are getting calmer, Sara thought, and I'm headed for a nervous breakdown. She slammed the gate to release unproductive energy.

Alana sped toward the Canadian goal and fired. The shot missed and Tara and Hayley Wickenheiser tangled. Zenk called a high stick on Mounsey. Tara skated to the box dejectedly while Sue, A.J., Vicki, and Shelley charged out to kill the penalty. The U.S. coaches tried to adjust their special teams, that is, make last-minute substitutions to face the Canadian power-play unit, but caught heat from Zenk. Colleen, Chris, Sandra, and Tricia, who made up the second shift of penalty killers, shut down the Canadian power play. But the Americans were caught on a bad line change as Tara came out of the box. Canada capitalized, rushing in on Sarah, who made a solid left-side save. Minutes later the Canadians broke in again on Teeter. Karen Nystrom released a laser-fast wrist shot, which Teeter stopped and smothered. Teeter's in the zone, Sara thought. She's hot.

With three minutes left in the first period, Cassie Campbell dragged down Tara. Team USA had its first power play. But American snipers couldn't score. Fiona Smith leveled Shelley while the Canadian men's team, in their formal red-and-white Olympic uniforms, rooted for the penalty killers. Steve Yzerman, Eric Lindros, and Wayne Gretzky cheered on their compatriots.

Sue shot. Manon saved. With each threat Rhéaume looked sharper. Manon's going for the gold, Sara thought. Both goaltenders are sizzling.

When the team returned to the locker room at the period's end, their emphasis was on remaining calm and sustaining the fast pace of the opening period. Sara found the peaceful atmosphere comforting. She sat down with Teeter and processed her performance in the net. Teeter had eight solid saves to Manon Rhéaume's nine.

Meanwhile their teammates ate Powerbars and fruit and rested for the second period. Cammi interrupted their repose and invited them to huddle. "Great first period. Let's stay calm. Let's play our best. Here we go, guys!"

When she reached the bench, Sara could sense increased excitement in the arena. The fans greeted the returning players with an enormous ovation and attendant flag-waving and horn-blowing. A Canadian woman wearing a white bra with a large red maple leaf painted on each cup paraded through the crowd waving an enormous Canadian flag. Canadian fans in red felt caps sewn in the shape of a maple leaf applauded her audacity.

The arena's cameras scanned the crowd and focused on Japanese children in "Snowlet" outfits. The Snowlets were four little multicolored creatures that served as mascots for the Nagano Olympics. The children loved seeing themselves on the giant video monitor and waved to the audience. Older kids in hockey shirts jumped up and down to attract the cameras' attention, but the cameramen passed over them and panned signs hanging from the balconies. One read, IT'S OUR GAME! Another said, USA ROCKS!

Amie, Bob Allen, and Tom Mutch, Sr., sat behind John Miller, Joe and Susan King, David and Sharyn Baker, and the rest of the American families and tried to stay calm. All of the American relatives were dressed for the occasion. The entire Ulion family wore T-shirts that said, THE GREAT GRETA. Many parents like Walter Dunn wore navy jackets with their daughter's name and number embroidered on the sleeve and chest. Others wore dark green jackets that were gifts from Olympic sponsor AT&T.

Tom Mutch, Sr., repositioned his navy blue baseball cap and Amie rubbed her eyes as the players lined up for the start of the second period. "Face-off! Face-off! Face-off!" the loudspeaker screamed. When the referee dropped the puck, Amie contorted her body to nudge the puck onto an American stick.

It worked. Cammi hit the puck to Angela, who passed up ice to a winger. Forty seconds later Nancy Drolet drew a Canadian penalty for tripping Tara. Team USA sent out its power-play unit while American fans cheered for a goal. "C'mon, Karyn! C'mon Alana! C'mon, Shelley!" the crowed roared. "Put it in, Katie! Bury it, Laurie!"

Sara opened the gate for the change-up. "Set it up, Whytie," she said. "Set it up."

Sandra and Colleen quarterbacked the action. Cammi, Gretchen, and Jenny dug in the corners and worked the puck around. Therese Brisson cleared the puck by sending it into the bench, stopping the clock.

The American coaches diagrammed a set play and sent the power-play unit back to execute it. Cammi carried the puck into the zone. "Go high! Get it up top!" the coaches yelled.

Cammi gave the puck to Gretchen, who fired it to Sue at the point. Sue made a quick pass to Sandra in front of the net. While the penalty killers moved toward Sandra, she passed to Gretchen, who was crashing in on Manon's left. Gretchen took the pass and, standing on one foot, sent the puck sailing over Manon's shoulder for a goal.

The audience and bench erupted. Sara jumped up and down and slapped players' backs as they returned to the bench. "Great goal, Greta!" she cried. "Awesome! Awesome!"

"U-S-A! U-S-A!" the crowd chanted. "Do it again! Do it again!"

"Good start," Smith said calmly on the bench. "Now settle down and let's get another one." He looked at Tommy Mutch and smiled. The skaters on the power play had done exactly what they had diagrammed.

"Okay, who's next?" Sara asked. "Who's got the second one?"

A second goal wouldn't come easy. Manon Rhéaume was not the least bit flustered by the American's perfect play. She made terrific saves on Tricia and Alana and forced turnarounds that went back toward Teeter. "Pinch it! Pinch it!" the crowd screamed. "Get it out of there!"

With music blaring after every icing of the puck—firing it to the opposite end of the ice and halting play—the fans yelled directions and Sara became increasingly nervous. When I'm in the game I can't hear all this stuff, she thought. I don't think about anything except stopping the puck. She looked at her coach. He was completely oblivious to the chaos around him. Stay calm, she thought. Follow his example.

With six minutes left in the period, Colleen was penalized for holding Kathy McCormack. The Canadian fans jumped out of their seats and called for a goal. *"Can-a-da! Can-a-da!"* they chanted.

"Get it out! Get it out!" the Americans responded. "C'mon, USA! Kill it!"

Sara heard cowbells, tooters, and harmonicas along with the screaming. The penalty killers did their job, but the noise increased. "Great job, USA!" the fans yelled. "Now get on her! Get on her! Watch your wing! Skate it out!"

Sara opened her gate and looked at the clock. Hang on, Teeter, she thought. Three more minutes.

Sue grabbed the puck. "Drill it!" the crowd screamed. "Drill it!"

Sue drilled a shot, which Manon saved. The puck came back to neutral ice. Jayna Hefford grabbed it and started a rush on Teeter. Vicki Movsessian slid to steal the puck from Vicky Sunohara and was called for tripping. Sara checked the clock—two minutes and thirty-eight seconds left in the period.

Again the Canadians had a power play. The camera scanned the U.S. and Canadian benches to monitor expressions. On the American side, Smith remained unflappable. On Canada's bench, Shannon Miller diagrammed a play. Miller wore black, as always, and patted her strongest shooters on the back as they jumped out to try to even the score.

Amie started humming as Bob Allen flipped his cap and Tom Mutch, Sr., yelled, "C'mon, Sarah Tueting! You can do it!"

The Canadian fans' bells and horns drowned out his voice. *"Can-a-da! Can-a-da!* Tie it up! Tie it up!"

Teeter braced herself for the onslaught. While the American penalty killers poked and stabbed to try to steal the puck, it popped out to Hayley Wickenheiser in front of the net. She got off a shot, which Teeter deftly deflected with her stick. Stacy Wilson released a flip shot, which Teeter caught in her glove. "Great job!" Sara yelled. "Way to go, Teeter!"

"Cool as a cucumber," Bob Allen said confidently to Amie, who continued her humming.

"Unbelievable!" John Miller added.

The American penalty killers were relentless. Tricia cleared the puck out of Teeter's zone and into the Canadian end. Sandra held it there as long as she could. "That's it! Good job!" Bob Allen cried.

"One minute left in the second period," a voice on the loudspeakers announced. "One minute."

The Canadians reclaimed the puck. The American spectators jumped to their feet. "C'mon, USA, get a bounce!" John Miller yelled.

Nancy Drolet threatened Teeter. Angela sent the puck back the other way. The Canadians recovered it, but Chris intervened and fired it toward the Canadian net. The American penalty killers hustled. With only seconds left on the Canadian power play, Zenk called a face-off in Manon's end. Lisa won the face-off and, with help from Colleen, Vicki, and Tara, protected the 1–0 score at the buzzer.

"Great period!" John Miller cheered as the entire audience applauded Team USA on its way to the locker room.

The shots on net flashed on the video screen: USA 11, Canada 4. "Hell of a period," Bob told Amie. "Hell of a game!"

CBS camera crews pursued Gretchen as she left the ice. "More goals are going to come," she told the interviewer. "We need a few more."

In the locker room, excitement was building. "We're playing well," Sandra said, "but we've got to get another goal."

"Yeah, no way the Canadians will let down now," Tricia added. "In the third, they'll come out flying."

Tara turned to Lisa as she sipped her water bottle. "I want this win so bad I can taste it."

"Me too. We're so close. We've got to get another goal," Lisa said.

"We can do it. I think we're peaking," Tara said. "Saturday's game helped."

"We had a great third period. Let's do it again," Lisa said.

Ben Smith walked in slowly, concentrating on maintaining his composure. "Super second period! You're all playing well. Stay out of the box and have fun!"

Cammi gathered her teammates around their mascot. "Okay, listen up. Let's stay in control and play our game. Let's make this period our best! Go USA!"

Twenty more minutes, Sara thought, remembering Tara Van-Derveer's advice: "It will feel like an eternity but it's all that's left between you and the gold medal." She hugged Teeter and said, "You're ready, Teeter. Go for it!"

As the women filed down the hallway, Ben Smith caught Bob Allen's extended hand and started laughing. "Like I told you, Bob, this is all your fault!" Bob squeezed his hand a little harder and grinned from ear to ear.

"Face-off! Face-off! Face-off!" the loudspeaker blared as the Americans did supercharged laps around the cages. The Canadians came out of the locker room late because they were listening to NHL stars Brendan Shanahan and Joe Sakic give an inspirational speech. Team Canada burst out of the gate so psyched they barely needed a warm-up. The audience roared as the two teams filed onto their benches and lined up for the puck drop.

Sandra and Stacy Wilson skated to center ice to take the face-off.

Both knew the period was going to be intense. The game would be decided the way all great contests should be, by the performance of the people on the playing field. Four world championships and emotional wins in Burlington, Lake Placid, and San Jose no longer mattered. All the posturing and psychological tactics became irrelevant. The final outcome now came down to the essence of the game, the players on the ice.

Sandra won the face-off and Cammi grabbed the puck. Hayley Wickenheiser fought for it and sent it sailing into Teeter's zone. Tara pursued the shot into the American zone. As Teeter moved behind the net to clear the puck, Nancy Drolet intercepted the clearing pass and fired a wrist shot. Scurrying back into the crease just in time, Teeter made a spectacular, just-in-time glove save. "Great hustle!" Sara screamed. "Keep it up!"

Jayna Hefford skated one-on-one with Chris toward Teeter and unloaded a backhand. Teeter stopped the puck with her pad and kicked the bouncing rebound away with her left skate. Holy cow! Sara thought. *What a save!*

With only seconds for recovery, Teeter faced Danielle Goyette, who turned the defense and attacked. Holding the post, Tueting stuffed

Canada's top scorer, but the puck kept moving. Therese Brisson grabbed it and fired a blistering shot. Tueting made a sparkling stop. "Great save!" Sara screamed. "Great save!"

Sara became vicariously involved in every move Teeter was making. She analyzed angles and instinctively anticipated the action Teeter should take. Sara was a bundle of nervous energy. She swung the door more often as the players became tired faster and the shifts became shorter.

With approximately fifteen minutes remaining, Gretchen picked up a loose puck and, using a Canadian defenseman as a screen, crashed the net and snapped a twenty-foot shot at Rhéaume. Manon deflected it with her blocker.

Moments later Nancy Drolet took a pass in the neutral zone. She broke in alone on Teeter, who sprawled to make the save. The puck trickled across the crease and, as Hayley Wickenheiser misfired, Vicki—on her knees and falling forward—batted the puck out of the American crease. "What a play!" Sara screamed as the noise in the arena became deafening.

A.J. moved the puck into the neutral zone and passed it to Shelley at center ice. As Shelley turned to accelerate, Danielle Goyette checked her so hard she landed on the ice. Zenk slammed her fist into the palm of her other hand to signal body-checking. The Canadians, down by a goal, were now shorthanded for two minutes.

Smith and Mutch sent out the Americans' first power-play unit and held their breath. Both knew that in the random, chaotic game of hockey there is very little a coach can do to influence the outcome once the game is under way. The one exception is the power play. A coach can insert a set power play into the chaos and hope that it works. That set play is a coach's primary offensive weapon. Its design represents a thorough analysis of an opponents' strengths and weaknesses, adjustments and strategies. The Americans' power play had already worked once in the game, when it was perfectly executed as diagrammed. Could the same skaters possibly execute it a second time?

The Canadians fought aggressively to prevent the Americans from entering their zone to set the play. Eventually Jenny and Gretchen traded passes in the corner to Manon Rhéaume's left, allowing other teammates to take their positions. When everyone was ready, Gretchen skated out of the corner and fed Sandra, who, dropping down into the high slot from her place at the blue line, one-timed the puck to Shelley. Waiting patiently at Manon Rhéaume's right, Shelley reached in and touched the puck just hard enough to send it fluttering over Manon's outstretched pad.

Smith's and Mutch's hearts skipped a beat. The bench and arena erupted! Sara embraced her teammates as they bounced through the gate. Team USA was ahead 2–0 with nine minutes to go in the game! Danielle Goyette dejectedly stepped out of the penalty box and skated to her bench.

Amie, Bob, and Tom Mutch, Sr., joined John Miller and other American family members in a communal celebration. They jumped up and down, hugging and hollering. Brothers and sisters, boyfriends and partners waved their flags and raised their signs. American Olympians seated around them—bobsledders, skiers, skaters, and jumpers—whooped and cheered while the arena camera scanned the spectators, who were standing and clapping.

Team Canada, like all great teams, however, was unwilling to concede defeat. The memory of their disastrous round-robin game three days earlier remained in their psyche, but the dynamic for tonight's contest was completely different. Saturday night's game was essentially a throwaway. Tonight's game was for a piece of Olympic history. The gold-medal contest was not destined to be a high-scoring shootout. For fifty minutes it had been a tight-checking, low-scoring affair highlighted by spectacular, acrobatic goaltending at both ends of the ice. The Canadians dug in to make their comeback.

Young star Hayley Wickenheiser led the charge. Hayley had a strained right knee and a suspected-fractured elbow bone. Nevertheless, she threatened with a shot to Sarah Tueting's left. The Americans weighed in with defense. Canada finally got the break it needed when Tara reached down to scoop the puck and put her shoulder into Jayna Hefford, sending her crashing into the boards. With only four minutes left in the game, the referee called Tara for body-checking.

Tara skated to the penalty box, sat down, and looked at the floor. Oh, my God, what have I done? she thought. I don't want to let the team down. If we lose now, it could be my fault.

Ben Smith calmly assessed the situation. This is a good time to take a penalty, he thought. We can ice it for two straight minutes. He believed that his team was no longer intimidated by Canada's power play. Canada had gone zero for three on power plays thus far in the game. One more would not be a problem.

But Shannon Miller and her assistant realized they had a critical opportunity to get back in the game. They diagrammed a set play for their Canadian aces. Both sides were getting tired, they surmised. Anything could happen. The Canadian fans chanted, *"Can-a-da! Can-a-da!"* as their power-play specialists faced off against the Americans.

Team Canada's special team didn't waste time. A fore-checking Geraldine Heaney tied up Alana behind the net, allowing the puck to slide to Wickenheiser. Hayley centered it to wide-open Danielle Goyette, who instantly buried it in the American net. Score! Nine seconds had elapsed.

Canada's players, coaches, and fans went crazy! Cowbells, horns, and tooters rattled the building. The Canadian men's team joined the cheers and waving of flags. Shannon Miller was ecstatic. She had just shown the unflappable Benjamin Smith that she, too, could orchestrate a lethal power play.

Ben Smith realized that Team USA was going to have to win the hard way. He looked at Sarah Tueting to assess her reaction. She was sweeping the crease with her stick and shaking off the psychological impact of Goyette's goal. Hang in there, Teeter, he thought. You're playing great. Finish strong.

Tara skated out of the penalty box and over to her bench dejectedly. Smith and Mutch both gave her a nod and sent her right back out to play defense.

Sandra took her seat on the bench and stared at the celebrating Canadians. "They are *not* going to get back into this," she said. "We will *not* fall apart. We will *not* let that happen." She then divined what her coaches were thinking: that in the last few minutes of a knotted game, with two great teams on the ice, adrenaline pumping, and emotions running wild, the end result would ultimately come down to two things: the people between the pipes—Tueting and Rhéaume—and the "hockey god," also known as "Lady Luck." Sandra knew that her good friend Sarah Tueting would stand on her head to win the game, and so would Manon Rhéaume. But the hockey god? Sandra wondered. Who will she help?

Then Sandra remembered Muhammad Ali, the witch doctor, and the woman with the trembling hand. This is about the inner circle and inner strength, she decided. We've come for a higher purpose. We are our own woman with a trembling hand. We will be master of ourselves and our fate.

The Canadians attacked and Hayley Wickenheiser barely missed tying the game when a centering pass slid under her stick as she broke open in front of Tueting. The crowd gasped.

The Americans recovered briefly, but Katie accidently pulled the skates out from beneath Cassie Campbell and was nearly called for a tripping penalty. Katie fortunately avoided the call by letting go of her stick. Booing and hissing, the Canadian fans called for the referee's head.

Gretchen and A.J. alternated keeping the puck deep in the Canadian zone in an attempt to prevent the Canadians from once again generating an attack.

With little more than one minute left, Danielle Goyette led a Canadian rush down the left-side boards. Karen Nystrom delivered a thundering check on Lisa, who was digging for the puck behind the net. The puck squirted loose to Teeter's left. Therese Brisson immediately returned the puck to Nystrom behind the net, who, without looking up, fired it to Stacy Wilson, wide open in front of Teeter. As Wilson's perfect wrist shot rocketed toward the lower right corner of the net, Teeter slashed out her right skate, denying the Canadian captain the equalizer. *"Oh my God, Teeter!"* Sara screamed. *"That was the gold-medal save!"*

Shannon Miller called a time out and pulled her goaltender. With fifty-four seconds on the clock and Team Canada huddled around her, she diagrammed what she hoped would be the tying goal.

On the other bench, Ben Smith and Tommy Mutch countered with a defensive strategy. Tom was responsible for the defensemen. He needed fresh legs and the best puck handlers on the team. He studied the six players Miller sent out on the ice and turned to Tara. "I'm using you now, Tara, but only if you are not too tired. You've played a shitload on your injured knee. If you're tired, you've *got* to tell me."

"I'm okay, Mutchie, I can go," Tara said quickly.

"Listen, Tara, are you *sure?*"

"I can go, Mutchie. *I can do it!*"

"Okay, Mounsey, you're a go-to girl. Bring it home."

Tara skated to her position, put her stick on the ice, and felt her heart pounding. I can do this, she said to herself. I can give it my best shot.

Smith looked at Miller's offense. She had put out her snipers and stars. With the gold medal hanging in the balance, he responded with his most defensive forwards. He needed speed, size, and reach—people who could win the face-off and take away the passing lanes. He knew which of his players could consistently neutralize the Canadians by closing their gaps or getting in their way. Shannon Miller was skating the same players over and over in a desperate attempt to score. Most were exhausted physically and emotionally. Every American was a role player who had skated in rotation during the game, preserving the team's collective energy. Smith wanted the skaters on the ice for the last fifty-four seconds to play their roles perfectly.

With the rafters of Big Hat shaking with the thunder of the crowd's supplications, A.J. won the face-off in the corner, forcing another face-off and, more important, taking valuable seconds off the clock. On the ensuing face-off, the Americans cleared the puck into the Canadian zone.

With thirty seconds left, Team Canada regrouped and rushed again, led by Wickenheiser. Hayley's wrist shot was deflected into the corner. Tara cleared the puck, but it was intercepted at the blue line. Karyn stole a Canadian's weak return and immediately shot toward Canada's empty net. As the crowd screamed, both teams scrambled for the puck.

Sandra seized the loose puck in front of the American bench and, playing it off the boards, turned on her speed and caught her own indirect pass. Everyone on the ice turned to chase her as she crashed the net. Smith saw her outskate the last Canadian defender in her path and felt his heart pounding in his chest. Turn out the lights, Sandra! he thought. *Turn out the lights!* When Sandra reached the Canadian blue line, she pulled back her stick, took careful aim, and fired the puck forty feet into the empty Canadian goal mouth. As the puck hit the back of the net, she raised her arms, pumped them in the air, and felt a profound sense of relief as she came to rest against the boards. Breathless, she looked at the clock and rejoiced. With eight seconds left, she had sealed the gold-medal victory for the United States!

Angela, Tricia, and an extremely elated Tara skated to the boards, threw their arms around Sandra, and squeezed her. She had produced the guarantee goal and two amazing assists! She had had the game of her life! At the other end of the ice, Teeter danced around her goal cage in absolute ecstasy.

Team USA went out of control on the bench. Colleen jumped up and ran down the line slapping every player's helmet. Tom embraced Cammi and, lifting her in the air, carried her the length of the bench to congratulate her teammates. Cammi and Sara hugged each player as they flew in the gate and hung on to Sandra. *"You did it, Whytie!"* they screamed. *"You did it!"*

Ben Smith tried to prevent pandemonium. "Let's settle down!" he cried. "Let's get a line out there!" His pleas were useless. Five players automatically skated to the face-off circle, but the celebration had started.

"U-S-A! U-S-A! U-S-A!" the Americans' fans shouted. *"U-S-A! U-S-A! U-S-A!"* Big Hat Arena reverberated. Every spectator stood to applaud and watch history in the making. Amie and Bob Allen, flushed with excitement, moved to the end of their row and prepared to dash to the bench.

Marina Zenk held the puck at center ice for the face-off. Sara felt everything begin to move in slow motion. Five smiling American skaters lined up against five stunned and defeated Canadians. Zenk dropped the puck as the audience started a countdown. *"Eight! . . . Seven!"* The coaches looked at the clock. *"Six! . . . Five!"* Sara opened the gate. *"Four! . . . Three!"* Team USA straddled the boards . . . *"Two! . . . One!"* . . . threw their sticks and gloves in the air . . . *"Zero!!!"* . . . and, filled with the thrill of victory, piled on their ecstatic goalies in the middle of the ice.

Ben Smith embraced Tommy Mutch and then gave Webby a bear hug. Jeanna grabbed Smith around the neck and, crying, gave him a kiss. Amie ran up to the bench and hugged the whole lineup. When she got to Smith she said, "I got my glass slipper!" Then she hugged him in jubilation.

Bob Allen arrived at the scene and was all but speechless. "It's all your fault!" Smith kidded. "I hope you're happy!"

Art Berglund, overcome with joy and aware that Ben's father had passed away a few years earlier, said, "I know your dad is proud of you, Ben, he's with you at this moment." Smith gave Art a bear hug, too, certain that it was true.

On the ice, while their teammates kissed and hugged, collapsed and cried, the two young goalies grabbed each other on the shoulders and, laughing through their tears, cried, *"We did it! We did it! We did it! We backstopped this team to the Olympic gold medal!"* Sandra threw her arms around both of them and, looking into the stands where the crowd was cheering euphorically, caught sight of Peter Haberl smiling.

The Toyota van rumbled down a dark mountain road from Turner Network Television's distant interview location and into the deserted streets of Nagano. Reaching the Olympic Village and moving through the security gate, the van sped up the quiet concourse to the International Zone. The driver unloaded his joking passengers, who hurried into the lobby. Removing their gold medals so as to pass through the metal detectors, the riders danced through the checkpoint and then scurried down the hallway. Several rushed to the Surf Shack to check what was sure to be great e-mail. Others headed to the cafeteria for coffee and ice cream. "No more training rules!" they cheered. "Time for something fattening."

Two ran to find the ten players going to CBS's Nagano studio at five A.M.—just two hours away—to tape a spot for David Letterman's show. Sara's line in the Top Ten List for the question, "What are the top ten reasons to win an Olympic gold medal?" was "You get to be President Clinton's intern." At eight A.M. Sandra, Gretchen, and Cammi were scheduled to join CBS's Olympic host Jim Nantz for a live broadcast from CBS's special studio beside Zenkoji Temple.

When all of the happy riders had hurried off in different directions, Cammi Granato and Ben Smith found themselves walking alone in the bitter cold to the entrance of USA House. They agreed that, while it had been sad hearing the Canadian players singing their national anthem in their locker room in tears, Team USA's rivalry with Team Canada had never been better served than when Shannon Miller, heartbroken at losing the gold, stated at the postgame press conference that she was moved when she saw the first women's gold medal in the sport placed around Cammi's neck. Her spirits were lifted by what had been achieved not only for the sport but for women athletes.

Climbing the Village steps in the moonlight, Smith turned to Cammi joyfully and said, "Well, Catherine, this turned out okay, huh?"

Cammi smiled affectionately and said, "Yeah, Coach, I think it did."

Smith shook his head in amazement and asked, "Who'd a thunk it?"

Cammi laughed and answered, "No idea, Coach. But next time we team up, do me a favor. Surprise me. Show me something special."

EPILOGUE

"The Spirit of the Game"

NEW YORK, NEW YORK ~ OCTOBER 19, 1998

The forty-three members of the Girls' Choir of Harlem—dressed in elegant gray blouses, floor-length black skirts, and pearl necklaces—gave an inspired performance of the song "Climb Every Mountain" to start the Women's Sports Foundation's nineteenth annual salute to women in sports. The October 1998 celebration was called "The Spirit of the Game." As the choirgirls stepped off the stage of the Waldorf-Astoria's Grand Ballroom, Donna Lopiano, executive director of the Women's Sports Foundation (WSF), walked to the podium to offer a warm welcome to the enormous audience. Patrons in black tie and cocktail dresses had paid $1,000 per plate to attend the sold-out affair. Sitting at tables decorated with autumn leaves, pumpkins, roses, and votive lights, the guests noticed how their jewelry and wineglasses sparkled above the candles' glittering flames.

When Lopiano finished thanking the foundation's many corporate sponsors and individual donors, she asked legendary long-distance swimmer Diana Nyad to the stage to call the roll for the "Grand March of Athletes." Approximately one hundred of the finest women athletes in the world, representing virtually every sport in which women compete, waited in the wings to hear Nyad call their names.

Diana Nyad greeted the crowd and then asked the audience to recognize the first women in the grand march, the representatives of the 1998 gold medal–winning U.S. Women's Olympic Ice Hockey Team. As nine women in elegant black cocktail dresses and high heels walked onto the stage, the audience arose from their seats in a standing ovation. When the clapping subsided, Nyad introduced the women individually. At her name, each player waved to the audience and placed a long-stemmed red rose in a basket.

In the eight months since they had competed in Nagano, Japan, the nine women introduced in New York, the eleven whose commitments prevented them from attending the WSF salute, and their Coach Ben Smith had learned what Art Berglund meant when he said "Olympic gold medals change lives." The athletes were congratulated in a White House reception, a U.S. Olympic Committee salute, and a USA Hockey celebration. They all became hometown heroes, and many experienced exciting changes in their personal lives.

Chris Bailey returned from the Olympics to a hometown parade and a series of speaking engagements including high school graduations. Throughout the spring she volunteered and spoke at philanthropic events for the Syracuse, New York, regional chapters of the March of Dimes and Make-A-Wish-Foundation. Chris conducted mini-clinics teaching hockey skills to children in Los Angeles and San Diego under the auspices of USA Hockey National Team sponsor Colombo Yogurt. In the fall Chris moved to Ohio to take a corporate sales position with the Columbus Chill men's team in the East Coast Hockey League.

Laurie Baker participated in many charity hockey and softball games across New England during the spring and summer including fund-raisers with the Old Time Boston Bruins and Celebrity Ice Sharks. In the fall she returned to Providence College for her junior year. While concentrating in the social sciences at Providence, Laurie continues to train with dreams of making the Olympic team that will compete in Salt Lake City in 2002.

After many public speaking engagements and traveling with her mother to the Mediterranean during the spring, Alana Blahoski worked at several sports clinics including the Gold Medal Camp in Spooner, Wisconsin, with Angela Ruggiero. In the fall Alana enrolled in a master's degree program in exercise physiology, sport, and nutrition at Minnesota State University at Mankato and became a graduate assistant. She also landed a position as an assistant coach for the university's women's hockey team, the Mavericks.

On August 25, in Ann Arbor, Michigan, Lisa Brown-Miller gave birth to Alexander Joseph Miller. Lisa and John did not know that Lisa was pregnant during the Olympics, leading to much teasing about "too many people on the ice" during the Olympic games. During the summer and fall, John and Lisa built and moved into a new home in White Lake, Michigan, while Lisa frequently spoke to young girls about overcoming adversity and setting goals. Lisa is considering coaching offers as well as opportunities to earn a teaching certificate in elementary education.

During the spring Karyn Bye threw out the opening pitch at the Minnesota Twins baseball game. As well, with the sponsorship of the National Hockey League, she shared her message and dream at over twenty schools in Wisconsin and dozens of hospitals and schools in ten cities across the Midwest. During the summer she organized a golf tournament that raised $25,000 in September for Habitat for Humanity's St. Croix Valley Chapter. A job promoting the NHL expansion team, the Minnesota Wild, arriving in St. Paul in 2002, allows Karyn time to train.

After a warm homecoming in Falmouth on Cape Cod, Colleen Coyne dedicated herself to visiting children in school classrooms throughout Massachusetts during both the spring and fall of 1998. She attended many humanitarian events, including numerous programs raising funds for cancer and cystic fibrosis research. Along with Sandra Whyte and Vicki Movsessian, she volunteered at the Massachusetts Special Olympics. In September she and Karyn were inducted into the University of New Hampshire's Hall of Honor.

After returning home to a heroine's welcome in Rhode Island, Sara DeCosta spoke at schools and organizations throughout the area before reenrolling at Providence College. Having preserved her amateur status and National Collegiate Athletic Association eligibility, Sara rejoined her teammates on Providence's women's hockey team. The governor's office, and later the Federal Highway Administration's Office of Highway Safety, selected Sara as their national spokesperson for seat belt use.

Tricia Dunn was inducted into her high school (Pinkerton Academy, Derry, New Hampshire) hall of fame. In addition to speaking at schools throughout New Hampshire and Massachusetts, she participated in raising $2 million for the Cambridge Family and Children's Services Group, which supports local social service agencies in the Cambridge, Massachusetts area. Tricia also joined Katie King in writing an instructional book, tentatively titled *Gold Medal Hockey for Women and Girls*.

Cammi Granato crisscrossed Illinois speaking with schoolchildren about her experience. With her mother's assistance and a generous donation from Visa, she established the Cammi Granato Golden Dreams for Children Foundation and awarded its first grant to the Brain Tumor Research Association. Cammi enjoyed the help of Team Illinois, her home state's girls' ice hockey team. A large demand for public speaking and guest appearances around the United States did not prevent Cammi from beginning a new job as a color analyst for the NHL's Los Angeles Kings radio broadcasts. She travels with the team and skates in their practices to stay in shape for what she hopes will be a hockey future.

After a joyous homecoming celebration in Salem, New Hampshire, Katie King participated in many school visits, charity events, and celebrity softball games throughout New England before writing an instructional hockey book with Tricia Dunn. She also was featured at opening day games for the New York Yankees (with her teammates), the Kentucky Thoroughblades, and Portland Pirates. Meanwhile Katie works out at Mike Boyle's new strength training facility in Burlington, Massachusetts.

Scoring the game-winning goal to win the Olympic gold medal generated many requests for talks and personal appearances for Shelley Looney. After a busy spring and summer of both, Shelley enrolled in computing and health administration classes in Boston to prepare for a health sciences career. In between attending classes and training for the 1998 Three Nations Cup and 1999 World Championships, Shelley works as a volunteer coach for the Northeastern University women's varsity ice hockey team.

The *Greenwich Times* (Connecticut) created an impressive twenty-page commemorative supplement to recognize and celebrate Sue Merz's remarkable athletic accomplishments. After numerous speaking engagements in her hometown and surrounding communities, Sue moved to Toronto, Canada, to join the Brampton Ontario Thunder in the Canadian Women's Senior Triple A Hockey League. Former teammate Jeanine Sobek also competes for the Thunder.

Nantucket islanders turned out en masse to welcome home A.J. Mleczko, who participated in many post-Olympic events and worked with her father during the spring and summer. In the fall, A.J. returned to Harvard College for her senior year. After a two-year leave of absence, she resumed her history studies and rejoined her teammates on the women's varsity ice hockey team. A.J. preserved her athletic eligibility so as to be able to play her final year for the Crimson. In October 1998, A.J., Sandra Whyte '92, and Ben Smith'68 were guest speakers at Harvard's celebration of twenty-five years of women's Ivy League athletics. A.J. will graduate in June 1999.

Tara Mounsey was given a parade through Concord, New Hampshire, and a state celebration on her birthday, March 12. She happily spoke to schoolchildren and social service organizations throughout the area before spending her summer on Cape Cod. In September, Tara, who also had retained her athletic eligibility, returned to Brown University for her sophomore year. She immediately registered for her premedical courses, rejoined the varsity field hockey team, and committed to play for the varsity ice hockey team. She hopes to graduate from Brown in 2001 and defer entrance to medical school to play on the 2002 Olympic team.

Three days after winning the gold medal, Vicki Movsessian became engaged to Chris Lamoriello in Nagano. Since returning to the United States she has been planning her wedding and considering job offers while also visiting schools, participating in charity events, and teaching in sports clinics like her Olympic teammates. During the spring and summer she corresponded with Serina Saito, the twelve-year-old Japanese girl who led the American delegation in the Olympic opening and closing ceremonies. On September 12, Vicki read at Erin Whitten's wedding to Tim Hamlen in Lake George, New York.

Angela Ruggiero returned to Choate Rosemary Hall in March, completed her high school degree, and graduated in June. During the summer she worked at various hockey camps and clinics across the United States. In August she trained at the women's National Camp in Lake Placid with A.J. Mleczko, Sara DeCosta, and Jenny Schmidgall, among others. In September, Angela started her first year at Harvard College, where she will play ice hockey with A.J. and former Canadian opponent Jennifer Botterill. Angela and Jennifer are also rowing crew.

Still eligible to play with her state's girls' select team, Jenny Schmidgall traded her Olympic uniform for a Minnesota Thoroughbreds outfit and competed in five games in the U.S. Girls' National Tournament in the spring. A parade in Edina preceded many public

speaking opportunities with schoolchildren and organizations including D.A.R.E. After training at the National Camp in August,
Jenny matriculated at the University of Minnesota where she is a
member of the women's varsity ice hockey team, now in its second
year.

Sarah Tueting traveled widely throughout Illinois and the United
States following her return. She participated in the Chicago Cubs and
White Sox home openers and volunteered for the Illinois Fatherhood
Initiative Program. Sara helped the KOHL Children's Museum with
a special exhibit and local fund-raisers with a project to assist a New
Trier High School student seriously injured in an automobile accident.
She also volunteered with the Elizabeth Glaser Pediatric AIDS Foun-
dation celebrity carnival in Los Angeles. After a summer vacation in
Wyoming, Washington, and Vancouver, Sara returned to Dartmouth
College to complete her premedical courses and graduation require-
ments.

Gretchen Ulion retired from international competition when she returned home from the Olympic Games. During the spring she participated in various public speaking engagements while completing the
plans for her summer wedding. On July 11, Gretchen married Steven
Silverman in Massachusetts with most of the members of the Olympic
team in attendance. Following their honeymoon, she and Steve moved
to Salinas, California, where Gretchen now teaches in an elementary
school. Gretchen has taken up roller hockey for fun.

After a joyful homecoming celebration in Saugus, Massachusetts,
Sandra Whyte made numerous school appearances and volunteered
with many social service projects including the Special Olympics. In
June she became engaged to John Sweeney and is planning an April
1999 wedding. During the late summer Sandra became a pharma-eco-
nomics research analyst at a Cambridge research firm. In the fall she
accompanied Colleen, Tricia, A.J., and Vicki—as representatives of
the 1998 Women's U.S. Olympic Ice Hockey Team—to a special event
sponsored by the New England Women's (NEW) Fund, an organization whose mission is to increase opportunities for women and girls
through sports. Eight hundred guests gave Sandra and her teammates
a standing ovation as the NEW Fund honored the players for their
"accomplishments, leadership, and courage."

When Diana Nyad had finished greeting all of the Olympic ice hockey players, she introduced ninety more elite women athletes. Among those who carried a long-stemmed red rose to the stage were Dominique Dawes (gymnastics), Jean Driscoll (athletics/paraolympics), Julie Foudy (soccer), Rebecca Lobo (basketball), Martina Navratilova (tennis), Lyn St. James (auto racing), Nikki Stone (freestyle skiing), Jenny Thompson (swimming), Grete Waitz (athletics/running), Teresa Weatherspoon (basketball), and Dee Dee Weiman (softball). When the one hundred stars had delivered their roses, a trumpet was blown and the athletes yelled, "Charge!" Then they moved off the stage to enjoy their dinner, while Nyad placed the roses in a crystal vase.

When the program resumed, the WSF president and gold medalist in her own right, Benita Fitzgerald Mosely, announced the awards ceremony. Dr. Linda Bunker, professor of education at the University of Virginia, received the Billie Jean King Contribution Award. Willye White, who participated on five U.S. Olympic track-and-field teams and enjoyed a long career in Chicago government administration, received the Wilma Rudolph Courage Award. Olympic great Jackie Joyner-Kersee was honored for her outstanding community service, which has raised over $12 million for the children of East St. Louis, Missouri. Broadcaster Lynn Scherr announced the new site of the WSF International Women's Sports Hall of Fame in Eisenhower Park, East Meadow, New York. Ellen DeGeneres congratulated Olympic basketball coach Tara VanDerveer, who was selected as the hall of fame coach. Marathoner Grete Waitz celebrated Australian track-and-field great Shirley Strickland de la Hunty as a pioneer in women's sports. American tennis great Margaret Osbourne du Pont received the other pioneer athlete designation from broadcaster Meredith Viera.

In a moving tribute by Ahmad and Phylicia Rashad, Al Joyner accepted the Women's Sports Foundation Hall of Fame award on behalf of his late wife, Florence Griffith Joyner, telling the emotional audience that "DeeDee" liked to say, "Believe, achieve, succeed." The audience blinked back tears as Joyner was handed the crystal vase with the one hundred long-stemmed roses carried by the women athletes in the grand march.

After world champion ice skater Michelle Kwan accepted the Individual Sportswoman of the Year award, basketball sensation Cynthia Cooper of the Women's National Basketball Association's Houston Comets received the Team Sportswoman of the Year honor. Cooper kiddingly told the audience that she had "raised the roof" (a congratulatory gesture made by pushing the palms of your upraised hands toward the ceiling) in her local supermarket when she saw the Olympic women's ice hockey team's pictures on the Wheaties box.

When all of the 1998 Women's Sports Foundation Awards had been announced, one of the most courageous leaders in the women's movement, Gloria Steinem, stepped forward to remind the audience of an event twenty-five years earlier, "when boys had sports and girls had gym." The Billie Jean King/Bobby Riggs tennis match, dubbed the "Battle of the Sexes," held what Steinem called a "transcendent message" for all women competing in a man's world. She said that because "poor societies value fat women and rich societies value thin women . . . but all male-dominated societies value weak women," King's defeat of Riggs before a worldwide audience of fifty million had had tremendous social significance.

When the winner of that historic contest, Billie Jean King, moved to the podium, everyone stood in reverence. King told them that when she was five years old doing the dishes with her mother, she had informed her mom that "something great would happen" in her life. After a free tennis lesson on a town court she started to sleep with a tennis racket under her arm and dream of winning at Wimbledon. Her later victories at Wimbledon were personal achievements, but her defeat of Bobby Riggs in 1973 was social change. She told the audience that fully implementing Title IX *now* was absolutely vital and that "every little girl born today has the right to dream her dream and have it come true."

King's stirring remarks signaled the end of the evening's celebration. After exchanging good-byes with the people at my table, I mingled with the crowd. First I spoke with Ben Smith, who had come to see his players receive yet another honor. Ben had also received numerous awards since his return from Nagano, including the U.S. Olympic Committee's 1998 Coach of the Year award. We joked about how much fun it was to see his skaters dressed so elegantly and associated with the world's finest women athletes. Then I spoke with one of the Olympic women hockey players in attendance, A.J. Mleczko. A.J. told me she was born in 1975, two years after the King/Riggs match, and was interested in learning more about Title IX and the legacy of women athletes like Billie Jean King and Donna de Verona— women who not only excelled athletically but had the social conscience and vision to create the Women's Sports Foundation.

As a women's studies professor, I found A.J.'s comment intriguing. I looked at the beautiful, intelligent, healthy young woman who was asking for a history lesson and felt a profound sense of hope. Here was a girl who, as a child, had done what Billie Jean King, as an adult, had done: She had dared to compete with boys and succeeded. Ten years later A.J. crashed the net with her female teammates and won an Olympic gold medal. Tonight she had swapped schoolbooks and computers, shoulder pads and skates for a cocktail dress and heels. Moreover, she had discovered that she was part of a remarkable legacy, what Donna de Varona and Benita Fitzgerald Mosley described as "a long journey strewn with hardship, personal sacrifice and long-fought battles for equality." I smiled, promised to send A.J. literature about what had and had not yet been accomplished to achieve sex equity under Title IX legislation, and happily felt confident that the legacy and progress would continue.

MARY TURCO

INDEX

Adobe Systems, 118

Ahlen, Annica, 159

Akebono, 155

Akihito, Emperor, 155

Ali, Muhammad, 127–30, 184, 194, 211

Allain, Keith, 81

Allen, Bob, 9, 176
 Christmas celebration (1997), 56, 57
 final Lake Placid game (1997) and, 72, 74, 78, 85
 as godfather of Team USA, 57, 58, 72, 74, 78
 gold-medal game (Nagano) and, 197, 203, 205–6, 207, 209, 213
 San Jose game (1998) and, 118

Amateur Hockey Association of the United States (AHAUS), 109–10

American Association of University Women (AAUW), xxii

American Basketball Association, xxiii

American Girls Hockey Association, 109–10

Andeberhan, Julie, 8

Apple, 118

Aqua Wing Arena (Nagano), 150–51, 154, 161, 165, 170, 185

Arlington Catholic High School, 173

AT&T Family Center, 159, 198, 203

auto racing, 223

Babson, Tom, 81

Bailey, Chris, 90, 91, 156
 aftermath of Olympics, 218
 in Burlington, Vermont game (1997), 26–27, 40, 41, 47, 48
 in final Lake Placid game (1997), 83
 in gold-medal game (Nagano), 202, 206, 207
 in gold-medal preview game (Nagano), 172
 at Olympics award ceremony, 11
 in San Jose game (1998), 120
 in USA v. Finland game (Nagano), 161

Baker, Bill, 3, 5

Baker, Laurie, 90, 97–98, 116
 aftermath of Olympics, 218
 in Burlington, Vermont game (1997), 40, 42
 family support of, 203
 in final Lake Placid game (1997), 83
 in gold-medal game (Nagano), 204
 in gold-medal preview game (Nagano), 174, 175, 177–78

Baker, Laurie (*cont.*)
  at Olympics award ceremony, 11
  in San Jose game (1998), 119,
    121–22, 124
baseball, xx, xxi, 96–97, 119, 219,
  222
basketball, xxiii, 79, 108, 113, 124,
  223, 224
"being there" concept, 2, 126–30
Berard, Bryan, xxv, 2, 68, 191
Berglund, Art, xx, 9, 38–39, 61,
  62–63, 114, 118, 193, 197,
  214, 218
Big Hat Arena (Nagano), 1–15,
  150, 153, 165, 185, 194–214
Blahoski, Alana, 32, 58–59, 84, 90,
  139–40, 147
  aftermath of Olympics, 218
  evolution as hockey player,
    140–41
  family support of, 140
  in gold-medal game (Nagano),
    202, 204, 210
  in gold-medal preview game
    (Nagano), 175, 183
  at Olympics award ceremony, 11,
    13–14
  in San Jose game (1998), 120,
    121–22
  in USA v. Finland game
    (Nagano), 161
  after winning Olympic game, 6
Blake, Deborah, xxi
Boston Bruins, 66, 81, 112–13,
  218
Boston University, 68–69, 81
Botterill, Jennifer, 46, 221
Boyle, Mike, 69, 73, 74, 120, 220
boys' teams, female athletes on,
  xv–xvi, xx–xxi, xxv, 3, 19–20,
  27–28, 36–37, 42, 68, 70,

    73–74, 77, 107–8, 119, 123,
    140, 173, 188–89
Brampton Ontario Thunder, 220
Brendan Byrne Arena, 113
Brisson, Therese, 24, 42, 43, 48, 84,
  171–72, 174, 204, 208, 211
Brown-Miller, Lisa
  aftermath of Olympics, 218–19
  in Burlington, Vermont game
    (1997), 36–39, 47, 48, 53–54
  Christmas celebration (1997),
    55–57
  evolution as hockey player, xxiv,
    36–39
  in final Lake Placid game (1997),
    59–62, 71–72, 76, 78, 83–85, 87
  in gold-medal game (Nagano),
    200, 202, 206, 211
  in gold-medal preview game
    (Nagano), 171, 175, 177, 183
  marriage, 38–39, 61, 218–19
  at Olympics award ceremony,
    xxvii, 10–11, 13
  Olympic selection process and,
    55, 63, 87–100
  as Princeton coach, 38, 61, 62–63
  Ben Smith's career and, 61–63
  warm-up routine, 116–17
  after winning Olympic game,
    4–5, 7–8
Brown University, xxi–xxii, 36, 40,
  54, 79, 221
Bunker, Linda, 223
Bush, Walter, Jr., xx, 9, 200
Bye, Karyn
  aftermath of Olympics, 219
  in Burlington, Vermont game
    (1997), 39–40, 43, 46, 48, 49,
    53
  Christmas celebration (1997),
    58–59

evolution as hockey player, xxiv, 3–4

in final Lake Placid game (1997), 62, 75, 76, 78, 82, 84, 85

"focused fun" and, 2–3

in gold-medal game (Nagano), 202, 204, 212

in gold-medal preview game (Nagano), 171, 175

injuries, 149

at Olympics award ceremony, 10–15

Olympic selection process and, 88, 90–91, 95, 99–100

petition of U.S. Olympic Committee, xxiv, 3

in preparation for gold-medal game (Nagano), 191, 196

in San Jose game (1998), 120–21

U.S. flag and, 4–5, 8, 15

USA v. Finland game (Nagano), 161–62, 163

after winning Olympic game, 1–15

Calgary game, 111, 149

Cambridge Family and Children's Services Group, 219

Cammi Granato Golden Dreams for Children Foundation, 220

Campbell, Cassie, 171–72, 202, 211

Canada. *See* Team Canada

Carlson, Tom, 117, 118

Carney, Keith, 68

Cavanaugh, Joe, 68

Celebrity Ice Sharks, 218

Chelsea Piers, 81, 113, 133

Chicago Blackhawks, 66, 104–5, 106, 133

Chicago Cubs, 222

Chicago Tribune, 5

Chicago White Sox, 222

China, 158–59

Choate-Rosemary Hall, 190, 221

"circle of control" concept, 125, 126, 184

civil rights, xviii, 37

Clay, Cassius, 128–29

    See also Ali, Muhammad

Cleveland game, 111

Clinton, Bill, 140, 214

Cohen, Amy, xxi–xxii

Cohen v. Brown University, xxi

Colby College, 33

college scouts, xvii

Colombo Yogurt, 118, 218

Colorado Springs training sessions, 111, 125–28

Columbus Chill, 218

Concord, New Hampshire game (1997), 18–22

Concordia University, 110

Connecticut Polar Bears, 119, 190

Cooper, Cynthia, 224

corporate sponsors, xvii, xxiii, 66, 101, 118, 123–24, 144, 149–50, 153–54, 198, 220

Courtenay, Bruce, 197

Coyne, Colleen, 7, 60, 90, 94

    aftermath of Olympics, 219, 222

    evolution as hockey player, 96–97

    in final Lake Placid game (1997), 84

    in gold-medal game (Nagano), 202, 204, 205, 206, 213

    in gold-medal preview game (Nagano), 175

    at Olympics award ceremony, 11, 14

    in preparation for gold-medal game (Nagano), 194

Coyne, Colleen (*cont.*)
   in USA v. Finland game
      (Nagano), 161, 163
Craig, Jim, 81
crashing the net, defined, xxvi
Cross, Jimmy, 41
cross-country, 140
cultural battleground image, xx,
   xxii, xxiii–xiv
Curley, Cindy, 8, 109
curling, 143

Dallas Freeze, 65
Dartmouth College, 61, 69–70, 71,
   76, 77, 195, 200, 222
Dawes, Dominique, 223
DeCosta, Sara, 22
   aftermath of Olympics, 219, 221
   in Burlington, Vermont game
      (1997), 26
   Christmas celebration (1997),
      55–56
   evolution as hockey player, xxv,
      67–69
   family support of, 68, 72, 83–84,
      97–98, 199
   in final Lake Placid game (1997),
      59–60, 66, 67, 72, 74–75, 78,
      82–86
   in gold-medal game (Nagano),
      200, 201, 203, 204, 205,
      207–8, 209, 213, 214
   in gold-medal preview game (Nag-
      ano), 171, 172, 174, 175, 177
   injury, 69, 71
   at Olympics award ceremony, 11
   Olympic selection process and,
      90–91
   in preparation for gold-medal
      game (Nagano), 187, 192–95,
      196, 197

   in San Jose game (1998), 118,
      119, 120
   strength training in Boston, 69
   after winning Olympic game, 2
DeFranz, Anita, 12–15
DeGeneres, Ellen, 223
DeGregorio, Ron, xx, 9, 85, 200
Devens, Sarah, 69, 195
de Verona, Donna, 225
Diduck, Judy, 171, 176–77
Difference, The (Mann), xxii
DiMaggio, Joe, 20
Downers Grove North High
   School, 108
Driscoll, Jean, 223
Driscoll, Maura, 41, 44
Drolet, Nancy, 43, 46, 47, 83, 204,
   206, 207, 208
drug testing, 139
Dunn, Tricia, 20, 90, 91, 115, 140
   aftermath of Olympics, 219, 220,
      222
   evolution as hockey player, 176
   family support of, 203
   in final Lake Placid game (1997),
      75–78, 83
   in gold-medal game (Nagano),
      202, 204, 206, 213
   in gold-medal preview game
      (Nagano), 171, 176
   at Olympics award ceremony, 11
   in USA v. Finland game
      (Nagano), 161, 163
Dupuis, Lori, 171, 174, 175
Dupuis, Nancy, 48, 71–72
Dyer, Kelly, 8

Eastern Collegiate Athletic Confer-
   ence (ECAC)
   All-Stars, 3–4, 21, 73, 76
   Co-Player of the Year, 141

Player of the Year, 79
Rookies of the Year, 26, 42, 73, 76
Eastman Kodak, 150
eating disorders, xv
Elliott, Helene, xxvi–xxvii
Emrick, Mike, 24–29, 35, 36, 39, 49–50
Eruzione, Mike, 40–41, 64, 81, 105, 127

Failing at Fairness (Sadker and Sadker), xxii
feeder programs, xx–xxi, 108
female athletes
  on boys' teams, xv–xvi, xx–xxi, xxv, 3, 19–20, 27–28, 36–37, 42, 68, 70, 73–74, 77, 107–8, 119, 123, 140, 173, 188–89
  cultural battleground image of, xx, xxii, xxiii–xiv
  feeder programs, xx–xxi, 108
  increasing opportunities for, xxv–xxvi
  number of, xx–xxi
  as role models, xvi, xxii, xxiii, 21–22, 66, 101, 123, 125
  Title XI and, xviii–xix, xx–xxii, 37–38, 110, 188–89, 224, 225
  Women's Sports Foundation and, xviii, 123–24, 217–25
femininity, xvii–xviii
field hockey, 3, 73, 79, 119, 221
figure skating, xxiii, 42
Financial World, xxiii
Finland, 9–10, 11, 14, 31, 36, 109, 161–64
Flaim, Eric, 156, 157
"focused fun" concept, 2–3, 4, 125–26
football, xx, 104, 188

Foreman, George, 129
Foudy, Julie, 223

gender stereotypes, 106–9
gender testing, 139, 148–49
Giguerre, Isabelle, 66, 201
Gilligan, Mike, 41
Glasson, Sandy, 9, 10, 117, 194
Gold Medal Camp, 218
golf, xx, 219
Gonzalez, Nancy, 145, 146
Good Morning America, xxiv
Gordon, Barbara, 8, 32–34, 88, 113
Goyette, Danielle, 39, 44, 46, 47, 75, 83, 171–72, 177–85, 187, 207–11
Grabarek, Brooke, xxiii
Granato, Cammi, vii
  aftermath of Olympics, 220
  in Burlington, Vermont game (1997), 29–30, 35–36, 43, 45–46, 53
  Christmas celebration (1997), 57–59
  evolution as hockey player, xxiv, 29–30, 104–5, 106–11
  family support of, 98, 102–5, 121, 122–23, 133, 174–75, 199
  final Lake Placid game (1997) and, 59–60, 62, 64–65, 84, 85
  in gold-medal game (Nagano), 200, 201, 204, 206–7, 214–15
  in gold-medal preview game (Nagano), 171, 175, 178, 181
  leadership role, 132–33
  at Olympics award ceremony, xxvii, 10–15
  Olympic selection process and, 88–89, 90–91, 93, 95
  in preparation for gold-medal game (Nagano), 196, 200

Granato, Cammi (*cont.*)
  and San Jose, California game
    (1998), 101–2, 105–6, 111–12,
    119, 120–21
  as spokesperson for women's ice
    hockey, 104, 105–6, 111, 132
  in USA v. China game (Nagano),
    158–59
  in USA v. Finland game
    (Nagano), 164
  after winning Olympic game,
    1–2, 4, 5, 6–7, 8
Granato, Natalie, 30, 104, 105,
    106–7, 108, 109, 111, 199
Granato, Tony, 6–7, 29–30, 102–5,
    107, 111, 121, 122–23, 133,
    174–75, 178
Greenspan, Bud, 126–27
Greenwich Blues, 119
Greenwich Times, 220
Gretzky, Wayne, 123, 133, 203
Griswold, Jason, 174, 198
Groger, Manuela, 201
Gummere, John, 81
Gurley, Joanne, xx
Gutterson Field House (University
    of Vermont), 22–31, 35–54
gymnastics, xxi, 113, 223

Haberl, Peter, 51, 52, 57, 80, 154,
    158
  "being there" concept, 2, 126–30
  "circle of control" concept, 125,
    126, 184
  "focused fun" concept, 2–3, 4,
    125–26
  "inner circle" concept, 125, 126,
    130–32, 141–42, 151, 161,
    163, 167–71, 180, 211
  in Nagano games, 181–84, 194
  role of, 115–23, 125–32

Haenninen, Krisi, 161
Hamlen, Tim, 221
Harvard College, 6, 29, 72–74,
    150, 220–21
Heaney, Geraldine, 43, 120, 210
Hefford, Jayna, 25, 39, 47–50, 83,
    84, 120, 152–53, 174, 175,
    205, 207, 209
Heiden, Eric, 63, 198
hell skate, defined, 133
Henie, Sonja, 64
Hilles, Amie, 1
  Burlington, Vermont game
    (1997), 32–33, 54
  Christmas celebration (1997),
    55–56, 57, 58
  final Lake Placid game (1997),
    85, 88, 89, 90, 98–99
  at Nagano Olympics (1998), 9,
    10, 140, 141, 142, 146, 152,
    153–55, 167, 168, 179–82,
    192, 193–94, 203, 204, 205,
    206, 208, 213
  San Jose, California game (1998),
    106, 111, 122–23, 130–31
Hong, Guo, 158
Hood, Sarah, 69
Houston Comets, 224
Howald, Sarah, 69
How Schools Shortchange Girls, xxii
Hull, Brett, 191

IBM, 149–50
IKON, 118
"inner circle" concept, 125, 126,
    130–32, 141–42, 151, 161,
    163, 167, 180, 211
International Herald Tribune,
    xxvi–xxvii
International Ice Hockey Federa-
    tion (IIHF), 109

International Olympic Committee (IOC), xxii, 12–15, 30, 109–10
Ito, Midori, 157
Ivy League Player of the Year, 79
Ivy League Rookie of the Year, 26, 69, 73, 76

Japan, women's ice hockey team, 109, 164–65
Joyner, Al, 223
Joyner, Florence Griffith, 223
Joyner-Kersee, Jackie, 223

Kale, Vicki, 35
Keillor, Garrison, 189
Kentucky Thoroughbreds, 220
King, Billie Jean, 224, 225
King, Katie, 20, 90
    admiration of coach Smith, 79–82
    aftermath of Olympics, 219, 220
    in Burlington, Vermont game (1997), 40, 42, 43, 46, 47, 48, 49
    evolution as hockey player, 78–82
    family support of, 97–98, 203
    in final Lake Placid game (1997), 78, 82–86, 85
    in gold-medal game (Nagano), 204, 211
    in gold-medal preview game (Nagano), 175
    at Olympics award ceremony, 11
    in San Jose game (1998), 119, 121–22
    in USA v. Finland game (Nagano), 161
Kipling, Rudyard, 80
Korpi, Rauno, 162
Kwan, Michelle, 224

Labore, Mark, 21
lacrosse, 73, 96
Lady Liberty mascot, 116, 118, 151, 191, 195, 200
LaFontaine, Pat, 2
Lake Erie College, xx
Lamoriello, Chris, 173, 221
Lawrence Academy, 42
Leech, Brian, 195
Leland, Ted, xxi
Lenczner, Sarah, 69
Letterman, David, 170, 214
Letterman, Dorothy, 170
Lifetime Television, 24–29, 40–41, 44–45, 49–50
Lindros, Eric, 115, 203
Lobo, Rebecca, 223
Looney, Shelley, 22, 34, 90–91
    aftermath of Olympics, 220
    in Burlington, Vermont game (1997), 42, 46, 47
    Christmas celebration (1997), 56–57
    in final Lake Placid game (1997), 75–77, 83
    in gold-medal game (Nagano), 202, 204, 208, 209
    in gold-medal preview game (Nagano), 171, 178, 181–82
    at Olympics award ceremony, xxvii, 11
    in preparation for gold-medal game (Nagano), 187–88, 190
    in San Jose game (1998), 119
Lopiano, Donna, 123–24, 217
Los Angeles Kings, 103, 123, 220
Louisville Hockey Products, xvii, 66
LSI Logic, 118

MacGregor, Jeff, xxiv
Madison Square Garden, 113
Magnuson, Keith, 106
Mann, Judy, xxii
Martello, Vincent, 116
McAuliffe, Christa, 21
McCarten, Jack, 127
McCormack, Kathy, 25, 47, 205
mentors, adult, xvi
Merz, Sue, 34, 90
   aftermath of Olympics, 220
   in Burlington, Vermont game
     (1997), 46, 47, 48
   evolution as hockey player,
     119–20
   in final Lake Placid game (1997),
     75–76, 83
   in gold-medal game (Nagano),
     202, 203, 204, 205
   in gold-medal preview game
     (Nagano), 171
   at Olympics award ceremony, 11
   in preparation for gold-medal
     game (Nagano), 187, 190
   in San Jose game (1998), 119,
     120–21
   strength training in Boston, 120
   in USA v. Finland game
     (Nagano), 161–62
Michaels, Al, 64
Michiko, Empress, 155
Milborn, Kirk, 145
Miller, John, 7–8, 39, 55, 61, 87,
    88, 89, 95, 99, 174, 203, 206,
    209, 218–19
Miller, Shannon, 31, 205, 210,
    214–15
   in Burlington, Vermont game
     (1997), 36, 41, 43, 48, 49, 50
   in final Lake Placid game (1997),
     84, 86

   in gold-medal preview game, 171,
     172, 173, 175–81
   San Jose, California game (1998),
     106, 118
Minnesota Gophers, 189
Minnesota North Stars, 105
Minnesota State University, 218
Minnesota Thoroughbreds, 221
Minnesota Twins, 219
Minnesota Wild, 219
Mleczko, Allison (A.J.), 90, 91, 97,
    133
   aftermath of Olympics, 220–21,
     222, 225
   in Burlington, Vermont game
     (1997), 43, 48, 49
   evolution as hockey player,
     72–74, 77
   family support of, 73–74, 97–98,
     170, 199
   in final Lake Placid game (1997),
     77–78, 83, 85
   in gold-medal game (Nagano),
     202, 208, 211, 212
   in gold-medal preview game
     (Nagano), 171, 176, 177
   at Olympics award ceremony, 11
   in preparation for gold-medal
     game (Nagano), 197
   in San Jose game (1998), 121
   strength training in Boston, 73,
     74
   after winning Olympic game, 6
Mosely, Benita Fitzgerald, 223, 225
Mounsey, Tara
   aftermath of Olympics, 221
   in Burlington, Vermont game
     (1997), 17–19, 22–26, 36, 39,
     41, 44, 45, 46, 49, 51–54
   in Concord, New Hampshire
     game (1997), 18–22

evolution as hockey player, xxv,
   19–21, 26
family support of, 19
final Lake Placid game (1997)
   and, 59, 64–65, 74–75, 84, 85
in gold-medal game (Nagano),
   202, 204, 206, 207, 209, 210,
   211–12, 213
in gold-medal preview game
   (Nagano), 171, 175
injuries, xxv, 17, 39, 41, 45,
   51–52, 64–65, 95, 149,
   195–96, 211–12
at Olympics award ceremony,
   11
Olympic selection process and,
   64–65, 90–91, 94–95
in preparation for gold-medal
   game (Nagano), 194
in San Jose game (1998), 120–21,
   123
in USA v. Finland game
   (Nagano), 161–62, 163
Mount St. Charles Academy, 68
Movsessian, Vicki, 7, 90, 98
   aftermath of Olympics, 219, 221,
   222
   evolution as hockey player, 173
   family support of, 173
   in final Lake Placid game (1997),
      72, 76, 84
   in gold-medal game (Nagano),
      202, 205, 206, 208
   in gold-medal preview game
      (Nagano), 172–74
   humor of, 152, 160
   at Olympics award ceremony, 11
   in USA v. Finland game
      (Nagano), 161, 163
Murphy, Margaret Degidio (Digit),
   36, 39

Mutch, Tom, Jr., 9, 10, 130
   in Burlington, Vermont game
      (1997), 48, 49, 50
   in final Lake Placid game (1997),
      83
   in Nagano Olympics, 137, 168,
      169, 173, 177, 204, 208, 209,
      210, 211, 213
   Olympic selection process and,
      89, 93–94, 95–96, 97, 98–99
   in San Jose game (1998), 121
Mutch, Tom, Sr., 203, 204, 205,
   209
M-Wave Arena (Nagano), 150
Myers, Mike, 122

Nagano Olympics (1998), xv, xx,
   xxiii, 135–215
   aftermath of ice hockey competi-
      tion, 1–15
   drug testing, 139
   family support during, xxvii, 6,
      7–8, 10–11, 13, 136, 198–99,
      203–4
   gender testing, 139, 148–49
   gifts for athletes, 136, 137–38,
      151–52, 153–54
   gold medal game, xxvii, 8–15,
      187–214
   gold-medal preview game
      (Nagano), 170–80
   Olympic Village, 142–51, 214
   Opening Ceremonies, 136–37,
      154–58
   team processing, 135–42
   Team USA practice sessions,
      150–51, 165–66, 167–71
   USA v. China game, 158–59
   USA v. Finland game, 161–64
   USA v. Japan game, 164–65
   USA v. Sweden game, 159

Nagano Skate Center, 154, 167
Nantz, Jim, 214
National Camps, xvii, xviin, 221, 222
National Collegiate Athletic Association (NCAA), xviii–ix, xxi, 108, 219
National Federation of High School Athletic Associations, xx
National Hockey League (NHL), 30, 68, 106, 108, 114, 115, 165, 219
National Hockey League Players Association, 7
Navratilova, Martina, 223
Neely, Cam, 66
Netcom, 118
New England Women's (NEW) Fund, 222
New Hampshire Sunday News, 21
New Jersey Devils, 113, 173
New Trier High School, 70
New York Islanders, 68
New York/New Jersey games, 113, 133
New York Rangers, 68, 81, 113
New York Yankees, 220
Nieminen, Riiki, 161
Nike Inc., vii, xxiii, 101, 153–54
Northeastern University, xix, 34, 56, 61, 63, 220
Norway, 109
Nyad, Diana, 217, 223
Nystrom, Karen, 39–40, 48, 171, 202, 211

O'Connell, Kathy, xxiii
O'Connor, Bob, 194
Ogrean, David, xx, 9, 123–24, 181, 200
Old Time Boston Bruins, 218

O'Leary, Kelly, 8, 91–92, 93, 95
  in final Lake Placid game (1997), 62, 75, 78, 83
Olympic Games
  Summer, 1960, 128–29
  Summer, 1972, xxii
  Summer, 1980, 12
  Summer, 1996, xxii, xxiii, 113–14, 124
  Winter, 1960, 127
  Winter, 1980, 57
  Winter, 1984, 126–27
  Winter, 1988, 30, 102
  Winter, 1994, xxiii
  Winter, 1998. *See* Nagano Olympics (1998)
Olympic Training Center (Colorado Springs), 18, 89
Olympic Training Center (Lake Placid), xviin, 18, 31–32
  described, 63–64
  final Lake Placid game (1997), 59–67, 71–72, 74–76, 82–87
Olympic Village (Nagano), 142–51
  International Zone, 144–46, 149, 163–64, 194, 214
  security measures, 144, 145–46
  USA House, 145, 146–51, 214
Ontario Women's Hockey Association, 110
Orenstein, Peggy, xxii
Orr, Bobby, 57
Osbourne du Pont, Margaret, 223
O'Sullivan, Stephanie, 8, 27–28, 44–45, 47, 67, 69, 78, 83, 91–93, 95, 97
O'Sullivan Hockey Academy Foundation, 28
Otos, Sally, xxi
Ozawa, Seiji, 157

Page, Margot, 66–67
Parece, Debra, 35, 66, 201
Park, Brad, 81
Parker, Jack, 81
Pasadena Maple Leafs, 190
patriarchy, xxii
penalty kill, defined, 44
Peterson, Dave, xix, 30, 102
Philadelphia Flyers, 56
Phoenix Coyotes, 68
Pinkerton Academy, 176, 219
Pipher, Mary, xv, xx
Pleimann, Kris, 9, 10, 32–33, 57,
    93, 106, 111, 122–23, 158–59,
    163, 181, 182
Portland Pirates, 220
postfeminist era, xviii, 224–25
Power of One, The (Courtenay),
    197
power play, defined, 44
Princeton University, 38, 61, 62–63
Providence College, 27, 28, 37–38,
    42, 68–69, 93, 108, 110, 116,
    140–41, 173, 196, 218, 219
Puputti, Tuula Katriina, 161

Ramaley, Judith, 30–31
Rashad, Ahmad, 223
Rashad, Phylicia, 223
Reddon, Lesley, 66, 171–72, 174–77
Reebok, xxiii
Reviving Ophelia (Pipher), xv
Rhéaume, Manon
  in Burlington, Vermont game
      (1997), 24, 40, 43, 46, 48, 49
  in final Lake Placid game (1997),
      66–67, 72, 75–78, 83–86
  in gold-medal game (Nagano),
      201, 203, 204, 205, 206,
      208–9, 210–11
  in San Jose game (1998), 121–22

Richter, Mike, 2, 81, 133, 191, 195
Riggs, Bobby, 224, 225
roller hockey, 222
Romanuk, Paul, 66–67
Root, Gary, 37, 39
Rosenbloom, Steve, 5
Rossi, Tony, xx
rowing, 12, 221
Roy, Patrick, 40
Ruggiero, Angela, 90
  aftermath of Olympics, 218,
      221
  in Burlington, Vermont game
      (1997), 43, 44, 47, 48, 49
  evolution as hockey player,
      189–90
  family support of, 189–90
  in final Lake Placid game (1997),
      72, 83
  in gold-medal game (Nagano),
      200, 202, 204, 206, 213
  in gold-medal preview game
      (Nagano), 171–72, 174
  at Olympics award ceremony, 11,
      14
  in preparation for gold-medal
      game (Nagano), 187–88, 190
  after winning Olympic game, 6
running, 223
Rutland Area Hockey Association,
    40

Sadker, David, xxii
Sadker, Myra, xxii
Saeger, Becky, 124
St. James, Lyn, 223
Saito, Serina, 156, 157, 221
Sakic, Joe, 207
Salem (New Hampshire) High
    School, 79
Salt Lake City game (1997), 71

San Jose, California game (1998),
  101–2, 105–6, 111–12, 115–22
San Jose Arena (Shark Tank), 102,
  105–6, 118, 121
San Jose Sharks, 30, 123
San Jose Sports Authority, 123
Satoya, Tae, 165
Savard, Dennis, 66
Schepman, Jeanna, 9, 10, 32–33,
  39, 52, 57, 60, 88, 117, 119,
  120, 130, 149, 163, 167,
  168–69, 194, 195, 213
Scherr, Lynn, 223
Schmidgall, Jenny, 32, 90–91
  aftermath of Olympics, 221–22
  evolution as hockey player,
    188–89
  family support of, 189
  in final Lake Placid game (1997),
    75, 84
  in gold-medal game (Nagano),
    202, 204, 208–9
  in gold-medal preview game
    (Nagano), 175–76
  at Olympics award ceremony, 11,
    14
  in preparation for gold-medal
    game (Nagano), 188, 193
  in USA v. China game (Nagano),
    158
Schneider, Matt, 68, 191
scholarships, athletic, xvi, xxi,
  188–89
School Girls (Orenstein), xxii
Schultz, Dick, 123, 124
Seagate Software, 118
Second Jungle Book (Kipling), 80
self-esteem, xv
self-loathing, xv
sex equity, xviii, 110
  guidelines for, xxi

opposition to, xxi–xxii
stereotypes and, 106–9
Title IX and, xx–xxii, 37–38,
  110, 118–89, 224, 225
sexism, xvi
Shanahan, Brendan, 207
Silverman, Steven, 222
Sinden, Harry, 112
skiing, 223
Small, Sami Jo, 118
Smith, Ben, xv
  aftermath of Olympics, 221,
    224
  Burlington, Vermont game
    (1997), 22–31, 35–54
  career history, xix–xx, 38, 61–62
  coaching technique, 20, 50–52,
    79–82, 114, 124, 162– 63,
    167–71, 191–92, 194–95
  in Concord, New Hampshire
    game (1997), 18–22
  described, xxv–xxvi
  in final Lake Placid game (1997),
    59–67, 71–72, 74–76, 82–87
  "focused fun" and, 3, 4
  in gold-medal game (Nagano),
    200–215
  in gold-medal preview game
    (Nagano), 170–85
  hired as Team USA coach, 38–39,
    61–63
  humor of, 81–82, 137
  Olympic gold medal ceremony
    and, 8–10, 15
  Olympic selection process,
    31–35, 63, 87–100
  personal relationships with play-
    ers/family, 86–87
  in preparation for gold-medal
    game (Nagano), 191–92,
    193–95, 197

in San Jose, California game (1998), 101–2, 105–6, 111–12, 115–22

Scandinavian tour, 38–39, 61–62, 81–82

Smith, Fiona, 24, 46, 47, 171, 202

Snouse, Sue, 148–49, 171

Sobek, Jeanine, 8, 22, 32–34, 88, 113, 220

soccer, xx, 42, 104, 108, 113, 140, 223

softball, 3, 42, 79, 104, 113, 119, 140, 223

Special Olympics, 219, 222

sponsors, corporate, xvii, xxiii, 66, 101, 118, 123–24, 144, 149–50, 153–54, 198, 220

sports medicine experts, xix

Stanford University, xxi

state championships, xvi

Steinem, Gloria, 224

stereotypes, gender, 106–9

Stone, Katie, 6

Stone, Nikki, 223

street hockey, 42

Strickland de la Hunty, Shirley, 223

Summers, Sumner, 3

Sunohara, Vicky, 174, 175, 205

Sweden, 109, 159

Sweeney, John, 167, 222

swimming, 3, 188, 223

Switzerland, 109

Tabor Academy, 96

Taylor, Timmy, 81

Team Canada, 2, 9–10, 11, 14
  in Burlington, Vermont game (1997), 22–31, 35–54
  descriptions of players, 24–25
  in final Lake Placid game (1997), 65–67, 71–72, 74–76, 82–87

in final Olympic game (Nagano), 198–214

in Olympic preview game (Nagano), 170–80

Princess mascot, 45–46, 116

San Jose, California game (1998), 101–2, 105–6, 111–12, 115–22

Team Finland, 9–10, 11, 14, 161–64

Team Illinois, 220

Team USA
  as athlete-ambassadors, 123–25
  in Boston Bruins demo game, 112–13
  in Burlington, Vermont game (1997), 22–31, 35–54
  Christmas celebration (1997), 55–59
  "circle of control" concept, 125, 126, 184
  Colorado Springs training sessions, 125–28
  in Concord, New Hampshire game (1997), 18–22
  family members in Japan, 6, 7–8, 10–11, 13, 159–61, 162, 170, 174–75
  in final Lake Placid game (1997), 59–67, 71–72, 74–76, 82–87
  in gold-medal game (Nagano), 198–214
  in gold-medal preview game (Nagano), 170–80
  humor of, 58–59, 81–82, 160, 162
  impact on women's sports, xv, 21–22, 66
  "inner circle" concept, 125, 126, 130–32, 141–42, 151, 161, 163, 167, 180, 211

Team USA (*cont.*)
  Lady Liberty mascot, 116, 118,
    151, 191, 195, 200
  media attention, 112–15,
    177–85, 187
  at Nagano Olympics, 8–15,
    135–215
  New York City/New Jersey
    games, 113, 133
  Olympic award ceremony, xxvii,
    10–15
  Olympic gifts to athletes, 136,
    137–38, 151–52, 153–54
  Olympic selection process,
    31–35, 63, 87–100
  Olympic Village and,
    142–51
  in San Jose, California game
    (1998), 101–2, 105–6, 111–12,
    115–22
  Scandinavian tour, 38–39,
    61–62, 69, 81–82
  showcase games with Team
    Canada, 111
  team processing in Nagano,
    135–42
  in USA v. China game (Nagano),
    158–59
  in USA v. Finland game
    (Nagano), 161–64
  in USA v. Japan game (Nagano),
    164–65
  in USA v. Sweden game
    (Nagano), 159
  after winning Olympic game,
    1–15
tennis, 3, 42, 108, 223, 224
Thompson, Jenny, 223
Three Nations Cup tournament
    (1997)
  award ceremony, 85–86
  Burlington, Vermont game,
    22–31, 35–54
  described, 31
  final Lake Placid game, 59–67,
    71–72, 74–76, 82–87
Title IX, Federal Education Amend-
    ments of 1972
  delayed compliance with,
    xx–xxi
  impact of, xviii–xix, 37–38, 110,
    188–89, 224, 225
  lawsuits under, xxi–xxii
Title IX brothers, 68, 70
Toledo Storm, 65
Toll Gate High School (Warwick,
    Rhode Island), 68
Toll Gate Titans, 68
Toyota Motor Corporation, 118,
    144
TSN, 66–67
Tueting, Sarah, 24, 60, 88, 90, 130,
    158
  aftermath of Olympics, 222
  in Burlington, Vermont game
    (1997), 26
  evolution as hockey player, 67,
    69–71
  family support of, 70, 199
  in final Lake Placid game (1997),
    67
  in gold-medal game (Nagano),
    200–203, 205–6, 207–8, 209,
    210, 211, 213
  in gold-medal preview game
    (Nagano), 171, 172, 183
  music and, 71
  at Olympics award ceremony, 11,
    14
  in preparation for gold-medal
    game (Nagano), 192–93,
    196–97

in USA v. Finland game
(Nagano), 161–62, 163
Turner Network Television, 214

Ulion, Gretchen, 40, 47, 90, 116,
156
aftermath of Olympics, 222
evolution as hockey player,
76–77
family support of, 203
in final Lake Placid game (1997),
75, 76, 85–86
in gold-medal game (Nagano),
200, 204, 208–9, 211, 214
in gold-medal preview game
(Nagano), 171–72
humor of, 152
at Olympics award ceremony, 11
in USA v. Finland game
(Nagano), 162, 163
United States Amateur Hockey Association, 57
U.S. Girls' National Ice Hockey
Championships, xvi–xviii
U.S. Men's Olympic Ice Hockey
Team, 2, 34–35
U.S. Olympic Committee, 218
debriefing of athletes, 138–40
gifts to athletes, 137–38
media relations of athletes and,
139
petitions for women's hockey
team, xxiv, 3, 30, 110
U.S. Olympic Women's Rowing
Team, 12
U.S. Women's Basketball Team, 124
U.S. Women's Olympic Ice Hockey
Team. *See* Team USA
University of Minnesota, 189, 222
University of New Hampshire, 3–4,
34, 96, 119, 141, 176, 219

University of Vermont, games of
1997, 22–31, 35–54
University of Wisconsin, 102
USA Hockey, Inc., xix–xx, xviin,
218
corporate sponsors, 218
final Lake Placid game (1997),
64, 85
first women's team, 109
gold-medal game (Nagano), 9,
200
hiring of Ben Smith as coach,
38–39, 61–63
history of, 109–10
Nike Town and, 153–54
Olympic selection committee, 35,
88
San Jose game (1998) and, 121,
123–24
team gift watches, 58
Woman Player of the Year, 29,
42, 111
USA Today, xxiii

Vairo, Lou, 34–35
Vanbiesbrouck, John, 66
Vancouver game, 111, 114–15
VanDerveer, Tara, xix, 124, 207,
223
VISA, xxiii, 66, 123–24, 220
Vogler, Sara, 69
volleyball, xxi, 108

Waitz, Grete, 223
Walsh, Duncan, 19
Washington Post, xxvii
Weatherspoon, Teresa, 223
Webster, Bob, 32–33, 52, 53, 87,
103–4, 120, 130
Christmas celebration (1997),
57–58

Webster, Bob (*cont.*)
  in Nagano Olympics, 137,
    150–51, 167, 168, 181, 191,
    192, 195, 213
  role of, 115–16, 117, 118
  after winning Olympic game, 4,
    8, 9, 10, 15
Weiman, Dee Dee, 223
Wellesley College Center for Re-
    search on Women, xxii
West Germany, 109
White, Willye, 223
White Ring Arena (Nagano), 150
Whitten, Erin, 8, 23–24, 26, 59, 60,
    65, 67, 68–69, 71, 84, 91–92,
    95, 97, 221
  in Burlington, Vermont game
    (1997), 36, 38, 39, 43–48,
    52–53
Whyte, Sandra, 73, 140, 194
  aftermath of Olympics, 219, 221,
    222
  in Burlington, Vermont game
    (1997), 28–29, 39–40, 48, 49
  Christmas celebration (1997),
    58–59
  evolution as hockey player,
    xxiv–xxv
  family support of, 159–61, 184–85
  in final Lake Placid game (1997),
    75–76
  in gold-medal game (Nagano),
    202, 204, 206, 207, 209,
    210–11, 212–14
  in gold-medal preview game
    (Nagano), 172, 174, 177–85,
    187
  incident with Danielle Goyette,
    177–85, 187

  at Olympics award ceremony, 11
  Olympic selection process and,
    90–91, 93
  Olympic Village and, 142–51
  Opening Ceremony and, 154–58
  in preparation for gold-medal
    game (Nagano), 187
  in San Jose game (1998), 121
  team processing in Nagano,
    135–42
  Valentine's Day in Nagano,
    166–71
  after winning Olympic game,
    6, 8
Wickenheiser, Hayley, 25, 36, 39,
    46–49, 75, 83, 87, 177, 202,
    205, 207–12
Wilbon, Michael, xxvii
Wilson, Ron, 2
Wilson, Stacy, 35, 43, 175, 205–6,
    207, 211
Winfrey, Oprah, 7, 175
Women's College Coalition,
    101
Women's Law Center, xxi
Women's National Basketball Asso-
    ciation, xxiii, 224
Women's Sports Foundation, xviii,
    123–24, 217–25
wrestling, xx

Xerox Corporation, 198

Yamada, Mizue, vii, xxvi
Young, Evonne, 35
Yzerman, Steve, 203

Zenk, Marina, 66, 84, 201–2, 206,
    208, 213